Language in Action

'The organization is excellent and I very much liked the insistent use of real talk, collected and properly transcribed by the author. This gives the book not only a cohesion and immediacy, but also applies the strong (and, to my mind) entirely appropriate test of real-world exchanges to approaches which sometimes slip by on armchair examples. A real plus.' **Charles Antaki, Department of Social Sciences, Loughborough University**

Face-to-face conversation between two or more people is a universal form, and perhaps the basic form, of social interaction. It is the primary site of social interaction in all cultures and the place where social and cultural meaning takes shape. Face-to-face conversation between children and parents can also be an important context for social and cognitive development. Given the universality, frequency and importance of conversation in social life, a psychological model of conversation is required for an understanding of central issues in social and developmental psychology. This book provides such a model.

Language in Action presents a critical examination of four models of conversation: the Code model based on Chomsky's linguistic views; the Speech Act model of Austin and Searle; the Inferential model of Grice and the Conversation Analytic model of Sacks and Schegloff. It also considers the Brown and Levinson model of politeness in conversation. Using many examples from natural talk and drawing on the positive aspects of the reviewed models, Turnbull proposes a new Social Pragmatic model of conversation as social interaction. He also describes the research paradigm of Social Pragmatics that experimental psychologists can use to study conversation. This book will be invaluable for advanced students in psychology, sociology, language and linguistics and communication. It will also make fascinating and lively reading for anyone wanting a greater understanding of this fundamental form of social interaction.

William Turnbull is Professor of Psychology at Simon Fraser University in Canada. He is an expert in the field of social interaction and conversation.

Language in Action
Psychological Models of Conversation

William Turnbull

Psychology Press
Taylor & Francis Group
HOVE AND NEW YORK

First published 2003
by Psychology Press
27 Church Road, Hove, East Sussex BN3 2FA

Simultaneously published in the USA and Canada
by Psychology Press
29 West 35th Street, New York, NY 10001

Psychology Press is part of the Taylor & Francis Group

Typeset in Times by Keystroke, Jacaranda Lodge, Wolverhampton
Printed and bound in Great Britain by Biddles Ltd, Guildford and King's Lynn
Paperback cover design by Terry Foley at Anú Design

British Library Cataloguing in Publication Data
A catalogue record for this book is available from the British Library

Library of Congress Cataloging in Publication Data
Turnbull, William, 1946–
   Language in action: psychological models of conversation /
   William Turnbull.
      p. cm.—(International series in social psychology)
   Includes bibliographical references and index.
   ISBN 0–415–19867–4 (alk. paper—ISBN 0–415–19868–2
   (pbk. : alk. paper)
   1. Conversation—Psychological aspects.   I. Title.   II. Series.
   BF637.C45 T86 2003
   153.6—dc21
                                                    2002012280

ISBN 0–415–19867–4 (hbk)
ISBN 0–415–19868–2 (pbk)

Contents

Preface

People spend a lot of their time talking: they chat, joke with one another, exchange recipes, ask for and receive directions and advice, discuss politics, negotiate the terms of a mortgage, and praise their friends, spouses and children, just to name a few of the activities that take place in talk. Talking is also the main way in which people get to know one another, become more or less intimate with one another, attain domination over others or become submissive with others, and enter into and out of long- and short-term relationships, just to name some of the many interpersonal activities that take place in talk. Indeed, if an extra-terrestrial anthropologist were to visit Earth, talking would certainly stand out as a frequent and universal activity of human kind.

The present book is about talk. For many years, in attempting to understand the nature and role of talk in human life, I equated talk with spoken language. Talk (conversation), then, seemed to be centrally a linguistic or psycholinguistic phenomenon. This turned out to be a serious mistake for reasons that I discuss in this book. Eventually, I came to the conclusion that talk is best understood as social interaction. From this perspective, talk is very much a psychological and sociological phenomenon. Once talk is recognized to be a form of social interaction, it is possible to construct a psychological model of talk that fits the data of everyday talk or conversation. Further, since the major way people interact is by talking, a model of talk can be used to study social interaction in, for example, personal relationships, psychological therapy, education, or child development. The book presents an argument for viewing talk as social interaction. I also explore how the model of talk developed in the book can be used to study issues in social interaction that interest psychologists.

The book is based on over fifteen years of teaching a psychology course on conversation. From the many hundreds of students I taught, I received lots of feedback. Often, the feedback showed me that I had not been clear about the points I was trying to make. At other times the feedback showed me that there is an ingrained way of thinking about conversation – it is nothing more than spoken language – that is very difficult to dislodge. Both types of feedback forced me to be clearer about the argument, to relate it to the taken-for-granted view, and to back up the argument at every point with examples from natural conversation. I owe a great deal to student feedback. I also thank those who allowed me to use their tape-recordings of natural conversation.

My research and the book have been supported with funding from Simon Fraser University and from the Social Sciences and Humanities Research Council of Canada. I thank them. Over the years I have been most fortunate to have supervised some superb students. They have taught me a great deal and they deserve credit for many of the merits of this book. In particular, I thank Sherrie Atwood, Shannon Gifford, John Kerkhoven, Peter Muntigl and Karen Saxton. Special thanks go to my colleague Jeremy Carpendale who has been supportive of the ideas presented here.

W. Turnbull
Vancouver, BC
August 2001

1

Introduction

The Conversing Organism

Who Is the Audience for This Book?

When preparing to write anything, it is important to know who is the intended audience. The title of this book may lead readers to assume the book is about language. Perhaps, then, the intended audience consists of psycholinguists and perhaps also linguists and sociolinguists. It may come as a surprise to learn, then, that in an important sense the book is not about language as one normally thinks of that term. In the course of the book the argument is made that conversation is social interaction. Thus, the book focuses on social interaction, not language.

To see how conversation could be considered social interaction, consider an example of a conversation in which the wife of a colleague asked him how he liked her new reading glasses. My colleague reported, and this was the point of him telling me the story, that he had paused too long before answering. What he meant by this is that his wife had taken his silence as indicating that he did not like her new glasses, an interpretation that was confirmed when his wife next expressed displeasure over her husband's negative evaluation of her glasses. In this situation, silence or failing to speak was a crucial part of the conversation: the husband used it to carry out a particular action, and the action was recognized as such by his wife. Silence is not part of the structure of English, nor of any natural language, but silence is relevant to an understanding of this conversation. Further, it was in and through conversation that the husband and wife carried out an episode of social interaction; and it was in and through conversation that interpersonal effects were produced. In other words, their conversation constituted a form of social interaction.

In this book, through the careful consideration of the positive and negative attributes of various models of talk, a model of talk-as-social-interaction is developed. In addition, a methodology for analysing talk-as-social-interaction, including a set of analytic categories, is also presented. The usefulness for psychological research of the model of talk-as-social-interaction is illustrated through research on important psychological phenomena, including mother–child interaction and couples counselling. Finally because conversation is centrally about meaning-making, implications of a model of talk-as-social-interaction for theories of action, meaning and representation are briefly discussed.

The psychological study of interaction, which includes the study of personal relationships, and of interpersonal, group and cultural processes, is the domain of social psychology. But it is also the case that developmental psychologists study the impact of social interaction, in particular of parent–child and peer interactions, on social and cognitive development. Accordingly, the book is directed primarily to social and developmental psychologists who should find the model of talk-as-social-interaction interesting because it provides them with a way of examining the structures of episodes of interaction and of characterizing the nature of interactions in various ways. Those analyses can be related, in turn, to such phenomena as the relation between the structure of arguing and the quality of long-term intimate relations, or the impact of styles of parent–child interaction on the child's social/cognitive development.

To demonstrate the relevance to social and developmental psychology of the material discussed in this book will take some time. The dominant, taken-for-granted models treat talk as relatively unimportant and, at most, merely a conduit by which one person conveys information to another. Further, those models are so entrenched that they have attained the status of fact rather than theory. But they are theories and I will try to convince you that they are seriously flawed theories. However, because of their taken-for-grantedness, to dispel the dominant view of talk requires a long and difficult argument. Until that argument is complete, the reader needs to be patient in waiting to see how the study of talk is centrally relevant to the study of social interaction.

In order to set the stage for the issues discussed in this book, it is necessary to first define some terms and set down some signposts.

What Is Conversation?

Conversation can be defined as the situation in which two socialized and co-present persons talk to one another as they go about their everyday informal lives. There are other types of 'conversation' that do not include one or more aspects of this definition. In particular, there is conversation involving more than two participants and conversation between people from different cultures. Also, there is conversation without visual interaction (e.g., conversation on the telephone), and there is conversation with varying degrees of formality (e.g., in formal situations such as the classroom, the courtroom and the therapy session). Although examples from various types of conversation are given in this book, the focus of the book is two person, everyday, informal, face-to-face conversation.

Examination of conversation reveals that it is composed of much more than spoken language as traditionally defined (this will become evident as you proceed through the examples presented in the book). Thus, it is preferable to use a term for this type of human social activity that does not have the connotation of conversation being equated with spoken language or speaking. Further, 'conversation' may refer to a form of social activity involving two or more participants ('having a conversation') and to the activities of each of the participants in creating this social activity ('speaking' or 'conversing'). Accordingly, the term 'talk' is used to refer both to the activities or ways in which people together construct this universal form of social interaction and to social interaction so constructed. Specific forms of talk are referred to as, for example, telephone talk, lecture talk, therapy talk and mother–child talk.

Aims of the Book: Why Study Conversation/Talk?

I have already suggested that the study of talk is relevant for psychologists interested in social interaction. The following are five additional reasons why talk should interest psychologists, practitioners of other social science disciplines (e.g., sociologists, anthropologists), cultural theorists, linguists, educators and educated citizens.

Everyday talk occurs in all cultures and involves all social categories of persons: ruler and ruled, rich and poor, literate and illiterate, male and female. Even people who are unable to talk or whose language is seriously impoverished, such as the very young and those with severe physical or mental impairments, engage in talk with others. It is because universal human activities may reveal something essential about the human experience that talk is of interest. Further, because talk is the most frequent form of social interaction, what is learned about talk will be useful in understanding other forms of interaction.

Second, talk is reflexively tied to personal identity, to human relationships, and to culture; that is, in talk participants co-construct their personal, social and cultural worlds, and participants' orientations to those co-constructed worlds influence the structure of talk (Ochs, 1988, 1992).

Third, the ability of persons to coordinate their actions bestows an adaptive advantage. It seems likely that talk evolved from the attempts of human beings to coordinate their own actions with the actions of others (Goody, 1995). Language, in turn, evolved from talk, and it is likely that the structure of language is greatly influenced by its origins as a solution to problems of coordination. It can be expected that grammar is adapted to the structures of talk (Ochs, Schegloff, & Thompson, 1996). A model of talk is, thus, relevant to an understanding of language.

Fourth, language is considered by many theorists to be a uniquely human achievement and, thus, central to a theory of mind. The influence of this belief is evident in claims about the relation of language and intelligence, both natural and artificial, and in the vast amount of philosophical debate about the relation of language and mind. By focusing on talk rather than language, a fresh perspective is brought to these concerns. For example, the philosopher Wittgenstein proposed a tight interconnection between talk and thought, one in which thoughts are not pre-existing entities to which words are then applied: 'Does a child learn only to talk, or also to think? Does it learn the sense of multiplication *before* or *after* it learns multiplication?' (Wittgenstein, 1970, p. 324, italics in original). Wittgenstein is expressing the belief that talk and thought develop together in a 'chicken and egg' sort of way. Focusing on talk rather than language also brings new perspectives to the Sapir-Whorf hypothesis that language determines or influences thought, that 'culture, through language, affects the way in which we think, especially perhaps our classification of the experienced world' (Gumperz & Levinson, 1996, p. 1).

Fifth, on a practical note, a model of how humans talk has implications for the possibility of developing artificially intelligent machines that can 'talk'.

How people accomplish talk is not obvious

The above reasons for studying talk may be convincing, and it might be wondered why psychologists have not devoted a great deal of research to the study of talk. One reason is there is a widely accepted model of talk (language use) and in that model, language is important but talk is not. That model is described in detail later in this chapter. A second reason is that talk may be overlooked as a central activity of human social life precisely because talk is a universal and ubiquitous form of human interaction. Just as fish might be the last organisms to discover water, so too might human beings be the last to discover what is all around them – talk. Another fate of extremely common, mundane activities is that even if they are recognized, they may arouse no interest and, instead, be dismissed as obvious. But one should be very cautious about the nature of phenomena deemed obvious. As long as 'obvious' is meant to signify only that there is considerable agreement about the existence, and perhaps also the prevalence, of some phenomenon, there is no problem. Unfortunately, 'obvious' is often used to signify that something is simple and explanations of it are readily available. It is not uncommon in the social sciences, however, to discover on careful examination that many mundane, everyday, 'obvious' activities are extremely complex and difficult to explain. Talk is just such an activity. The central goals of this book are to reveal some of the complexities of talk and to examine critically some of the models/theories of how humans accomplish talk in their everyday lives.

Psychological Study of Talk

As noted previously, because people speak when they converse, one might be led to the conclusion that the study of talk is the study of language and, therefore, part of the discipline of linguistics. Research in linguistics has contributed to the study of talk, but so too has research in anthropology, communication studies, psychology and sociology. Whereas research from all these disciplines is considered in the present book, the primary focus is the psychological analysis of everyday talk. From a psychological perspective, I examine various models of how it is that people carry out talk, of how they are able to understand one another when they talk, of how understanding sometimes goes wrong and how such misunderstandings are corrected, of what people do when they talk, and of how it is that they can do all these things. In other words, the focus of this book is on the nature of everyday talk and the psychological models and theories, the psychological explanations, of such behaviour.

Appropriate data for research on talk

Research psychologists agree that if a theorist makes a claim about any aspect of human behaviour, that claim must be backed up with empirical data. The requirement that researchers back up their claims empirically means that they must observe, measure and describe the phenomena they wish to study. These observations, measurements and descriptions constitute the data of psychology. Psychologists then try to explain what processes people must be employing in order for them to act as they do. Explanations ultimately derive from theories and researchers choose the theory that most closely fits the data and does so in the simplest, most parsimonious way. Thus, in order to evaluate theories of how people accomplish talk, it is necessary to compare these theories with the data of talk.

Given a focus on talk, it seems clear that what needs to be carefully observed, the empirical data that ought to be collected and examined, are instances and fragments of natural talk. On the surface, this would seem to pose no problem. After all, there is a vast amount of talk all around us, so all one has to do is listen to some of it. The trouble with that approach, however, is that talk tends to pass by very quickly, leaving little time for any close examination. To help make the task of examining actual talk easier, researchers make audio or videotapes of talk, and then create a written record, or *transcript*, of it. Because the transcript is a written record of talk, it is easy to examine it carefully and repeatedly, and portions of transcripts can be included in research reports.

Transcription

In this book, all examples of talk are presented in a transcription system based on the notation of a brand of sociology known as Conversation Analysis (c.f., Atkinson & Heritage, 1984, pp. ix–xvi). Each example is numbered; the first number refers to the chapter of the book in which the example is presented and the second number refers to the number of the example in that chapter. In some cases, a brief description of relevant background information about the talk, such as whether it occurred on the telephone, in a classroom, between a mother and her child, etc., is presented in parentheses immediately below the example number. Each line of the transcript is numbered sequentially, and these line numbers are presented at the far left of the transcript. Except for these notations, everything else in the transcript refers to something that is evident in the tape-recorded talk. The goal of transcription is to capture the sounds and the sequence of turns that occurred as the interaction proceeded (as occurs on the tape recording). Accordingly, contributions to the interaction are presented sequentially turn by turn, with an upper case letter identifying the speaker, followed by a colon, followed by the speaker's turn. Further, the words the speaker uttered are spelled as the speaker pronounced them, as are vocalizations that are not words (e.g., backchannels such as 'ums' and 'ahs'). Table 1.1 presents a description of all other symbols used in transcription.

The following examples of talk illustrate the use of the majority of symbols in the transcription system.

Example 1:1

1　A:　i just have one small question

2　B:　okay one small question ((laughs))

3　A:　do you agree that um (0.7) well (.) so you think all clearcutting is

4　　　(.) is bad↑

5　B:　clearcutting (.) personally (.) yes

Example 1:2

1　A:　she kinda makes you feel important too

2　B:　[yeah]

3　C:　[mhm]

4　A:　like you're (.) you're kind of <u>one of her</u> [ya know like]

5　B:　　　　　　　　　　　　　　　　　　　[yeah exactly]

6　A:　like well we're all in this together and [ya know]

7　C:　　　　　　　　　　　　　　　　　　[mhm]

8　A:　you're important to me (.) and when they do that you feel good=

9　C:　=mhm

Example 1:3

(mother, M, and child, C, making up a story based on a picture book)

1　M:　um:: so he know how does he know that she took it↑

2　　　(1.0)

TABLE 1.1 *Symbols used in transcription*

Symbol	Meaning of symbol
(.)	Pause too brief to count
(0.5)	Minimum countable pause
(2.5)	Length of pause (greater than 0.5 seconds)
hh, hh	Speaker's in-breath and out-breath
hehh, hahh	Laughter, with attempt to capture sound
((sniff)) ((cough)) ((laughter))	Non-speech sounds
wo(h)rd	(h) denotes non-speech sounds
cu–	Dash denotes a sharp cut-off
lo:::ng	Colons denote a drawn out sound; more colons, more sound drawn out
(transcriber's guess)	Transcriber's guess as to speech on tape
(syll syll)	Unclear speech or noise with approximation of number of sounds
( )	Unclear speech or noise for which no guess could be made
=latching=	Equal signs link sequential utterances not separated by a pause. Also used in the case of overlap to link speaker's present turn back to his/her previous turn
word↓	Falling intonation
word↑	Rising intonation. DO NOT USE QUESTION MARK as the issue of whether something is a question is an analytic decision
underline for emphasis	Underlining indicates emphasis
CAPITALS	CAPITAL LETTERS indicates speech noticeably louder than surrounding speech
soft	Degree signs (° °) or (* *) indicates speech noticeably quieter than surrounding speech
>fast<	Faster than surrounding speech
<slow>	Slower than surrounding speech
over[lap] [over]lap	Square brackets between adjacent lines of concurrent speech denote the start and finish of over-lapping talk
. . .	Material left out of transcript (e.g., for brevity or confidentiality)
((gesture))	Describes relevant types of visual behaviour; used with videotape only

3 M: hm::↑

4 C: maybe she found out he found out

5 M: he found out (.5) so he's very upset isn't he (.) and she doesn't

6   look too upset (.90) hu:hh *what did he do↑*

7   (1.2)

8 M: what did he do↑

9 C: i don't know

Details in the structure of talk: relevant or irrelevant?

To produce a transcript containing the level of detail illustrated in the above examples takes a great deal of time and effort. It might be argued that this effort is wasted since much of that detail contributes nothing to one's understanding of the talk and, indeed, might make the task of understanding it more difficult. Consider Example 1:1 lines 3 and 4 where A says 'do you agree that um (0.7) well (.) so you think all clearcutting is (.) is bad↑'. A critic might argue that what is important about A's turn is that A is asking B and proposing that B believes that all clearcutting is bad. That A produced an 'um' followed by 0.7 seconds of silence, and then continued with 'well', a slight pause '(.)', 'so', 'you think', and another slight pause between a repetition of 'is', 'is (.) is', is irrelevant to what A was doing in his turn. Indeed, the critic continues, these attributes are verbal disfluencies, errors of performance, that have nothing to do with A's message and only make it difficult, for both participants and analysts, to arrive at a clear understanding of A's message. The conclusion the critic reaches is that this 'irrelevant detail' should not be included in the transcript. Certainly, it would make transcripts much easier to produce and to read if these details were ignored.

Whereas this view may seem reasonable, it is misguided. To appreciate why this is so, consider examples of students refusing (Example 1:4) or granting (Example 1:5) a request to participate in a psychology experiment (Turnbull & Saxton, 1997). For brevity, only the end of the request is reproduced. The examples were chosen because they are very typical instances of refusals and grantings.

Example 1:4

1 R: . . . takes place up at the university this saturday from seven

2   o'clock in the morning til about ten thirty

3   (1.6)

4 S: uuh (1.2) hum (1.5) until ten thirty↑ i i have an exam that day

5   (1.3) so:::: (0.8) i don't think i should

6 R: alright then

7 S: yep

8 R: okay

9 S: thanks

10 R: thank you bye bye

Example 1:5

1   R: . . . takes place up at the university this saturday from seven

2   o'clock in the morning til about ten thirty

3   S: yeah sure

The refusal (Example 1:4) is longer, more round-about and hedged, and contains many more details than the granting (Example 1:5). The differences between the refusal and the granting reflect a general pattern. Silence before the turn begins, periods of silence (unfilled pauses) within the turn, 'uuhs' (filled pauses), the presence of excuses and apologies, the use of hedges ('i i don't think'), and the tendency to push the critical action (in this case, refusal) back later into the turn are typically present when a speaker refuses a request, turns down an invitation, disagrees with the prior speaker, rejects advice, admits blame, and fails to answer a question as expected. Moreover, these details are usually absent when speakers grant a request, accept an invitation, take advice, deny blame, and answer a question as expected (Levinson, 1983; Pomerantz, 1984; Sacks, 1992). Obviously, in response to a request someone could, and on occasion people do, say clearly and without hesitation 'No'; that is, a refusal can have the structure of a typical granting. That refusals typically do not have this structure while grantings do suggests that these details are important and that they fulfil some function.

The important point is that these details of talk are orderly, they are regularities of talk. Because such details are regular, it is extremely unlikely that they are irrelevant to how participants accomplish and interpret actions. Furthermore, although people have strong intuitions about how actions are performed, intuitions do not match the actual structure of action in talk. For example, intuitions about refusals typically fail to contain a turn initial pause, a turn initial 'well' or 'oh', 'ums' and 'ahs', interpolated pauses, and elements such as 'I think' or 'possibly' that weaken the refusal (Turnbull, 2001). If theories of talk are going to be advanced, it is important that those theories account for the actual structure of talk. Since people's intuitions about talk do not accurately reflect what real talk is like, the data used in the study of talk must consist of or be based on examples of natural talk and detailed transcriptions of such talk. Due to ethical concerns, it is often difficult to collect natural, everyday talk, and it takes a great deal of time to transcribe such talk. It is much easier to use talk that is made up, recalled, or taken from novels, plays, or movies. Nevertheless, the easy way out must be avoided. In sum, models or theories of talk must be based on recordings of natural talk, and on transcriptions of those recordings. Further, the transcriptions must capture the detailed structures of talk. It is for these reasons that the transcription system is so detailed and, as a result, why transcribing is such a labour-intensive activity.

Standards against which claims about talk are assessed

The critical analysis of talk presented in this book is, of course, based on logical argument. Any claim made about talk is backed up in two additional ways. First, every claim is supported by an example(s) from natural talk in English which illustrates that claim. These examples are drawn from a corpus of tape- or disk-recordings of telephone and face-to-face talk collected in British Columbia by the author and his students over the past twelve years. In all cases the persons recorded gave their permission to be recorded and to have their talk used in research, with the condition that their names be changed to guarantee anonymity. Typically, talk was collected by giving participants a tape or disk recorder and asking them to record occasions on which they would normally talk with others. Most of the recordings ended up being made during or after mealtimes, and at parties, school, work and while playing (usually only when children were participants).

The second way in which the claims made in this book are supported is by reference to participants' meaning. In particular, when examples are used, an attempt is made to support the claim at issue by reference to the meanings of the talk for the participants in the talk. For illustration, imagine the analyst claims that utterances with the form of an interrogative can be used to do the action of inviting, and the following example is presented in support.

Example 1:6

(telephone talk)

1   H: interested in goin' to a wine tasting october twelvth↑

2   D: love to but we're away that weekend

3   H: that's too bad (.) maybe next time

H's first turn has the form and intonation pattern of a question; in particular, it is the yes/no question (revised for grammaticality and spelling) 'Are you interested in going to a wine tasting on October the twelfth?' If H and D treat it as that question, then D should answer 'yes' or 'no'. In fact, D responds with a truncated form of 'I would (or 'we would') love to go to a wine tasting on October 12', following which D gives what looks like an explanation for why he/we cannot go. D has treated H's line 1 utterance as an invitation, and D has turned down that invitation and given a reason for doing so. Support for this interpretation is provided also by H's next turn in which H expresses regret that D cannot accept the invitation and proposes that an invitation can be accepted at some other time.

As can be seen in the analysis of Example 1:6, what makes possible the determination of participants' meaning is that the speaker displays in every turn at talk how she treated the prior turn. Hutchby and Wooffitt (1998) refer to this way of determining participants' meaning as the 'next-turn proof procedure', a procedure used throughout this book. It is important to note that using the next-turn proof procedure allows for the determination of participants' meaning without requiring that participants explicitly name the actions they are performing. For example, H does not say explicitly that he/she is extending an invitation, nor does D say explicitly that he/she is turning down that invitation. Rather, D responds to H in a way that displays that D *treats* H's utterance as an invitation (i.e., by thanking H for inviting D and by giving a reason why D cannot accept the invitation), and H responds in a way that displays that H treats D's utterance as a rejection of the invitation. In other words, evidence for claims about participants' meaning is based on observation of the way participants manifestly treat utterances in sequence.

TWO CONCEPTIONS OF TALK: COGNITIVE AND SOCIAL PRAGMATIC

Cognitive Model of Talk

The dominant psychological conception of talk, the cognitive model, is based on central tenets of Noam Chomsky's model of language combined with the perspective of cognitive psychology. The central assumption of the cognitive model is that talk is spoken language, a perspective that is so widely accepted that it tends to be treated as the truth rather than a set of assumptions. An alternative conception of talk is based on the assumption that talk is social interaction. The arguments to be presented in this book lead to the conclusion that a social pragmatic view of talk-as-social-interaction is the more appropriate model of talk. However, in order to develop that argument, it will be useful to first describe in some detail the cognitive model of talk-as-spoken-language that continues to dominate conceptions of talk.

Cognitive Model: Talk-as-Spoken-Language

Chomsky's model of language

One strand of the talk-as-spoken-language view derives from the influential model of language described initially by Chomsky (1957, 1965, 1968). Chomsky based his views on two abilities of competent speakers; namely, that every competent speaker of a human language can produce and understand a potentially infinite number of sentences – the ability to be linguistically *creative*; and judge whether a sentence is a possible sentence in the language, and judge whether a sound combination is a possible sound combination in that language – the ability to have appropriate *linguistic intuitions*. Importantly speakers can make these judgments on sentences and sound combinations they have never encountered before.

Chomsky's answer to the question of how it is possible for people to do the above is that speakers must know a finite set of rules and a finite set of elements, and they must be able to recursively apply the rules to the elements to produce a potentially infinite set of sentences. As an analogy, think of how it is possible to play a game of chess when each game is different from any other game you have ever played. Your ability to play chess is not based entirely on remembering certain games and repeating what you remember. Following Chomsky, the only explanation of your ability to play chess is that you must know the rules of chess and you must be able to apply those rules on specific occasions. Depending on the placement of the chessmen on the board, your options of what to do are determined by the application of the rules to that specific placement of chessmen on the board.

In sum, on Chomsky's view, knowing a natural language is equivalent to knowing a system of rules and their appropriate application. The knowledge speakers must possess is referred to as linguistic competence. A grammar (e.g., a transformational grammar like that of Chomsky) describes the elements and rules that constitute a natural language; that is, a grammar is a description of linguistic competence (for a dissenting view see Baker & Hacker, 1984; Robinson, 1975).

Relation between linguistic competence and linguistic performances

Writing and speaking are linguistic performances that, according to Chomsky, are based on the underlying linguistic competence. Writers and speakers sometimes make mistakes, perhaps due to distractions, slips of the tongue, carelessness or whatever. Thus, linguistic performance is an imperfect reflection of linguistic competence. The competence–performance distinction is highly compatible with the cognitive psychological perspective on human functioning.

Cognitive Psychology

The common, everyday conception of behaviour is that mental phenomena such as beliefs, values, goals, plans, intentions, etc., are the causes of overt behaviour. Mental phenomena, however, are not directly observable, which poses a problem for the empirical study of mental life. Eventually, a cognitive psychology emerged with a set of assumptions and an associated methodology that allowed for the empirical study of mental life (Neisser, 1967). Briefly, the cognitive model is as follows: an external or internally-generated stimulus elicits neural activity in the organism's central nervous system; this neural activity triggers certain mental states consisting of mental representations and mental processes; the mental processes act on the mental representations, thereby transforming them in some way; finally, the organism responds either overtly or covertly. In sum, the essence of the cognitive model is that thinking (cognition) consists of the processing of a stimulus by mental processes acting on mental representations such that the mental representations are transformed (changed) in some principled, orderly and lawful way.

The transformation by mental processes of mental representations is the main assumption of the cognitive model, and thus it is necessary to clarify the concepts of 'mental process' and 'mental representation'. A representation is something that stands for something else, and a good representation is one that mirrors objective reality. For example, representations of you include your photograph, your portrait, a written description and a verbal description. What is assumed in the cognitive model is that the world is represented not only in directly observable ways (as in the above examples of representations of you), but is represented also symbolically inside people's heads (as, for example, a friend's mental image of you or her beliefs about you). These 'inside the head' symbolic representations are what is meant by the concept of 'mental representation'. Just as with a directly observable representation, a good mental representation is one that mirrors reality.

A representation, directly observable or mental, must be acted upon in order to be of use. Persons use directly observable representations to accomplish certain tasks. For example, if I want you to know what my friend Richard looks like, I could show you his photograph. To attain the goal of getting you to know what Richard looks like, I applied the observable action/process of 'showing' you the photographic representation of Richard. After showing you Richard's photograph, if he were to walk into the room you probably would recognize him. According to the cognitive model you are able do this because, given the photograph of Richard, you stored a mental representation/image of Richard in your brain. When Richard entered the room, you looked at him and compared your present visual experience with your mental image of Richard. When the visual stimuli matched the mental image, you then recognized Richard.

To summarize: when people act in the world, they employ directly observable processes, such as showing Richard's photograph, dividing a pie into six pieces, tracing out a route on a map from Vancouver to Seattle or mixing paint to get a desired colour. The cognitive model assumes that analogous processes are carried out mentally; for example, recognizing Richard may involve storing a mental image of Richard in memory, searching for that image, comparing the image to a present stimulus, and deciding whether or not there is a match between the present stimulus and the image. Other cognitive activities include those involved in doing mental division, following a mental map of the route from Vancouver to Seattle or imagining what colour will result from mixing several colours of paint.

Given this conception of mental representation and mental process, consider a cognitive description of the task of adding the number 18 to the number 24. To carry out this addition you must have a mental representation of the numbers 18 and 24, a mental representation of the whole numbers from 0 to 9, a set of mental processes for doing addition, and you must apply these processes in the correct way to the specific numbers. Once these processes have been applied, a new mental representation results; namely, the number 42. This resultant mental representation can either stay inside your head, or you can express it overtly by, for example, saying 'forty-two', writing the number '42', or placing 42 sticks on the ground.

A second assumption of the cognitive perspective is functionalism, the view that the human organism, including the cognitive systems that are now extant among *Homo sapiens*, has evolved in ways that ensure the organism's survival. Thus, the functions people must perform will influence the kind of cognitive system they possess, and the cognitive system people possess will influence the kinds of functions they can perform. The relevance of the functional perspective for the study of talk is that any cognitive model of talk will have to account for the kinds of use to which talk is put. It will, therefore, be important to examine carefully just what it is that people do with talk, what kinds of function are accomplished in talk.

The third assumption of the cognitive perspective is that experience is subjective (i.e., a phenomenological position). This assumption is a direct implication of the assumptions of information transformation and functionalism. Over a lifetime no two people ever experience the exact same stimuli and, except for identical twins, no two people have the same genetic endowment. Although some mental representations and processes may be innate, most develop as the individual matures. Thus, no two people will share identical mental representations and processes. Since stimuli are transformed by mental processes acting on mental representations, even when two people are exposed to the same stimuli their interpretations of the stimulus will be different. In other words, since experience is an interpretation based on our unique mental representations and mental processes, no two people ever have the identical experience. I refer to the uniqueness of every individual's interpretation of reality as *subjectivity*.

The cognitive perspective also predicts that there will be a great deal of overlap in the interpretations of people who are exposed to the same stimulus. There are two main reasons for this. First, we are all human beings and our nervous systems and our sensory-perceptual systems are identical for all intents and purposes. Second, people from the same culture speaking the same language are likely to have developed similar types of mental representations and mental processes. Given considerable overlap in the neural 'hardware' and in the 'software' that runs on that hardware, similar experiences of a situation should be the norm rather than the exception. When interpretations of reality are highly similar, I refer to this as *intersubjectivity.*

Methodology of cognitive psychology

Cognitive psychologists base their research methodologies on the following argument. The mental work of accessing a representation and acting on it involves neuro-chemical processes in the central nervous system. Because these processes are material (i.e., occur in the physical world), mental work consumes energy and takes time. For example, just as shuffling through a deck of cards looking for the ace of spades takes time, so too does searching through memory for a mental image of the ace of spades. Since mental work takes time, researchers can measure how long it takes for people to do specific mental tasks. In this way reaction time can be used as an observable index of non-observable mental work.

But how, precisely, is reaction time related to non-observable thinking? The assumption is that if Task A requires M mental 'steps' and Task B requires the M steps of Task A plus at least one more, then Task B will take longer to perform than Task A. If people are presented with Tasks A and B and asked to carry them out as quickly as possible, a measure of how quickly they do the tasks, their reaction time, can be used as a measure of the mental work performed. With modern technology very small units of time can be measured with extreme accuracy and, accordingly, reaction time is the major dependent variable in cognitive psychological research. Another implication of the view that mental work is analogous to physical work is that the more processes one has to perform to complete a task, the more likely one is to make an error. Number of errors (error rate) is, therefore, the other major dependent measure in cognitive psychology. (On simple mental tasks, in order to increase the error rate so that it is more easily observable, researchers often stress subjects, perhaps by rushing them along or distracting them in some way.) Type of error is also used as a dependent variable on the assumption that the more similar two mental representations or mental processes are, the more likely a person is to confuse one with the other.

When the cognitive approach is applied in developmental and social psychology, or in disciplines other than psychology, typically the major dependent variable is language (actually, writing or speaking). The rationale for using language in this way is that in many situations people overtly present the output or results of their mental processing by writing or speaking. For example, if I were interested in gender differences in autobiographical memory, I might ask male and female members of long-term intimate relationships to tell me all they can recall about their first date. Differences in what males and females said would then be used as a measure of gender differences in the mental representations and/or processes that underlie memory for autobiographical events. Or, if I wanted to know how the experience of a near miss or close call affected you, I might expose you to a near miss and then ask you to write out a description of how you feel or ask you to complete a set of self-report scales on which you report your feelings. And if I wanted to know if you had acquired the concept of transitivity, I might show you three sticks, A, B, and C; show you that A is longer than B; show you that B is longer than C; and then ask you whether or not A is longer than C. In these examples, language (writing and speaking) was employed as an observable indicator of mental life.

It must be stressed that most psychologists who adopt the cognitive model have no real interest in reaction times, error rates, types of error, writing or speech. The important assumption that underlies all research based on the cognitive model is that these observable behaviours are direct causal consequences of non-observable cognition. Thus, reaction times, error rates, types of error and spoken or written language are of interest *only* because they are observable manifestations of important mental processes that cannot be observed directly. The inference from such observable responses to covert mental states lies at the heart of cognitive analyses.

Cognitive model of talk

Combining Chomsky's competence–performance theory of language with the cognitive perspective results in the following cognitive model of talk: Talk consists of spoken language or speech. Talk (spoken language) is the overt manifestation of covert thought. Thought is the manipulation of symbolic representations. Persons use a linguistic grammar (i.e., linguistic competence) to transform their thoughts into words. Words can be expressed internally (i.e., private speech) or can be expressed externally in writing, speaking or sign language. In each case, a linguistic performance occurs.

There are three major implications of these assumptions for a model of talk. Thoughts contain information and information is useful to persons. But thoughts cannot be observed directly by others and, thus, the function of language is to put thoughts into a form that can then be overtly expressed and observed. Accordingly, the first implication is that the function of talk is to convey information. The second implication is that a model of language is mainly a model of linguistic competence. The cognitive psychologist focuses on mental objects and mental processes involved in the transformation of thoughts into language. Those mental objects and processes constitute linguistic competence. As empiricists, however, cognitive psychologists need observable evidence to support claims about non-observable linguistic competence. Since linguistic performance is an observable though imperfect expression of linguistic competence, talk is important only to the extent that it reveals thought and/or linguistic competence. The third implication is that talk is an activity of an individual person. In order for talk to convey information, someone has to hear it. But both the production of talk and the understanding of talk are activities that occur in the minds and bodies of individual persons.

Social Pragmatic Model: Talk-as-Social-Interaction

An alternative to the cognitive model treats talk as a form of social interaction. A particular view of talk-as-social-interaction, the *social pragmatic* model, is developed in this book. As you proceed through the book, it will be useful to have some familiarity with the social pragmatic view.

According to the social pragmatic view, talk is a form of social interaction. The words used in talk do not primarily reflect thought; rather, people together create talk by uttering and responding to words. As participants in talk co-construct (construct together) their interaction by using words, they also co-construct images of themselves, the other, their relationship, and their culture; that is, participants in talk co-construct their personal, social, and cultural worlds. This is the social aspect of the social pragmatic perspective. The pragmatic aspect is the claim that people do things together when they talk; for example, they ask for or give directions, they accuse or excuse, they request or refuse. I next very briefly consider each of these assumptions of the social pragmatic conception of talk in more detail.

Talk and the coordination of human interaction

Across all cultures, people typically talk to one another in face-to-face visual contact as they work together on tasks such as repairing a plough, building a wall, or deciding where to eat dinner. To accomplish such tasks, people need to coordinate their activities so that one person's actions dovetail with those of the others. People can coordinate their actions without talking to one another, but coordination is facilitated by talk. Indeed, talk is the major way through which humans coordinate social life; that is, talk is a practical activity used mainly so that two or more people can coordinate their activities. The practical, pragmatic orientation of talk has implications for the requirement of intersubjectivity. In particular, all that matters is that there is intersubjectivity for all practical purposes.

The basic unit of talk is the turn: speaker A responds to speaker B's previous turn, B responds to A's turn, and so on. In turns and sequences of turns, participants accomplish actions together. For example, A may do the act of inviting B to dinner, and B may respond by accepting the invitation, turning it down, or trying to negotiate a different time. Not only does B respond to A's prior action with, for example, an acceptance, but in so doing B affirms that A's action was interpreted as an invitation. Thus, both A and B are involved in the doing of an invitation by A; that is, A's invitation is co-constructed by A and B. In sum, speakers primarily use words not to reflect their thoughts but rather to accomplish actions and to dovetail their own actions with those of the partner. Words are constitutive of talk; that is, by using words (and other devices) speakers together create talk.

Interaction and talk require that each participant coordinate his/her own actions with those of another. Accordingly, the individually-oriented, intrapersonal, cognitive model of talk needs to be replaced by a model of talk as a co-constructed, interpersonal, and dialectic process. Recognizing that talk is interaction has additional implications for psychological models. Certain criteria must be met in order for interaction to occur; for example, each participant in an interaction must be responsive to the prior contribution of the other. An important consequence is that interaction must unfold in a sequential, turn-by-turn manner. If A and B make their contributions concurrently rather than sequentially, there is no possibility of them being responsive to one another. To be responsive, A must wait for B to finish his contribution and *then* A can make her own contribution; that is, talk can only be constructed sequentially. The structure of talk is in large measure determined by the requirements for interaction, rather than by the nature of our cognitive systems.

Comparison of Cognitive and Social Pragmatic Perspectives

Thought, word and action

Cognitive: talk is the verbal expression of thought; the purpose of talk is to convey information; this is accomplished through the use of language.

Social pragmatic: people do things with words; words/language are constitutive of talk; people coordinate their actions in talk.

Processes by which talk occurs

Cognitive: talk is the product of mental processes located in individual brains; talk is an intrapersonal process.

Social pragmatic: talk is a co-constructed, interpersonal, dialectic process; talk is the most common form of human interaction.

Structure of cognition or structure of interaction

Cognitive: the structure of cognition determines the structure of talk, but is not influenced by talk; the structure of talk is merely a reflection of cognition.

Social pragmatic: the structure of talk influences the structure of cognition, and vice-versa; the structure of talk is not a direct reflection of cognition but rather is determined by the criteria that must be met in order for interaction to occur.

Overview of the Book

Chapter 2 focuses on the most prevalent model of talk, the Code Model. The Code Model conceptualizes talk as the use of language to encode thoughts; specifically, speakers encode their thoughts into words/language and addressees decode thoughts out of words/language. The model is applied successfully to infra-human communication. Serious deficiencies of the Code Model as a model of talk are detailed. Chapter 3 considers Speech Act Theory, an approach that emphasizes the actions speakers accomplish in talk. It is argued that Speech Act Theory appropriately focuses on action rather than information/thoughts. However, examples from natural talk are used to reveal serious deficiencies of Speech Act Theory accounts. Chapter 4 presents the philosopher Paul Grice's theory of non-natural meaning and his related claims about the Cooperative Principle that underlies all human interaction. Based on this discussion, an Inferential Model of talk is outlined, a model that has a strong action/pragmatic emphasis. One important problem with the Inferential Model is that the role of talk in the creation of personal, social and cultural identity is ignored. Chapter 5 begins to explore this social aspect of talk through a consideration of Brown and Levinson's (1987) model of politeness. Examples are used to illustrate how participants in talk use many of the orderly structures of talk to orient to the interpersonal dimension. Several revisions of and extensions to the Brown and Levinson model are considered. Chapter 6 presents a discussion of Conversation Analysis and, in so doing, identifies important structures of talk and the orderly practices participants employ both to produce and interpret talk. Both the positive aspects and the deficiencies of Conversation Analysis for a model of talk are discussed and illustrated. In Chapter 7 the various strands in the discussion of an appropriate model of talk are pulled together, and a social pragmatic model is proposed. An appropriate methodology for social pragmatics is described. To illustrate the nature and advantages of the social pragmatic approach to research on talk/social interaction, three examples of social pragmatic research are described in detail. The chapter ends with a discussion of the positive aspects and the deficiencies of social pragmatics. Chapter 8 presents a summary of the models reviewed. Following this summary, I explore some implications of social pragmatics for psychological models of social interaction, meaning, minds and persons.

Throughout the book the terms 'Speaker' and 'Addressee' (for brevity, S and A) are used repeatedly. If participants in an example identify their gender, I use the appropriate pronouns (e.g., he or she, his or hers) when referring to them. Otherwise, in the interests of both the nonsexist use of language and parsimony, I refer to the Speaker as 'she' and the Addressee as 'he'.

2

The Code Model

Overview

Code Models are based on the assumption that talk is a means by which people convey their thoughts to one another. The essential claims of Code Models of talk are: (1) talk involves the encoding of thoughts into words/language by the speaker and the decoding of thoughts from words/language by the hearer; and (2) the encoding of thoughts to words and the decoding of thoughts from words is a one-to-one relationship (i.e., there is a unique encoding for each thought and a unique decoding for each word/set of words.) The Code Model was derived from the General Comunications Model, a model of the transfer of information that was developed by engineers interested in machine communication. Accordingly, the chapter begins with a brief description of the General Communication Model, and then proceeds to describe the Code Model in detail. The Code Model is applied to communication in infra-human species; in particular, I discuss research by von Frisch on the 'language' of bees. Following this, aspects of talk are described that seem to be accounted for by the Code Model. The chapter ends with a discussion of deficiencies of the Code Model as a model of talk. Both the pros and cons of the Code Model are illustrated with examples from natural talk.

THE GENERAL COMMUNICATION MODEL

The first formal depiction of a general model of communication came not from psychology but from engineering. In the 1930s, systems of communication were developing at a rapid rate and engineers needed to understand the nature of communication to improve on these systems. Two electrical engineers, Shannon and Weaver (1949), proposed a model of communication which they referred to as the General Communication Model. The proposed model was 'general' in the sense that Shannon and Weaver claimed it applied to any system of communication, whether it be a biological system or a system that is an artefact of human technology. The General Communication Model has the following components and properties. There is a Source, and the Source has a Message to send. The Message corresponds to the information that is to be transmitted or sent. The Message is encoded into some format that can be transmitted. Once encoded, the Message is now a Signal. The Signal is transmitted across some Channel. The Channel can be influenced by Noise which consists of signals other than the one being sent from the Source. The Signal is received at some Destination. Depending on the Noise in the Channel, the Signal sent may or may not be identical to the Signal received. At the Destination the received Signal is decoded and a Message is received.

Consider an example of the Code Model in action. In the typical 1950s western movie a telegraph clerk is sitting before a telegraph machine in a railway station. In Morse Code the clerk is tapping out 'Outlaws are coming to town at noon – get out'. The thoughts that correspond to this warning, the Message, have to be sent to the sheriff in the next town. The Message is encoded into Morse Code, a code in which each letter of the alphabet is associated with some unique combination of dots and dashes. When the Message in Morse Code is tapped out on the telegraph, the Message becomes a Signal. That Signal is a series of electrical impulses. The electrical impulses are transmitted along a telegraph wire, which is the Channel. At the other end of the Channel sits sheriff John Wayne, the Destination. John also has a telegraph machine and a Signal is received at that machine. The Signal consists of a series of clicks corresponding to the dots and dashes of Morse Code. With his understanding of Morse Code, John is able to decode the Signal and receive a Message: 'Outlaws are coming to town at noon – get out'. Being John Wayne, he does not leave, but instead prepares to face the bad guys in a showdown to the death. Of course, John has a quirky old sidekick, a fallen woman who secretly loves him, and a virginal and beautiful girl who will become his wife. The plot thickens . . .

Various themes that relate to the General Communication Model can be played out in such movies. Perhaps the outlaws know that the telegraph clerk intends to send a warning to the sheriff. They prevent this by killing the clerk, possibly before he can send his warning, or, better still, in the middle of his warning 'Bad guys ar–'. Alternatively, knowing that a warning is or will be sent, the outlaws cut the telegraph wires or destroy the telegraph machine in the sheriff's office. In these scenarios, either the Message is not encoded in its entirety into a Signal or the Signal is not received in its entirety at the Destination. If there is no Signal received at the Destination, then no Message can be decoded from it. If the received Signal is damaged or incomplete in some way, then the decoded Message will not correspond to the Message sent. If the sheriff does not have a telegraph machine compatible with the machine used to encode the Message into a Signal or if there is no one around who is sufficiently fluent in Morse Code to decode the received Signal, then the sheriff will not get the warning. In all these cases the communication between the telegraph clerk and the sheriff has been either completely prevented or severely impaired.

In sum, according to Shannon and Weaver's General Communication Model, what is communicated is a message which consists of information; the message/information gets encoded or transformed in a variety of ways into a signal; the signal is transmitted across some channel; the signal is received at the destination;

various aspects of the environment can interfere with the transmission of the signal so that the signal that is sent and the signal that is received may or may not be the same; the received signal is decoded; and if everything works out, the message/ information that was sent is the message/information that is received. When the General Communication Model is applied to communication among organisms (as opposed to communication among machines), the resulting model is referred to as the Code Model.

The Code Model of Infra-Human Communication: Communication in Bees

The Code Model is a General Communication Model. Thus, according to this view, in order to communicate organisms need: (1) some device by which to encode their 'thoughts' into a form that makes a change in some perceptible modality in their environment; and (2) some device that can perceive such changes and decode 'thoughts' out of those changes. For humans, the typical perceptible modality of communication is sound; that is, thoughts are encoded into speech, into a series of changes in sound to which the human system is sensitive. Other organisms use different perceptible modalities to communicate, including visual, tactile, olfactory, or electrical modalities, or different ranges within those modalities (whales and dolphins, for example, use certain sounds that are beyond the perceptible range for the human auditory system).

One system of infra-human communication that has been studied extensively that seems very much to fit with the Code Model is that of the European honeybee.

Communication in the European honeybee

Innovative research on communication of European honeybees was carried out by the biologist von Frisch (1966). Briefly, von Frisch observed that on days with little cloud cover, worker bees leave the hive and fly off in all directions, apparently searching for a source of food. When a bee locates a source of food, it samples the food and then flies back to the hive. Once inside the hive, the bee performs one of two types of 'dance' on the honeycomb. In the round dance, the bee goes round and round in a circle. As the bee does this, other bees gather as an audience. The faster the worker bee dances, the more worker bees gather to watch. The 'audience' of bees also touches the dancing bee and experiences the smell of a sample of the food source. After watching for some time, the other worker bees start to leave the hive and they fly to the food source. Careful observation and experimentation revealed that the round dance communicates that there is a food source within ten metres of the hive. The direction in which the food source is located is not communicated by the round dance. However, given that a circle with only a ten metre diameter needs to be searched, bees can detect the source by sight and possibly also by olfaction. The scent of the food sample also communicates the type of food source.

The second type of dance, the tail-wagging dance, communicates distance and direction of the food source. The dancing bee performs a figure eight pattern in which it travels up a straight line then loops in a circle to the left, back up the straight section again, around on a loop to the right, and so on. The time taken to traverse the straight line segment communicates the distance from the hive of the food source. The direction of the food source is determined by the angle of the straight-line portion. When the straight line segment is oriented vertically on the honeycomb, the food source is located in a straight line to the sun. Deviation from the vertical, measured in degrees either right or left of the vertical, corresponds to deviation from a straight line to the sun. So, for example, if the straight line portion is 33° to the right, the food source is 33° to the right of a straight line to the sun.

The Code Model provides a good account of communication among bees. Consider, in this regard, communication and the tail-wagging dance. A foraging bee locates a source of food and translates or encodes relevant stimuli – the quality of the food source, its direction from the hive relative to the sun, its distance from the hive – into a mental representation or message. That message/representation is then overtly displayed or turned into a signal, not by the bee talking or drawing a diagram, but by performing some physical motions in space. The other bees have identical encoding and decoding devices. Thus, when witnessing the dance, bees decode information about the food source and its location from the physical display. In brief, 'dancing' in honeybees is a classic instance of a code model of communication: a foraging bee encodes information and sends it over a channel, which in this case is a visual channel; other bees then receive that visual signal and decode the information back out of the signal; given no interference with the channel or the encoding/decoding devices of the bees, communication is successful.

There is no reason to believe that bees learn to communicate in this way. Bees do not live long enough to learn much at all, and their ability to communicate seems to be something that is innate. One important piece of evidence that the bee communication system is innate is that bees of different species cannot communicate with one another; colloquially, different bee species have different 'languages', their encoding/decoding devices are different. Additional evidence comes from studies in which European honeybees were cross-bred with Italian honeybees. The offspring of this cross-breeding looked either like the mother or the father bee and, importantly, the physical appearance of an offspring corresponded to the type of code that it used.

The case of the honeybee seems to fit the Code Model absolutely perfectly, as does the evidence about systems of communication of many other organisms. Typically, communication systems are more likely to be found in social organisms. To survive, organisms that live together in groups must coordinate their activities. A system of communication is a very useful means of coordinating activity. Systems of communication may, therefore, have evolved primarily as mechanisms for the coordination of activity, as a solution to problems of coordination. (Interesting analyses of human coordination problems may be found in Lewis (1969) and

Schelling (1960)). Accordingly, it may be advisable to retain some doubt about the assumption of the Code Model that the primary goal of communication is the transfer of information. Before considering that possibility, I next consider the Code Model as a model of human talk.

The Code Model of Talk

The model consists of several related claims: that people converse in order to communicate; that communication primarily involves the transfer of information from speaker to addressee; that information consists of speakers' thoughts; that conversation consists of people using language; that language is a code that associates sounds to thoughts in a one-to-one relationship; and that a speaker's thoughts are encoded into language, the language is spoken, and the hearer gets information (speaker's thoughts) back out of the words by decoding thoughts from the words. In brief, the essential assumptions of Code Models of talk are: (1) that natural languages are codes which associate sounds to thoughts in a one-to-one relationship; and (2) that conversation consists of the encoding of thoughts (information) into language by the speaker and the decoding of thought from language by the hearer.

Consider how the model may be a description of human talk. In the basic case, talk involves two people who take alternative turns at being a Speaker and an Addressee. (I refer to Speaker and Addressee, not Speaker and Hearer, because Speakers direct their talk to specific persons, even though someone else might listen in or overhear.) The Speaker, the *source*, has some thoughts, the *message*, that she wants to convey to the Addressee. In accordance with the standard cognitive view, as discussed in Chapter 1, thoughts are conceptualized as a-linguistic, symbolic representations. Through use of a linguistic device, typically conceptualized as some sort of grammar, the Speaker encodes her thoughts into words and then utters these words, thereby transforming her signal into a *signal*.

The production and reception of words is a very complicated business, but in brief what is involved is expelling air, using lips, tongue, vocal cords, and so on to produce sounds. In the normal case of talk, the sounds that are produced compact molecules of air or they spread them out, and these waves of compacted and spread out air molecules travel across a *channel* of air. The *receiver*, in the case of human oral conversation, consists of several interrelated systems beginning with the ear drum. The wave of air molecules that arrives at the receiver hits the receiver's ear drum, causing that membrane to move back and forth. The ear drum is attached to a series of three small bones, the malleus (hammer), incus (anvil) and stapes (stirrup). The stapes, which is last (i.e., furthest from the eardrum) in this series of three bones, is attached to a membrane called the oval window. The oval window seals off the end of a tube, the cochlea, that is filled with liquid. Movement back and forth of the stapes on the oval window sets up waves in this liquid. Running the length of the cochlea is a membrane, the basilar membrane, above and below which are hair cells. The hair cells are auditory receptors. Waves in the liquid in the cochlea produce waves in the basilar membrane. Movement of the basilar membrane bends the hair cells, thereby firing auditory neurons. These neurons are connected to the auditory nerve, which has projections to the brain. The final result is the subjective experience of hearing a sound.

This complicated series of events that was initiated by the uttering of some words by the Speaker finally produces a flow of electrical energy to the brain of the receiver, and this neural event constitutes the *received signal*. Given that the process proceeds correctly, the received signal will correspond to the signal sent by the Speaker; that is, the Addressee has the experience of hearing the words the Speaker produced. The next and final step of the communication process involves the decoding of the received signal into a *received message*. This process is accomplished by the Addressee using his linguistic device to decode thoughts from words. If the whole process proceeds correctly, the Addressee understands what the Speaker has said, what thoughts the Speaker tried to convey.

Why the Code Model is so popular as a model of talk

The Code Model is a cognitive model and, at present, the dominant perspective in psychology is the cognitive perspective. The Code Model fits very well with the cognitive perspective and this is probably the major reason why the Code Model is so popular as a model of talk. Essential to the cognitive view are the assumptions that meanings are stored 'inside the head' of individuals and that this information must be transformed in order to be communicated. Talk, according to a Code Model, consists of many transformations of inside-the-head information – from speaker's thoughts to words, to sounds, to movements of a membrane (eardrum), to movement of bones, to a wave moving through a liquid, to movement of hairs at a particular location in a tube of liquid, to electrical activity in neurons, and to thoughts. Further, this type of communication should be successful since, according to most theorists, all members of the species *Homo sapiens* have identical (for all practical purposes) encoder–decoder linguistic devices, identical perceptual and neural systems, and live in the same type of physical environment (where, for example, there is air which is necessary for the system to operate since sound cannot travel through a vacuum).

An important assumption of the Code Model, and of the cognitive model of language, is that thoughts do not travel from head to head. After all, if people could project their thoughts, there would be no reason for them to speak. Thus, according to the Code Model, since people cannot project their thoughts, in order to communicate they must transform their thoughts into a form that makes a perceptible difference in the environment of the addressee; that is, into a form that is overt and noticeable to the addressee. The relevance of this claim is that the Code Model is not restricted to oral encoding: any medium of encoding that *can* be perceived by the communicating organisms will do. Because of this, proponents of the Code Model believe that it has wide applicability. It accounts for human oral communication; communication via sign language by the deaf or mute, who encode their thoughts into a visual signal according to the conventions of American Sign Language (or other sign languages); communication between sailors in passing ships who can encode their thoughts into sets of flags or hand signals (semaphore); and communication between writer and reader as they encode thoughts into marks on paper or electrons on a computer screen and decode these marks into thoughts. In all these cases the encoding/decoding device acts on a transformation of what was originally some set of auditory or visually perceptible stimuli, and in all cases the communication system fits with the Code Model.

(It is interesting to speculate why sound became the medium of human language. A number of theorists have suggested that sound is a particularly useful medium because it leaves one's hands free to do other things and because sound can be perceived in the absence of visual contact.)

Code Model accounts of intersubjectivity and subjectivity

As noted in Chapter 1, all models of talk must account both for intersubjectivity and subjectivity; that is, they must account both for shared understanding and for breakdowns in shared understanding. The Code Model readily accounts for intersubjectivity. Given that Speaker and Addressee share encoding/decoding devices, and given the typical circumstances of talk (e.g., the Addressee can hear what the Speaker says), in general the signal that is sent will be the signal that is received. Furthermore, since there is a one-to-one relationship between thoughts and message, intersubjectivity should be the norm; that is, Addressees should typically decode the information that the Speaker encoded into the signal.

Although shared understanding is most common in talk, various types of problems of shared understanding (i.e., understanding 'errors') do sometimes occur. As will be seen, when such errors occur, they are often oriented to and, by various means, corrected or repaired. The term 'repairable' is used to refer to such errors and the term 'repair' is used to refer to sequences in talk in which participants negotiate the correction of such errors. The Code Model of talk has an account of certain types of repairables, including problems such as S's mispronunciation, incorrect word choice, difficulty in 'finding' a word, inability to produce/understand an appropriate word because it is not part of S's or A's vocabulary; and A's failure to hear a word correctly, to decode a word correctly, or to know what a word means. To account for such repairables, Code Model theorists point to problems in the environment in which talk occurs and to imperfections in the encoding/decoding system.

An example of an environmental factor that could lead to a misunderstanding is background noise. For example, if a train were to go roaring by just as my wife spoke to me, I might mishear what she said, or not hear some or all of it. In the former case, the signal decoded would not be identical to the signal sent. In the latter case I might try to guess at the missing words, and my guessing could be wrong. Examples of Code Model accounts of problems of understanding due to encoding–decoding include mispronunciations due to errors in the process of going from the mental representation of the sound of a word to actual production of the word; incorrect word choice or incorrect decoding of a word due to errors in 'looking up' the word in the 'mental dictionary'; and vocabulary problems, for both S and A, due to the absence of a word in the mental dictionary. Further, although rare, neurological abnormalities in the brain due to genetics, trauma, or drugs can lead to oddities of linguistic encoding or decoding, as is seen in various types of aphasias.

The next section of the chapter presents examples of repair sequences in natural talk that are consistent with Code Model accounts.

Examples of repairs that are consistent with the Code Model

(In all examples in this book, unless the participants in an example of talk have been identified by the transcriber in some particular way, for simplicity the first participant in each segment of talk is referred to as S(peaker) and the other as A(ddressee).) Example 2:1 illustrates a case in which S corrects his/her own inappropriate word choice.

Example 2:1

1 S: (.) hhh um but i said well i w- i i i w- would not volunteer

2   because . . .

S starts to say 'will' ('w-i i i w-') and then self-corrects with 'would'.

In the next example, S corrects his/her own mispronunciation.

Example 2:2

1 S: well i didn't know what you [wanted you have a spatic]

2 A: [yeah, right]

3 S: you have a particular order for these things=

In line 1 S produces the non-word 'spatic'. Following A's line 2 overlap, S continues in line 3 by self-repairing 'you have a spatic' to 'you have a particular' (i.e., 'spatic' becomes 'particular').

Whereas the previous two examples are of self-repair, in the next example the repair is made by the other participant.

Example 2:3

1 S: (.) hh you can tell the difference because this still has if you look

2   at it closely [it's still squared off]=

3 A: [it's <u>blocked</u>]

4 S: =<u>blocked</u>=

5 A: yes it is

In line 3, A overlaps with S's prior 'it's still squared off' and, with emphasis, makes the correction 'it's <u>blocked</u>'. In line 4 S repeats the repair, and A confirms the repair in line 5. Apparently, S had produced an incorrect term 'squared off' for something for which the term 'blocked' is the correct technical term.

In Example 2:4, the repair arises when A fails to hear all of what S has said.

Example 2:4

1 S: but <u>the:n</u> at the end of it all you know the day after i finish my

2   course it's my birthday

3   (1.6)

4 A: it's your wh<u>a:t</u>↑

5 S: birthday

Following 1.6 seconds of silence (attributable to A), A indicates that he/she has failed to hear all of what S said. In line 5 S makes the repair by repeating 'birthday'.

It is important to note that the above analysis of Example 2:4 is not quite correct. I stated that the repair arises when A indicates that he/she 'has failed to hear all of what S said'. In fact, I do not know that A failed to hear what S had said. The only person who could know that is A. And it is possible that A actually did hear what S had said but, for some reason, acted as though he/she did not hear what S had said. Thus, the appropriate statement about the repair is that A acted in a way that, in this specific case, would be a way of displaying that A did not hear what S had said. Or, briefly stated, A *displayed* that he/she did not hear what S had said. S's response is also consistent with the view that S treated what A had done as a display that A did not hear what S had said.

The advantage of this more conservative description of A's action is that it does not commit the analyst to making any claims about what A actually perceived, thought, believed, imagined, felt, etc. The conservative description is also supported by how S treated what A did. Throughout this book, I try to avoid making assumptions about what speakers meant and, instead, focus on what meanings participants manifestly display in their talk. It will be very useful for the reader to adopt the same approach to the analysis of transcripts.

PROBLEMS WITH THE CODE MODEL AS A MODEL OF TALK

In spite of the wide acceptance of the Code Model, there are many reasons to believe that it is a completely inadequate account of talk. The Code Model cannot account for most cases in which people understand talk, nor for most cases in which people experience problems in understanding talk. Further, the Code Model fails completely to take into account some of the most basic features of talk. The next three sections explore these deficiencies of the Code Model by focusing, respectively, on understanding talk, on failing to understand talk, and on the nature of talk.

Understanding Talk: Achieving Intersubjectivity

The Code Model conceptualizes talk as primarily the transmission and encoding/decoding of information. In the present section I examine three claims about intersubjectivity in talk, all of which contradict the Code Model. In particular, I use examples to demonstrate: (1) that intersubjectivity is not the result of decoding operations, but rather that intersubjectivity is something participants achieve through a process of interpretation; (2) that intersubjectivity involves participants' meaning not sentence or literal meaning; and (3) that participants' meaning is better conceived of not as the conveying of information, but rather as the carrying out of actions.

Interpretation not decoding

When an Addressee understands a Speaker's talk, the Addressee does not do so by decoding the Speaker's thoughts from her words; rather, the Addressee relies on processes of inference.

Consider five examples from natural talk that illustrate the central role of interpretation in understanding talk. In each example, a speaker produces an incomplete utterance which he/she then corrects (repairs) later in the sequence. The addressee, however, overtly displays understanding of the incomplete utterance *before* the speaker self-corrects. This would suggest that the addressee responds to something projected but not said; put colloquially, the addressee responds to what he believes the speaker meant or means to say. Since what someone 'meant/means to say' has not been said, it cannot be decoded but must be inferred/interpreted.

Examples 2:5 through 2:9 are all instances in which a participant acts in a way that displays his/her interpretation about what the other is about to say or meant to say, not what the other actually said.

Example 2:5

1   S: =for the the ehhmmm

2   A: oh of <u>cou:rse</u> [you (.)hhh]

3   S: [the bridal shower]

In line 2, A treats S's incomplete utterance as comprehensible and A proceeds to complete that utterance. However, before A can do so, S interrupts and completes it him/herself.

   In the next example, A in line 4 answers an incomplete question, something A could not do unless he/she were anticipating what S intended to or was about to say.

Example 2:6

1   S: .hh in which case if they a::re you didn't see an paternayen yarn

2   did you down at the:

3   (1.0)

4   A: no: no no [no]

5   S: [the place] you went [to

In the next example, one participant completes the other's incomplete utterance.

Example 2:7

1   S: (.)hh especially as [it]

2   A: [i-]

3   (0.9)

4   S: it oh actually i was going to say especially as it doesn't as it

5   A: has to go to <u>russia</u> but it's only going to toronto

6   S: ya . . .

After producing only a partial utterance in line 1, S continues in line 4 but still fails to produce a complete utterance. In the next line, A completes S's incomplete utterance, and S in line 6 acknowledges and thereby ratifies A's completion.

The next example illustrates a longer sequence over which one participant's incomplete utterance is repaired by the other.

Example 2:8

1   S: and <u>oh</u> <u>oh</u> did you get the: um

2   A: (0.5) no

3   S: express post [envelope for]

4   A: [no no] no

5   S: (0.8) for [uh]

6   A: [no] i didn't but i can get some . . .

In lines 2, 4 and 6, A answers a question that S never completes. Further, A in line 6 also offers to do an action that S might request given that the answer to S's question is 'no'. Thus, A responds not only to what S has said, but also to A's interpretation of what S was trying to accomplish by her utterances. There is no encoding–decoding account of this sequence.

Because an interpretation is an intelligent guess, there is always the possibility that an interpretation is incorrect, as is illustrated next.

Example 2:9

1   S: but i'm gonna do my next projects [on some fine]

2   A: [on linen↑]

3   S: not necessarily linen . . .

In line 2, A in overlap with S completes S's utterance. However, S in the next line manifestly treats A's completion as incorrect.

Speaker and Addressee meaning, not sentence meaning

According to the Code Model, sentences are encoded and decoded. By contrast, as the following fragments of talk illustrate, participants together use sentences/

utterances and other resources of talk to create meaning. Thus, meaning is not 'in' sentences from which it is mechanistically extracted, but rather meaning is achieved (or not) by participants who together use the resources of talk, including 'sentences'.

Example 2:10

(M picks up phone and then calls to her son, Sam)

1　M:　sam↑ john is on the phone

2　S:　okay

The literal or sentence meaning of line 1 is that there is a particular state of the world in which John is on the phone. However, M in line 1 is making an assertion in order to carry out the act of requesting that Sam come to the phone and start talking with John. Sam's line 2 'okay' conveys that he will grant the request: it is not an agreement with a statement about M's assertion. Thus, M and S use language to create meaning and it is the meaning they try to create, not the literal meaning, to which each orients. (Note also that John is not 'on' the phone, though this apparently causes no problems of interpretation for S).

The next example illustrates how something that has no literal meaning, the failure to speak (i.e., silence), is nevertheless interpreted by participants.

Example 2:11

(In the talk leading up to this segment, T claims to have been bitten by a mosquito, but C claims T has been bitten by a spider. They now talk about getting rid of spiders.)

1　C:　spiders are good they're just like bats (.) they get rid of

2　　　mosquitoes

3　　　(3.0)

4　T:　well what's the point of getting rid of mosquitoes if <u>they</u> bite us

5　　　<u>themse::lves</u>

After C's first turn, there is three seconds of silence. Since C had finished his/her turn, the silence is attributable to T. When T does take a turn, it is evident that the silence displays T's disagreement with C's prior claim.

The next example illustrates how participants use and interpret laughter.

Example 2:12

(R and G, an intimate couple, are concluding a somewhat aggressive argument)

1 R: so how are you↑

2 G: good

3 R: i'm stressed too my hands are still breaking out ((sigh)) are we

4   done↑

5 G: i don't know ((laughs)) are we done↑

6 R: ((laughs))

7   ((taping terminated))

In line 6, R uses laughter to agree with G that they have completed the discussion, after which the interaction comes to a close. Laughter may also have been used to realign participants, to re-affirm the positivity of their relationship despite the unpleasantness of the prior interaction.

The next example, which comes from an earlier part of the discussion of the same couple as above, illustrates how a word with the literal meaning of disagree ('no') is used to do an act of agreeing. In this example, then, the act accomplished by a word is opposite to the literal meaning of the word.

Example 2:13

(G has been warning R that they may get into a bad debt situation if R keeps spending too much money)

1 G: . . . i don't wanna slide into a situation where i'm still paying for

2 R: no i don't want you to do that either [i me]an because i don't

3   want to feel that way

4 G: [kay]

In line 2, R responds to G's prior assertion with 'no'. On the basis of literal meaning, R seems to be negating something. However, R then agrees with G's assertion and

G, in overlap, acknowledges R's agreement. Thus, R has used 'no' at a particular moment in talk to agree with G, and that is how both R and G treat R's use of 'no'.

The next example illustrates how a word with a literal meaning of agreement ('yeah') is used to do disagreement.

Example 2:14

1 A: the week after i'm going to stay with ken probably and

2 B: i i don't think i know ken

3 A: yeah you know ken

4 B: who's [ken↑]

5 A: [you've] seen him around

6 B: who is he↑

In line 3, A disagrees that B does not know Ken, and A does so in part by use of the word 'yeah'. As can be seen by the rest of the transcript, both A and B treat A's line 3 turn (that begins with 'yeah') as displaying A's disagreement with B.

Speaker meanings are actions and action sequences

Sentence meaning consists of assertions, interrogatives, or imperatives. Participants' meanings consist of the actions that are accomplished by the production of 'sentences'/utterances, actions such as invite, request, reject, apologize, assert, excuse, etc. The action-orientation of participants in talk is illustrated in Examples 2:15 through 2:19. These examples also illustrate that a turn at talk may consist of one or more utterances, each of which can accomplish one or more actions.

Example 2:17

(from Schegloff, 1984, p. 31)

1 A: why don't you come up and see me some[times↑]

2 B: [i would] like to

In this example A utters what, linguistically, is a question and B responds with an assertion. However, what A and B are doing here is making an invitation and accepting that invitation. It is the action of invitation to which B responds, not the linguistic question. Further, B's response is interpretable to participants and analysts as an acceptance, not a declarative, in part because it is a response to an invitation; and A's initial turn is interpretable as an invitation in part because it is responded to by B with an acceptance. Thus, participants' meanings are actions and action sequences.

In the next example, what the participants orient to are the sequential actions of invitation and rejection.

Example 2:18

(from Pomerantz, 1984, p. 101)

1	C:	uh if you'd care to come and visit a little while this morning i'll
2		give you a cup of coffee
3	D:	hehh well that's awfully sweet of you. i don't think i can make it
4		this morning. .hh i'm running an ad in the paper and and uh I
5		have to stay near the phone

The meaning of actions that participants orient to may be revealed (and sometimes actively negotiated) over a sequence of turns, as is illustrated next.

Example 2:19

1	T:	[(((laughter))] we always used to have butter on everything too
2		even our [(((inaudible))]
3	C:	[you <u>still</u> have butter on everything]
4		(0.8)
5	T:	what↑
6	C:	you do
7	T:	like what↑
8	C:	like all your toast and cereal

C in line 3 utters a declarative sentence, to which T responds with silence and the question 'what↑'. Although there may be uncertainty at this point about what T is doing, it is clear by line 7 that C in line 3 made an accusation that T is challenging, and thus denying.

The next example illustrates the case in which a turn at talk is oriented to as performing several actions.

Example 2:20

(C and T are preparing a meal)

```
1  C:   aren't we gonna get any onions from the garden to put on here

2  T:   oh:::hhh oh:::h you shudda told me that earlier

3       (1.0)

4  C:   well i thought you would think about it
```

C's line 1 linguistic interrogative is treated by both participants as the doing of a request. In line 2, T performs three actions; in particular, T displays that he/she did not realize that C wanted T to get onions from the garden (accomplished by 'oh:::hhh oh:::h'), T refuses the request, and T gives a reason for doing so in the form of an accusation. In lines 3 and 4, C displays recognition that T has done a refusal and C also responds to and rejects T's accusation with an accusation of his/her own.

The final example in this section, Example 2:21, illustrates how participants work together to maintain agreement on the actions that each is performing. This demonstrates participants' orientation to action and to shared understanding of action.

Example 2:21

(M and C are talking about a nightclub that C has been to on several occasions. C has been trying to describe the nightclub to M)

```
1  C:   yeah it's like it's like the orpheum sort of but the same (.) it's

2       very old be:::autiful old building beautiful

3  M:   it is↑

4  C:   like a big chandelier and stuff it's it's more it's not as um fancy

5       as the orpheum (.) but it's that old style of like balcony seating

6       and and then that-

7  M:   oh::::h

8  C:   it's a theatre it's a theatre
```

9 M: oh so it's like sit down seating

10 C: yeah and [there's a small area at the front]

11 M: [oh i didn't realize that at all]

In line 7, M uses 'oh' to display that he/she now understands something not previously understood. C responds to M's turn by confirming M's understanding. In line 9, M also uses 'oh' to carry out a similar action, but in this case M overtly displays what it is that he/she now understands ('so it's like sit down seating'). Again, C in line 10 confirms M's understanding and provides additional information. Overall, C is providing information to M, M is displaying that the information is new and that, as a consequence, M now understands, and C is checking and confirming M's understanding.

Failures to Reach Shared Understanding: Subjectivity in Talk

Earlier in the chapter, examples of repairs were presented that could be interpreted as involving interference with the signal (e.g., due to background noise) and problems in the encoding–decoding system. As noted, such repairs can be accounted for by the Code Model. However, many repairs involve problems of interpretation that cannot be accounted for by the Code Model. There are a variety of repairs of the 'problematic interpretation' sort. One such type arises when S uses a word for which A is unable to find or is unsure about having found the appropriate referent. Other types arise when A believes he has not understood or is not sure that he has understood what S intended to convey by saying what she said; or when S believes A has not understood or S is not sure that A has understood what S intended to convey by saying what she said. In each of these types of repair, the problem is not one of encoding–decoding, but rather is one of interpretation. The following illustrate such repairs.

In Examples 2:22 and 2:23, an addressee has difficulty in identifying the referent of a word or expression used by a prior speaker.

Example 2:22

1 S: so:::::, we'll do that tomorrow

2 A: do what tomorrow↑

3 S: go to seattle

In line 1, S uses the pronoun 'that', and A in line 2 displays a lack of understanding about what 'that' refers to. S in line 3 clarifies that the referent is 'go to seattle'.

Example 2:23

1 S: plus we could probably finish off this last dribble or two

2 A: what (.) the ribena↑

3 S: no this

In line 2, A displays uncertainty about what the referent of 'this last dribble or two' is, and A proposes 'the ribena' as a possible referent. In line 3, S rejects A's proposed referent and points to the correct referent.

In Example 2:24, A cannot identify a person that S has referred to by first name only.

Example 2:24

1 S: i::: got a:: um:: (0.8) ((tongue click)) card today from teesha

2 A: (.)hhh

3 S: byurestrum

4 A: oh byurestrum

After A in line 2 conveys a lack of understanding about who Teesha is, S provides further identification of Teesha by providing a surname. In line 4, A displays a change of state ('oh'), in particular, that A now understands whom S is talking about.

Example 2:25 illustrates how participants display their recognition that problems of understanding are occurring and how they attempt to resolve such problems.

Example 2:25

1 B: where's kristi↑

2 R: at work

3 B: no: last night (1.0) what (.) did she do [last]

4 R: [work]

5 G: until one thirty

6   (2.0)

7 B: <u>ser</u>iously!

8 R: yup

In line 3, B both rejects R's answer to B's line 1 question and clarifies that B was asking about last night, not this night. R and G then assert that R was indeed answering B's question; that is, R and G assert that R had understood and answered B's question. In line 7, B checks that this really is the answer to her intended question, and R confirms that it is. The problems of understanding are problems of interpretation, not encoding–decoding.

Examples 2:26 and 2:27 each involve several problems of interpretation that the participants have to work through together to reach mutual understanding.

Example 2:26

(A and B are talking about a court-imposed restraining order put on a man who had been terrorizing his neighbour).

1 A: he's not allowed to come (.) within five hundred metres of his

2   house

3 B: whose (.) their house↑

4 A: <u>his</u> house (.) well cause he lives right next door

5   (2.0)

6 B: wh- oh he's not allowed to go five hundred metres off his

7   property↑

8 A: no no no no he's not allowed to come within a radius of five

9   hundred metres (.) he has to stay

10 B: oh okay

11 A: five hundred metres (.) away from his house

12 B: he lives in the house right↑

13 A: he he wa- he did he doesn't anymore

14 B: o:h okay i see what you mean okay

15 A: yeah (1.2) so (0.7) um (2.0) he's had this campaign of terror going

16   for years but he's like [escalated]

17 B: [so (.) so where's] he living then↑

18 A: i̲ dunno

In line 2, B shows lack of understanding about whose house A was referring to by 'his house'. A clarifies that it was '<u>his</u>' (stressed) house; that is, the house of the man who was under the restraining order. The two second pause (line 5) and B's turn in line 6 convey that B still does not understand. After several more turns in which A and B continue to demonstrate that there is a problem of understanding, B in line 12 checks on something that apparently she had assumed. A in line 13 provides B with new information, thereby clearing up B's confusion, as evidenced by B's line 14 and the smooth flow of the rest of the segment. Most of this example involves A's and B's recognition of problems of understanding and their attempts to achieve mutual understanding.

Example 2:27 illustrates similar sorts of problems of understanding.

Example 2:27

 1 A: the funny thing was that we parked in the library (0.6) so when

 2   we left

 3   (0.4)

 4 B: the library↑=

 5 A: =yeah (.) the new library down basically we went down and spent

 6   five bucks for the night (.) and you just walk like it's like two

 7   blocks

 8 B: are we talking about the pacific coliseum [or]=

 9 A: [uh huh]

10 B: =b c place↑

11 A: the one with the white and the dome on top

12 B: that's b c place

13 A: oh b c place sorry [pacific]

14 B: [((laughs))]

15 A: coliseum in:

16 B: yeah (.) it's just [down the road]

17 A: [that's just right down here] whoops right yea:h

18   that's b c place (.) [anyways]

19 B: [oh well]

20 A: we parked at the library and walked from there but . . .

In line 4, B displays a lack of understanding. That turn sets up a sequence consisting of various attempts to create understanding and displays a lack of or only partial understanding. Finally, by the end of the segment of talk, the participants are successful in achieving mutual understanding.

THE NATURE OF TALK

The latter part of this chapter has focused on certain deficiencies of the Code Model of talk. These deficiencies, illustrated by examples of natural talk, stem from an inadequate conceptualization of talk. Careful consideration of the examples presented reveals important and essential attributes of talk. Since the central purpose of this book is to develop a good model of talk, it is worth summarizing just what has been learned about talk from this critical examination of the Code Model.

The major attribute of talk is that it consists of the sequential alternation of turns. This is a defining property; that is, for talk to occur, it must be the case that one person takes a turn and then another person takes a turn that orients to the prior turn and projects forward to a next turn of the first participant, and so on. In other words, talk consists of at least two participants who take alternate turns which are responsive to the prior and project forward to a next turn. Sequential and alternating turn-taking combined with the responsiveness of a turn to the prior turn constitute what it means to socially interact. Thus, talk is a form of social interaction. A model of talk is a model of interaction. Accordingly, the impact of turn-taking on the production and interpretation of talk must be central to any model of talk.

There are several important implications of the above basic attribute of talk. One implication is that since it takes at least two persons to interact ('it takes two to tango'), a model of talk must be a model of interpersonal behaviour, not a model of individual, intrapersonal behaviour. A second implication concerns the relation between the turn-taking structure of talk and the ways in which shared under-standings occur. In responding to S's prior turn, A manifestly reveals how he/she understood that prior turn. Given the displayed understanding, S can accept it or orient to it as problematic by initiating a repair. In this way, intersubjectivity is monitored by participants on a turn by turn basis. Further intersubjectivity is monitored in the manifest or observable details of talk; that is, the data on which intersubjectivity is created are available in the moment-by-moment sequentially unfolding details of a segment of talk. In other words, participants together construct (i.e., co-construct) the meanings of their talk in and from the manifest details of their talk. Accordingly, a focus on the manifest details of talk is required for an adequate model of talk.

The final implication to be discussed here is that in order to engage in talk, S must tailor what she does to a specific A at some specific moment in some specific sequentially unfolding situation. This feature is referred to as recipient design (Sacks, 1992). Recipient design not only influences how talk is produced by also how it is interpreted. Specifically, in order to engage in talk A must interpret S's talk on the assumption that S tailored what she said to A at that specific moment in that specific sequentially unfolding situation. Talk, then, does not involve speakers and those who just happen to hear what has been said. Rather, talk involves speakers and their addressees both of whom proceed on the assumption that each utterance is specifically designed for that specific other at that specific moment. A further implication of the recipient design nature of talk is that both the production and interpretation of talk are *indexical*, based on the specifics of the interaction at hand. Thus, even on the assumption (which I do not grant) that S 'puts her thoughts into words' and A 'decodes S's thoughts from those words', the words S uses are directed to a specific A at some specific moment in some specific sequential environment, as too is the interpretation that A constructs from those words.

The examples in this chapter may not clearly provide support for the claim that contributions to talk are recipient-designed. Fortunately, there is relevant research which is highly supportive of this claim. Schober & Clark (1989; see also Clark, 1992; Clark & Schaefer, 1987, 1992) created a situation in which an overhearer listened in on the talk between a speaker and addressee. Even though in each case the overhearer heard precisely what S said to A, results revealed that speakers and addressees understood their talk better than overhearers. Further, talk directed to addressees is different from talk directed to both addressees and overhearers (Clark & Shaefer, 1992). If recipient design applies both to the production and interpretation of talk, the above results are to be expected. By contrast, on an encoding–decoding view, given a certain set of thoughts, there is one way to encode it; and given a certain encoded set of thoughts, any competent speaker should be able to decode it. Thus, understanding by addressees and by overhearers should be the same and there should be no difference in how utterances are produced for addressees or overhearers. The research of Clark and his colleagues clearly contradicts that claim.

On the basis of the above discussion, the following description of central attributes of talk can be presented:

a) Talk consists of the sequential alternation of the responsive turns of two or more participants.
b) The production and interpretation of talk is evident in its manifest details.
c) Intersubjectivity is monitored and co-constructed by participants from the manifest details of sequential turns at talk.
d) Recipient-design influences both the production and interpretation of talk.
e) Talk is indexical.

In sum, talk is a sequential, manifest, co-constructed, recipient-designed, and index-ical accomplishment. The Code Model is based on assumptions about talk that deviate greatly from the actual structure of talk. Because of this, Code Models are bound to fail as models of talk.

3

The Speech Act Model

Introduction

The great appeal of the Code Model of talk is that it gives a clear and straightforward explanation of how intersubjectivity occurs, of how people can understand each other's talk. Specifically, it is assumed by Code Model advocates that each word in a language corresponds with a specific thought/bit of information; that a grammatical combination of words has a meaning, the literal meaning or sense; and that understanding occurs through the decoding of the literal meaning of what someone said. Because words and the sentences in which they occur stand in a one-to-one relation with information/thoughts, language and meaning have a very close relation. In particular, words represent or correspond to attributes of the world and a 'good' word/sentence is one that matches (is true of) the world. Accordingly, from this perspective, the most important issue about the meaning of what someone said is whether it is true or false, whether it does or does not correspond to the world it purportedly describes.

A central reason for rejecting a Code Model of talk is that participants' meaning (i.e., the meaning of utterances in sequence) does not necessarily correspond to the meaning of the words in the utterances participants produce. If this claim is accepted, there are two important issues that must be addressed by any model of talk. One concerns the relation between a set of words/an utterance and what speakers use those words/utterance to mean; namely, how do the specific words/ utterances used by participants to create meaning relate to the specific meanings created? Another concerns recognition of the actions participants in talk accomplish by using words/utterances; namely, how do addressees understand the meaning a speaker attempts to accomplish by producing words/utterances? These issues are complex and closely related. The present chapter examines one answer to each of these issues based on a model of talk referred to generally as the Speech Act Model.

Chapter Outline

The chapter begins with a description of the views of the philosopher John Austin (1962) on what people do with words/language and how they do so. John Searle (1969) extended and formalized Austin's conception, and the resulting model of talk came to be known as Speech Act Theory. Though based on Austin's original insights about what people do with language, Speech Act Theory differs from Austin in some important respects. Thus, a critical examination of Speech Act Theory must distinguish between the versions of Austin and of Searle. Following the presentation of these two perspectives on talk, the positive features of Austin's perspective are summarized and segments of spontaneous talk are presented to illustrate those features. The reader will recognize these features of talk since they were identified and illustrated in the previous chapter. Next, the focus moves to an examination of the various deficiencies of Searle's version of Speech Act Theory as a model of talk. It is argued that Speech Act Theory is a variant of a Code Model and, thus, Speech Act Theory inherits all the deficiencies of Code Models. Examples of spontaneous talk are used to illustrate these deficiencies.

Austin: How to Do Things with Words

In a very influential series of lectures, later published as 'How to do things with words', the philosopher John Austin (1962) emphasized the pragmatic nature of talk. The prevailing view of language among philosophers and linguists was that of language as an abstract system, the central function of which is the description of states of affairs. Austin, by contrast, proposed that language is a human activity, a human practice, a form of life (see also Wittgenstein, 1953). Accordingly, the focus of analysis should be the activities that can be accomplished by using words and the ways in which those activities are constructed.

To develop this claim, Austin began by distinguishing between utterances that make statements about the world (e.g., 'Vancouver, British Columbia is north of Seattle, Washington', 'There are three cows in the barn', 'I am tired') and utterances that make a change in the world (e.g., 'I sentence you to life in prison', 'Guilty!', 'I bet you ten dollars', 'I object to you smoking in my house'). Given the first kind of utterance, a *statement*, we can ask whether or not the utterance corresponds to some reality, whether it is true or false; for example, is there a place called 'Vancouver' and is it to the north of a place called 'Seattle'? Given the second kind of utterance, a *performative*, we can ask whether or not the utterance successfully carries out the action in question. For example, is it the case that when the performative utterance 'I sentence you to life in prison' is produced that the person to whom it is addressed is, as a result of that utterance, incarcerated in a state-controlled penal institution for a length of time corresponding to the legal definition of 'life'?

Although Austin began by distinguishing utterances for which issues of truth and falsity are paramount (statements), and those for which issues of the successful or unsuccessful carrying out of action are paramount (performatives), in the course of exploring this idea more fully, he came to the conclusion that *all* utterances have both a true/false component and an action component. For example, the statement 'Vancouver, British Columbia is north of Seattle, Washington' can be judged as to its truth or falsity. However, it can be rephrased as 'I state that Vancouver, British Columbia is north of Seattle, Washington', thereby becoming a performative that does the act of stating. In other situations, uttering those same words would accomplish other actions, such as giving directions (in response to the question of which direction to go to get to Vancouver), disagreeing (in response to the claim that Vancouver is south of Seattle), or informing (in response to a question in a geography class). Further, whereas uttering 'I sentence you to life in prison' in certain situations performs the action of sentencing, it also has aspects relevant to truth. In our culture there would, for example, be something false about 'I sentence you to life in prison' if a trial had not taken place, if the person doing the sentencing was not a judge of the court, or if the person being sentenced had been found not guilty.

In sum, Austin concluded that every utterance makes truth claims *and* carries out action (more properly, that persons who produce utterances make truth claims and carry out action). Austin used the term 'Speech Act' to emphasize the action component of all utterances, and it is this term that gives the name Speech Act Theory to the model of talk based on Austin's views.

Locutionary, illocutionary and perlocutionary acts

According to Austin, when someone makes an utterance, three distinct types of act occur; namely, a locutionary act, an illocutionary act and a perlocutionary act. The *locutionary act* consists of the production of utterances either orally, as with speech, or visually, as with a sign language. There is also the *illocutionary act*, the act(s) we perform by talking to one another, such as greeting, persuading, disagreeing, assessing, informing, etc. Finally, there is the *perlocutionary act*, the intended and unintended effects of the illocutionary act on the addressee.

Austin's analysis was fundamental to the development of the approach to the analysis of language called pragmatics, the concern of which is, to borrow a phrase from Austin, how people do things with words. Pragmatics has been concerned mainly with illocutionary acts, the social actions we perform by speaking, such as agreeing, blaming, excusing, granting, requesting, etc. In spite of this emphasis on illocutionary acts, it is also important to consider the perlocutionary acts and effects of utterances, the intended and actual effects of action, such intentions based on speakers' desires, wants, goals, etc. Many of these perlocutionary effects are inter-personal; for example, an addressee may be afraid of and try to avoid future interaction with a speaker who threatened the addressee.

Felicity conditions

The production and understanding of illocutionary acts/speech acts (in this book referred to as 'social actions' or 'actions') is central to Austin's model of talk. The issue then arises as to how participants in talk are able to produce and understand action. Austin proposed that every action in talk is produced and interpretable within the total speech situation consisting of who is talking to whom, on what occasion, at what point in their talk, in what social and cultural setting and for what purposes.

Within this total speech situation, there are certain conditions that an utterance must meet to count as the doing of some specific action X; otherwise, action X goes wrong in some way. Austin referred to these conditions as *felicity conditions*. Although the total speech situation and the felicity conditions for an action will vary from action to action, a general description can be given. Briefly, in order to produce a specific action X, the agent must behave in certain ways, while at the same time having certain states of mind. Put differently, the agent must behave and believe as follows (adapted from Levinson, 1983, p. 229):

1 The agent must carry out a conventional procedure with a conventional effect in the appropriate speech situation of persons and circumstances.
2 The agent must carry out the procedure in 1 correctly and completely.
3 Typically, (i) the agent must have certain thoughts and intentions, as specified in the procedure, and (ii) if certain conduct is specified, the agent must act accordingly.

As an illustration of what is meant by these conditions, imagine the situation in which a young teenager promises her mother that she will be home before her midnight curfew. Conditions 1 and 2 involve the teenager saying something to her mother like 'I promise I'll be back before 12'. Uttering these words conventionally carries out the action of making a specific promise, and this occurs in a situation in which the teenager is planning to leave the house when she knows she has a midnight curfew. Since a promise is an interpersonal action, it is also relevant that the mother acknowledges and, thus, ratifies, that a promise has been made. Satisfaction of Condition 3 requires the teenager to intend to, be morally committed to, and at some later point actually attempt to be home by midnight.

The requirements of Conditions 1 and 2 specify the speaker's (agent's) observable behaviour occurring under the observable circumstances that hold at the time at which some particular action is attempted. If any of these observable conditions are violated, both the speaker and the addressee/analyst will recognize that the action has not been produced. For example, uttering 'I promise to be home by 12' to the family dog will not result in a promise having been made, and nor will uttering to her mother 'I may be back by 12'. Condition 3 requirements, by contrast, specify which non-directly observable thoughts, beliefs, and feelings the speaker must hold at the time at which the action is attempted, plus future behaviours of the speaker. If Condition 3 is violated, a promise may appear to have been made but it is, in fact, an insincere promise. For example, if the teenager has no intention of actually returning home by midnight, although her mother may not know this, the promise is insincere.

To summarize, as can be seen from this example, uttering certain words in the right sort of circumstances with the right sort of thoughts and feelings will accomplish the action of sincerely 'promising to be home by midnight'. An agent who fails to behave in accordance with certain of these conditions will fail to bring off the action in question; and an agent who fails to behave in accordance with other of these conditions will fail to carry out the action sincerely.

Austin's claims about the felicity conditions for actions provide an explanation of how utterances can be connected to the social actions that are produced by making utterances in the total speech situation. It can be assumed that felicity conditions are shared by competent members of a culture (i.e., felicity conditions are cultural conventions). Thus, to produce Action X, a speaker must produce an utterance in accordance with the conventional felicity conditions for Action X in that specific total speech situation. To recognize that an utterance has brought off Action X, an addressee must identify the conventional felicity conditions to which the utterance conforms in that specific total speech situation. Given that speaker and addressee are from the same culture, they are likely to share the felicity conditions for each type of action and to be aware of the same total speech situation in which specific actions are produced. Thus, the production and recognition of action should normally occur. However, as previously noted, addressees may sometimes be fooled into believing a particular action has been produced when, in reality, it has been produced insincerely.

Searle's Speech Act Theory

The conception of talk that Austin advanced was extended and specified by the American philosopher John Searle (1969) into a full model of talk called Speech Act Theory. Searle began by arguing that each type of speech act has a unique set of felicity conditions that specify the preconditions that must hold in order for the action in question to be produced. Consider, for example, the speech act of promising, which according to Searle has the felicity conditions below. In order to understand what these felicity conditions are, it is helpful to relate them to the above discussion of the teenager who promises to be home by midnight.

Felicity conditions for the action of promising:

Propositional content
– about a future action, X, of the speaker, S
(teenager will be home by midnight)

Preparatory conditions
– S believes he/she can do action X
(teenager believes she can be home by midnight)

– S believes H (hearer) wants or is willing to have S do action X
(teenager believes her mother wants her home by midnight)
– S would not ordinarily do action X
(teenager would rather stay out well after midnight)

Sincerity condition
– S intends to do action X
(teenager intends to be home by midnight)

Essential
– S is obligated to do action X
(teenager is morally obligated to be home by midnight)

Given that the teenager follows these felicity conditions in making her utterance, the teenager will have accomplished the action of promising.

Searle's Speech Act Theory account of the production and understanding of action in talk

Having provided a description of the felicity conditions for actions, Searle went on to propose that there is a close relation between the literal meaning of a sentence and the action that is accomplished by producing that sentence in some context. In other words, Searle linked the linguistic form of a sentence to the action that is produced when that sentence is spoken. In order to be clear about exactly what Searle is claiming, several terms need to be defined. First is the distinction between 'utterance' and 'sentence'. A sentence is a formal linguistic object composed of a set of words with a certain structure, whereas an utterance is the production by a participant in talk of a sentence or a partial sentence (e.g., a word or phrase). An utterance consists of one or more utterance units, each of which can be used to produce an action. Consider Example 3:1 as an illustration. R has telephoned S to request S's participation in a psychology study. The transcript begins at the point at which R has identified herself and is completing her request.

Example 3:1

1 R: . . . and i was just wondering if you would be interested in coming

2   in for one↑

3 S: ahhm when↑

4 R: sometime this week preferably

5 S: oh no (.) i have a big exam this week

6 R: you do (.) how about next week↑

7   (1.5)

8 S: ummm (1.0) let me see (1.5) i don't think i have time for this

9   two weeks

10 R: okay

11 S: sorry

Examples of utterances consisting of one utterance unit include line 3 'ahhm when↑' and line 11 'sorry' that accomplish the actions, respectively, of questioning R to receive more information about the request and apologizing to R for the refusal. Line 5 is an example of an utterance composed of two utterance units, 'oh no' and 'i have a big exam this week' that accomplish the actions, respectively, of refusing the request and making an excuse for that refusal.

Searle's claim that sentence form (i.e., literal meaning) is related to the actions that are accomplished by uttering those sentences (i.e., by producing those utterance units) is also illustrated in Example 3:1. In particular, S does the action 'question' by using an interrogative sentence; the action 'apology' by using a member of the conventional set of declarative sentences for apologies (i.e., a set of conventional forms consisting largely of 'sorry' and its variants; Owen, 1983); the action 'refusal' by using a conventional negative declarative sentence; and the action 'excuse' by using a declarative sentence of a conventional form for excuses. In all cases, the sentence that is produced has a conventional meaning corresponding to the action accomplished by producing that sentence in context. Thus, all these examples support Searle's claim of a correspondence between sentence form (form of utterance unit) and the action accomplished by uttering that sentence.

It is now possible to describe how Searle's claims about the felicity conditions for acts can be built into a formal model of how speakers accomplish and recognize actions in talk. Such a model of talk rests on three central assumptions of Speech Act Theory. In particular, Speech Act Theory posits: (1) a unique and specifiable set of felicity conditions that must be met in order to perform action X; (2) felicity conditions are conventional constitutive rules acquired by all native speakers; and (3) these rules are used for the one-to-one encoding of actions onto utterance units and the decoding of utterance units onto actions. In other words, felicity conditions are conventions that speakers and addressees use as a code to produce and recognize actions. Speakers use the felicity conditions for actions as a device for encoding their actions into sentences with a particular linguistic structure that speakers then utter (i.e. they produce the appropriate utterance unit). Hearers, in turn, use the same set of felicity conditions for actions as a device for decoding the speaker's actions from the linguistic structure of the sentences the speaker produced (i.e., from the speaker's utterance units). Given this description it is evident that Searle's Speech

Act Model is a variant of a Code Model, the main difference being that in the Code Model thoughts are encoded into and decoded out of sentences/utterances, whereas in the Speech Act Model actions are encoded into and decoded out of sentences/utterances.

EVALUATING SPEECH ACT THEORY AS A MODEL OF TALK

Although Searle based his model of speech acts on Austin's pioneering work, the two approaches are significantly different in certain respects. In particular, Austin did not present a set of formal felicity conditions unique to each type of speech act, nor did he propose a strict and formal set of rules for the production and interpretation of action. Importantly, Austin also stressed the relevance of the indexical nature of speech act production and interpretation, which he alluded to as the 'total speech situation'. By contrast, Searle proposed a formal model in which rule-based procedures are applied similarly across different speech situations to unique sets of felicity conditions. The total speech situation is, therefore, of little relevance in Searle's model. Further, felicity conditions are conceptualized as the necessary and sufficient conditions for the production and interpretation of each type of speech act, rather than as guidelines for how actions might 'be brought off' or 'go wrong'. And, finally, Searle argues for a close correspondence between sentence form (i.e., literal or direct meaning) and the action accomplished by uttering that sentence (and it is not clear just how close Austin believed this correspondence to be).

Because of these large differences between the positions of Austin and Searle, in evaluating models of speech acts it is necessary to be clear about whose version is at issue. In the next section I examine the positive aspects of Austin's views, following which I examine the negative aspects of Speech Act Theory, most of which I attribute to Searle's version of the theory.

Positive Aspects of Austin's Views

The following important claims derived from Austin's analysis of language/talk are supported by observation of actual talk. It should be noted that the claims about talk made in this section were presented also in our discussion of attributes of talk that cannot be accounted for by a Code Model.

Participants' meaning

Austin emphasizes the meaning-making behaviour of participants in talk. Words, phrases and sentences do not have meaning; rather, participants in talk create or negotiate meaning, in part by using words, phrases and sentences. A model of talk cannot be a model of 'sentences', which are abstract, de-contextualized entities. Rather, a model of talk must be a model of participants' meaning, where participants' meanings are actions.

Example 3:2 illustrates the use of explicit performatives (e.g., in lines 6, 7, and 10), which tend to be infrequent in talk.

Example 3:2

(A, B, and C are children engaged in pretend play)

1 A: oh mighty king do we praise you (.) for eveh (.) and eveh

2 B: oh [mighty king]

3 C: [i'm the guard] i'm the guard

4   (1.4)

5 A: oh mighty king

6 C: ((growling noises))

7 A: we praise you

8 B: we praise you oh mighty king (.) oh

9 A: may i help you in any way↑

10 B: if we can help you in any way

11 A: [plea:se tell us]

12 B: [we will] (.) we will

Note, also, that A in line 9 uses an interrogative that B responds to by producing the antecedent of a conditional. As is evident from turns 10 and 11, A and B treat the interrogative and the incomplete conditional as the action of making an offer. In other words, participants' meaning differs from sentence meaning.

Example 3:3 presents another illustration of the distinction between sentence meaning and the action carried out by uttering a sentence (i.e., participants' meaning).

Example 3:3

(Two linguistic students discussing from which universities a professor received her degrees)

1 C: yeah (.) her other one's from manitoba

2   (2.0)

3 S: i thought she had one in europe and one in illinois

4 C: oh (.) she did post doctoral stuff in the states (.) yeah

From C's response in line 4, it is clear that C treated S's line 2 utterance as the action of disagreeing with C's line 1 claim. It is not evident how the illocutionary act accomplished by the line 3 utterance is related to the literal meaning (locutionary act) of the utterance. What is clear, however, is how participants treat the utterance. Further, the meaning of the utterance is determined in part by its location in sequence.

The importance of the total speech situation: the on-line and local negotiation of meaning

Austin (1962) emphasized that 'the total speech act in the total speech situation is the *only actual* phenomenon which, in the last resort, we are engaged in elucidating' (page 147, emphasis in original). In other words, talk is indexical, and the action accomplished by making an utterance depends not only on the utterance and its construction but also on the placement of the utterance in a specific sequence of utterances and turns. Referring to the determination of meaning as indexical stresses the importance of the specific moments of talk, of the specific details of an utterance and its location in some specific sequence.

To clarify the indexical nature of talk, the following examples illustrate how the structure of the utterances/turns and the particular sequence of turns in instances of talk are central to the production and recognition of action.

Example 3:4

(Halls is a type of cough candy)

1 B: oo: (.) halls=

2 A: =they're not all for you

3 B: can i have one↑

4 A: certainly you can have one (.) i got halls centers

5 B: mm

B in line 1 makes a statement of surprised and pleased recognition ('oo: (.) 'is stressed, elongated and followed by a brief pause) of a type of cough candy, to which A in line 2 responds immediately with a statement. B then proceeds to ask permission to eat one candy only, and A agrees to this request. Given the whole sequence, we (and the participants) can see that A in line 2 treated B's statement of recognition as preliminary to B's eating the candy, and A objected or warned B not to do this. B's request to eat one candy, in which B stresses that she only wants to eat one, displays B's recognition of and response to that warning. Without the sequential relations obtaining between the turns, it is not evident how, for example, 'oo: (.) halls' could be interpreted as the display of an intention to eat the Halls. Thus, the specific structure of turns and turn sequences, the on-line and local details, are central to understanding this segment of talk.

Example 3:5 illustrates how, in a specific sequence of turns, stressing a word can be used to initiate a repair.

Example 3:5

1 B: it was good↑

2 A: yeah

3 B: whaddid he have↑

4   (1.0)

5 A: lasagna

6 B: you both had lasagna

7 A: oh what did he have (.) he had (.) chicken and uh (.) mushroom

8   tortellini

In line 6, by putting stress on the word 'both' in 'you both had lasagna', B treats as problematic A's claim (not all of which is present in the segment) that both A and 'he' had lasagna. In lines 7–8, A treats B's turn as a repair initiator, as is evident by the fact that A makes a repair. In another sequence of turns, the line 6 utterance could be used to produce very different meanings; for example, it could be used to do an accusation or to make a negative assessment. The specific sequential placement of the utterance is, thus, central to its interpretation.

Examples 3:6 and 3:7 illustrate how the production of question–answer pairs in different sequential environments can be used to accomplish very different actions.

Example 3:6

1 A: o:h speaking of crazy neighbors

2 B: ye[ah↑]

3 A: [you]'ve got nuthin you've got <u>no</u> problems did i tell you (.)

4   about my aunt and uncles' crazy neighbor↑

5 B: no

6 A: oh my god the guy's a total nutbar (.) okay (.) they live . . .

In line 1, A begins with 'o:h', a change of state token (Heritage, 1984b) that manifestly displays that something B just said has triggered some new topic. The new topic is then introduced. In line 2, B produces an agreement with a questioning intonation. In appears that B is asking 'what about the crazy neighbors?'. At the beginning of line 3, A again connects the topic of crazy neighbors to something B had previously discussed, following which A asks a question to which B responds 'no'. In line 6, A then proceeds to tell a story. It is not clear how the question–answer sequence is connected to A's telling a story. However, if A's question is interpreted as asking permission to tell a story (if it is interpreted as a pre-story or pre-announcement), then B's line 5 performs the action of giving A the go-ahead to do so. The subsequent telling is consistent with this interpretation. Thus, it seems that from the beginning of the talk, A was projecting the telling of a story. Clearly, question–answer sequences do not always prefigure story-telling. That they do so in this example illustrates again how meaning is determined in part by the local, indexical aspects of the talk.

The next example involves a discussion about the upcoming wedding of B (the bride) and G (the groom). Prior to this segment, G has argued that B's mother, who is wealthy, should help pay for the wedding rather than place all the costs on B's father, who is not particularly well-off.

Example 3:7

1 A: yeah but at the same time is it really fair for dad to have to cough

2   up that dough↑ [i mean]

3 B: [yeah] when your mom's sitting on a huge bank

4   account of tons of money [course it is]

5 A: [well yeah] but the thing is is that

6 B: she has so much money [((inaudible))]

7 A: [it's not] gonna be her it's not gonna be

8   her paying for it

9 B: yeah that's what bugs me and then she tries to get involved and

10   everything

11 A: well

In lines 1–2, A's utterance is, linguistically, an interrogative. However, although A may have produced a question, that question functions as the claim that it is not fair for dad to have to cough up that dough. Apparently, A makes this claim by producing a question in order to manipulate B into admitting she holds a position that A can then attack. In other words, A uses an interrogative to state a particular version of B's position. Thus, in this sequential environment, what is linguistically a question is used as a rhetorical device to characterize B's position in such a way that it can be readily attacked.

The interpersonal effects of action

As Austin noted, a speaker's intent in producing an action typically is not simply to have it recognized, but rather to have the action produce certain desired effects. For example, if I request you to close the door, I certainly want you to recognize that I have made a request but I mainly want you to close the door. The intended effects of a speaker's action (other than the intent to have the action recognized as such) are referred to as perlocutionary effects. Some readings of Austin lead to the conclusion that both intended and unintended effects of a recognized action also fall into the category of perlocutionary effects. Regardless of this complication, Austin has introduced an interpersonal aspect to language.

It can be expected that speakers may construct their actions in ways that they believe will optimize the bringing about of desired effects and minimize the bringing about of undesired effects. Thus, there should be a relationship between how actions are constructed and which perlocutionary effects participants in talk attempt to bring off. Consider a situation in which Mary blames Harry. Mary may blame Harry in order to get him to accept responsibility and change his behaviour in the future. Both of these effects might occur. Alternatively, Harry might reject the blame, make no changes in his future behaviour, and feel negatively about Mary. Which of these two sets of reactions Harry might have to being blamed is likely to depend on how Mary constructed the action of blaming.

In Example 3:8, a student (S) is talking to her professor (P) about an upcoming midterm examination.

Example 3:8

1 S: i just need to ask you (.) um (.) a question about the midterm

2 P: m[hm↑]

3   S: [i] i uh i have to go to lethbridge (.) that weekend like we leave

4   on the wednesday

5   P: mhm

6   S: i wonder if it would be possible if (.) i could take the exam early

S knows that P generally allows exams to be written only at the scheduled time. Thus, S knows that the chances her request will be granted are not great. Presumably, however, it is very important to S that her request is granted. There are various features built into S's request that seem oriented to getting P to grant it. In line 1, S begins by asking permission to ask a question, a question she just 'needs to' ask. After being given the go-ahead to ask her question, S instead presents circumstances that will justify the question she has not yet asked. Those circumstances are framed as ones over which S has no control – 'i have to go'. Finally in line 6, S asks her question, which it turns out is a request. This request is made in a very hesitant way ('i wonder', 'if', 'it would be possible', 'if', 'i could take') that places S as subservient to P but very much reliant on P. Overall, then, rather than coming right out and making a request, S sets up the upcoming request with reasons to grant it, she frames those reasons as beyond her control, and she displays subservience and hesitancy about making the request. As the low power person in this interaction, S has structured her request in ways that increase its likelihood of being granted.

The impact of intended perlocutionary effects on the structure of action occurs even with relatively young children, as is illustrated in the following example.

Example 3:9

(A and B are ten year old girls, and C is the eight year old brother of A)

1 A: come on let's find two capes for us (.) or two (.) two capes we can

2   use a dress and a skirt

3 C: i have a cape [i have a cape]

4 B: [i'll use this one]

5 A: awright

6 C: [i have a cape]

7 A: [can you help me find] another one↑

8 B: yuh

9 C: this is my cape (2.0) I'm a [bad guy]

10 A: [can you] help me find one↑

In lines 1, 7, and 10, A makes a request of the other children. On one occasion A phrases her request as something they will all do ('let's find') and on two other occasions she requests help ('can you help me'). Commanding peers to do one's bidding is not likely to be an effective way of attaining one's goals, whereas including them in the request and asking for their help provides a much more effective strategy. Perlocutionary effects may have influenced how the action of requesting was produced.

Example 3:10 is another illustration of the impact of intended perlocutionary effects on the way in which action is structured. At the point at which the example starts, A is tracing around the picture on a card used in a game.

Example 3:10

(a father, F, and his ten year old daughter, A, the same girl as in the previous example, are playing a card game)

1 A: [and i'm gonna go like this] i'm gonna go like (.) i'm gonna trace

2   around it

3 F: yeah

4 A: then I can (.) maybe you trace a bit more here↑

5 F: yeah

In line 4, A makes a request of F, which F grants. It is unlikely that F would grant A's request were it phrased as a command, such as 'trace here!'. Perhaps because of this knowledge, A instead structures her request in ways that display her reluctance to tell her father what to do: her request is hesitant ('maybe'), minimized ('a bit more') and is phrased as a question. In our culture, these are generally effective strategies for getting a more powerful other to grant the request of a less powerful person.

Problems with Searle's Speech Act Theory

There are many reasons to think that Searle's Speech Act Model is an inadequate account of how participants produce and understand talk. In the following section, I discuss five major deficiencies of Speech Act Theory as a model of talk.

Action in general versus situated action

Speech Act Theory lays out the necessary and sufficient conditions for categories of actions, such as the category 'promising'. However, when a promise, for example, is produced, the promise is a specific promise occurring in a specific total speech situation. To put this differently, the general category 'promise' is not produced but rather a specific instance of that category. Thus, to explain how speech acts are accomplished and recognized is to explain situated action rather than action in general. Accordingly, if Speech Act Theory is a good model of the production and recognition of situated action, then it must be possible to derive specific felicity conditions for the specific situated action X_s from the general felicity conditions and the rules of their application for the action category X. There are, however, reasons to believe that it is impossible to provide a complete specification of just what is required in order to produce some specific action in some specific total speech situation.

Consider as an illustration of the difficulty of specifying the felicity conditions and their rules of application for specific actions in specific settings the example of the young teenager who promises her mother that she will be home before midnight by saying 'I promise to be home by 12'. According to Speech Act Theory, the propositional content of this promise, one of the felicity conditions, is that the teenager will be home by 12. The teenager will have satisfied this felicity condition if she is home by 12. But what does 'being home by 12' amount to? What is it precisely that the teenager has committed herself to? The following sorts of conditions seem to be part of what the teenager has committed herself to: '12' refers to midnight, that 'midnight' refers to the time that is conventionally referred to in that culture as 'midnight' (i.e., the daughter cannot take 'midnight' to be a magical time she and her friends have created), that the promise is for midnight on the day on which the promise is uttered, that it is for midnight in the time zone in which the promise is produced, that 'back' refers to the house in which she is making the promise, that it is a promise to be inside the house rather than on the roof or in the garage, that the daughter will return of her own accord (i.e., that she will not be forced to return home by others), that she will be alive when she returns home (i.e., her corpse will not be delivered before midnight), that the daughter will be physically present in the house by 12 (i.e., she will not simply be mentally present), that she will arrive before midnight and not immediately leave (i.e., she will spend the night in her house once she has returned), that 'I' refers to the teenager not some other person named 'I', and so on. Further considerations of this sort, perhaps involving other felicity conditions, make it clear that 'and so on' never stops.

It should also be noted that by changing the total speech situation in which the promise is made, the conditions that must hold in order for the teenager to be sincerely promising to be home by midnight also change. Suppose, for example, that rather than talking to her mother face-to-face, the teenager is telephoning from a relative's house, that her relative lives in a different country in a different time zone than that of her mother, that the teenager lives with her father who is separated from her mother, and that her father and mother live in different residences. In this situation, 'back' refers not to where she is when she makes the promise but rather to her father's house; that 'midnight' is midnight in her mother's or father's time zone, not the time zone the girl is phoning from; that she is promising to be back at her father's house by midnight, not at her mother's house. In sum, what counts as a felicity condition action X in one situation often will not count as a felicity condition for the same action in a different situation.

The complications outlined above stem from the difficulty of how to generate specific, situationally-relevant conditions from general conditions and rules for their application. Both Garfinkel (1967) and Wittgenstein (1953) have argued convincingly that it is not possible given an abstract category or principle/rule to enumerate an exhaustive list of conditions that satisfy that category or rule for any specific situation. Human situated action is based on a mass of unstated and unstatable assumptions and, thus, any specific use of an abstract category always involves 'et cetera' and 'let it pass' provisions. (For a fascinating account of the inadequacy of abstract rules as the causes of behaviour, see Suchman, 1987). According to Garfinkel (for a clear exposition of Garfinkel's claims, see Heritage, 1984a), abstract conditions and the rules for their use (of the sort exemplified by felicity conditions) are *not* descriptions of the causes of human action; rather, persons use such abstractions to render their actions intelligible and accountable.

In order to clarify Garfinkel's claim that abstract conditions (e.g., felicity conditions and their rules of application) are not the causes of situated action but rather are used to make action intelligible and accountable, imagine that the teenager who promised her mother to be home by 12 instead arrives home at 2 a.m. When challenged by her mother, what might the teenager do? One possibility is that she might explain her action by claiming that she really tried to get home but her car broke down and, thus, she was late. In other words, in excusing or accounting for her conduct, the teenager points to a felicity condition of promising that did hold (i.e., her intention and commitment to be home by 12) and to a mitigating circumstance beyond her control that interfered with the satisfaction of the felicity condition. Another possibility is that she might claim that she never really intended to be home by 12, but that she said so only because she knew her mother would not let her go out without that assurance. In this case, the teenager is accounting for her action by claiming that a felicity condition for promising did not hold and, therefore, that she did not really promise. In each case, the teenager has oriented to a felicity condition of promising in order to account for her actions. But this, of course, is not equivalent to the claim that the felicity conditions for promising (whether or not they 'held') caused her to act as she did.

The role of mental states

According to Searle, in order for an addressee (A) to recognize the action a speaker (S) is performing, A must identify those mental states of S that are part of the relevant felicity conditions. However, S's internal states are not directly observable to A. Thus, to claim that A 'recognizes' S's internal states is really to claim that A infers them from S's overt behaviour. This leads to circularity. Specifically, in order to understand what S's internal states are, A needs to recognize what action S is performing; but to recognize what action S is performing requires that A recognize what S's internal states are. Given that A's recognition of S's action depends on A's prior recognition of S's internal states, and that A's recognition of S's internal states depends on A's prior recognition of S's action, then it would be impossible for A to recognize either S's action or internal states. Since participants do recognize one another's actions (i.e., intersubjectivity in talk occurs with great frequency), the recognition of internal states cannot, therefore, be a prerequisite for the recognition of action.

A related problem concerns S's recognition of his/her own mental states. When I decide to apologize, for example, I do not first examine my internal states to be sure that they fit with the relevant felicity conditions for apologizing. Instead, what I do when I apologize is apologize. It is not at all clear what role, if any, my internal states play when I produce that action. This is not to deny that I have internal states; indeed, I may truly feel sorry and contrite. But I do not examine my internal states to decide whether I feel sorry and contrite before I produce an apology. Feeling sorry and contrite is something I might appeal to if I were asked why I apologized. But, again, I do not check to see if I have the requisite mental states and, having discovered I do, then produce an apology. In sum, specific inner or mental states cannot play the constitutive role in the production of action nor in its recognition that Searle envisages.

Sincerity in talk

Another problem with Searle's claims, one related to the issue of internal states, concerns the claimed importance of S's sincerity in the production and recognition of action. The issue is whether or not the sincerity condition needs to be met in order for action to be recognized.

To illustrate what is meant by sincerity conditions, consider the actions of promising and apologizing. Someone who sincerely promises is someone who intends to do the action he/she has promised to do, and someone who sincerely apologizes is someone who feels sorry for what he/she has done. If S is insincere A may not recognize this and, as a consequence, A would erroneously recognize S's actions as, for example, apologizing. In other words, if S's observable behaviours are such that, in that total speech situation, S conventionally produces an apology, A will treat what S has done as an apology. And this would be the case regardless of S's actual feelings, of S's sincerity.

(It is interesting to note at this point that Austin distinguished two general ways in which actions can 'go wrong'. 'Misfires' occur when S's observable behaviours fail in some way to meet the conventional standards. 'Abuses' occur when S's observable behaviours do meet conventional standards but S's mental states do not. Austin noted that if an 'abuse' occurs, it may be hard to detect and, if not detected, A will nevertheless 'recognize' S's actions.)

Given that insincerity may be present, not be detected, and yet A can still recognize action, then it must follow that sincerity cannot be a prerequisite for the recognition of action. The analyst of talk needs, therefore, to be careful about claims made about talk. Recall, in this regard, the caution made in Chapter 2 about making assumptions about the mental states of participants in talk. The issue was raised in a discussion of a participant whom I described as having 'failed to hear' what the other person said. It was noted that a more accurate description is that the participant 'displayed' that he/she failed to hear what the other person said. In a similar vein, rather than describing someone as having apologized, which invokes assumptions about specific mental states, it is more appropriate to describe someone as having 'done an apology' or 'displayed an apology'. These latter descriptions remain agnostic about the mental states of the agent.

A final point to be made in this context is that, unless there are good reasons to believe otherwise, sincerity seems to be something that participants in talk take for granted. Participants in talk do not automatically orient to and try to determine whether the other is being sincere, but rather sincerity becomes an issue that is oriented to only when there is observable evidence to suggest that sincerity may not hold.

Mapping utterances onto speech acts, and vice-versa

Perhaps the most serious deficiencies with Speech Act Theory as a model of talk largely involve three problems of speech act assignment.

Mapping problem 1

Consider, first, the assumption that there is a one-to-one mapping of sentence form onto function/action, and apply that assumption to declarative, interrogative and imperative sentences, the three basic sentence forms of English. From a Speech Act Theory perspective, it should be the case that declaratives are used to make statements or assertions, that interrogatives are used to ask questions, and that imperatives are used to issue commands. Examples from natural talk seriously undermine that expectation.

Participants in talk can accomplish many actions in addition to assertions by using declaratives. In Example 3:11, M in lines 2–3 uses the declarative 'they go back inside the jar or they go outside' as a command.

Example 3:11

(Mother, M, and young daughter, R)

1 R: look (0.2) look mom carrot sticks

2 M: no no (.) i doewanth mine here (.) they go back inside the jar or

3   they go outside

4   (2.0)

5 R: why mama↑

6   (1.0)

7 M: because that's just the way it is

In the next example, L in line 1 uses the declarative 'we'll do that tomorrow' to make a suggestion.

Example 3:12

1 L: so:::: we'll do that tomorrow

2   (1.5)

3 C: do what tomorrow↑

4 L: go to seattle

5 C: okay (.) yes that'll be fun (.) i'm looking forward to it . . .

Declaratives can, of course, also be used to make assertions or state opinions (complain), as is evident in lines 1 and 3 of the next example.

Example 3:13

1 J: that ones i don't like

2 R: oo:::::

3 J: you keep on using the same holes

The assumption of a close form–function mapping also finds no support from a consideration of interrogatives. As is evident in the next set of examples, participants in talk use interrogatives to do a variety of actions, not only questioning. In Example 3:14, an interrogative is used to do the action of making an invitation.

Example 3:14

1   H: interested in goin' to a wine tasting october twelvth↑

2   D: love to but we're away that weekend

Ervin-Tripp (1976) found that interrogatives, rather than imperatives, are the typical way to accomplish commands or polite requests, as illustrated in the next two examples.

Example 3:15

(father, F, and his young daughter, D, are playing a game neither have played before)

1   F: there's five different ways to play this game

2   D: kay which okay can i s- okay can you read out the ways↑

3   F: one of the simplest ways is just like a maze (.) you just have to . . .

In line 2, D says 'can you read out the ways↑', which F treats as a request, as is evident by F reading out one of the simplest ways to play the game.

Example 3:16

1   B: can i bum a cigarette offa ya↑

2   K: mmhumm

The next example contains two interrogatives, one used to do the action of making a suggestion, the other to do the action of asking a question.

Example 3:17

(K and B have been talking about possibly dying their hair)

1　K:　why don't we go really <u>dark</u> before we go black↑ (1.0) i <u>have</u> a

2　　　dark dye here

3　B:　((sniff)) dark what↑

4　K:　it's like a dark dark brown

The claimed one-to-one mapping of form onto function is not supported by imperatives either. The next example illustrates the use of an imperative to do the action of giving someone permission to go ahead with his/her projected action.

Example 3:18

(talking about a vase B received as a wedding gift)

1　B:　d'you wanna see it

2　A:　sure (.) d'you mind

3　B:　no go ahead

In line 3, B uses the imperative 'go ahead' to give A permission to see the vase.

The next example involves a customer, C, and a salesperson, S, for a cellular phone company. C wants S to check that C's telephone service is not about to be disconnected.

Example 3:19

1　C:　. . . so:: can you just check it for me and make sure they don't cut

2　　　it off

3　S:　uhmm (.) do you have your cell with you

4　C:　no

5　S:　just use my [phone]

In line 5, S uses an imperative to do the action of offering C help.

In the next example, which involves the same salesperson as in the above example, C wants to know what he/she needs to do to change to a new telephone plan.

Example 3:20

1   R: so the best thing to do is (1.0) your phone still works (.) right

2   C: yeah

3   R: just call customer service

4   C: uh hum

5   R: and just tell them that you're moving up to . . .

In lines 3 and 5, S uses imperatives to give C directions on how to find out if C has been switched to the new plan.

In the next example, the imperative 'have a good day' is used to display positive feelings and begin the closing of the telephone call.

Example 3:21

1   A: well thanks anyway

2   B: no problem

3   A: have a good day

4   B: you too

5   A: bye

6   B: bye

Mapping problem 2

The converse of the assumed one-to-one mapping of linguistic form onto action (discussed above) is the one-to-one mapping of action onto linguistic form. This is the second major mapping problem. To illustrate this problem, the discussion focuses on the action of refusing a request. From the perspective of Speech Act Theory, the action of refusing should be accomplished by uttering a negative declarative sentence, such as 'no' or 'I can't do that'. Although this does occur, the examples illustrate other linguistic forms commonly used to do refusing.

Examples 3:22 through 3:28 consist of segments of telephone calls containing request–refusal sequences. In all cases, the situation involved a research assistant,

R, telephoning students S, and requesting them to volunteer as research participants. For brevity, only the end of the request is presented.

Examples 3:22 to 3:25 involve the same R making the same request. There are a variety of ways in which negation is used to accomplish a refusal.

Example 3:22

1 R: and I'm just calling to see if you'd be interested in participating

2   in a short study next week

3 S: ahhh no (.) this week's pretty bad for me

4 R: yeah

5 S: yeah (.) it's pretty busy

6 R: awright (.) okay i know how it feels . . .

Example 3:23

1 R: . . . I'm just calling to see if you'd be interested in participating in a

2   st- short study next week

3 S: ahh next week↑ ah ah how much per hour↑

4 S: ahhm doesn't it pay any[thing]

5 S: [oh]

6 R: it takes about half an hour

7 S: oh (.) i'm not interested in dat

8 R: okay (.) thanks anyway

Example 3:24

1 R: and I'm just calling to see if you'd be interested in participating

2   in a short study next week

3 S: ahhmmm i'm afraid not

4 R: awright

5 S: alright (.) thank you

Example 3:25

1 R: . . . if you'd be interested in taking part in a ah short study this

2   week

3 S: well how long does it take first of all↑

4 R: ahmmm half an hour or less (.) it's just a questionnaire ahm

5   that's assessing your reactions towards an interpersonal

6   situation↑

7 S: ((laugh)) well if i had the time i'd say yes (.) but i'm gonna have

8   to say no

9 R: o-

10 S: bit bogged down with stuff

11 R: okay (.) ahmmm sure no problem (.) thanks anyway

These examples illustrate some of the different types of utterances that can be used to do refusals, including 'no', 'i'm not interested in dat', 'i'm afraid not', and 'i'm gonna have to say no'. All four refusals are accomplished through the production of a negative declarative sentence. However, as is illustrated next, refusals can be accomplished without any negative element.

Example 3:26

(telephone talk)

1 R: . . . takes place this saturday from seven o clock in the morning

2   'til about ten thirty

3   (10.9)

4 S: oh (.) i'm working on saturday

5 R: oh (.) i see

6 S: yeah

7 R: oh well maybe some other time

Example 3:27

(telephone talk)

1 R: . . . takes place this saturday from seven o clock in the morning

2   'til about ten thirty

3   (1.1)

4 S: oh:: i have a soccer tournament this weekend

5 R: oh i see

6 S: so sorry about that

Example 3:28

(telephone talk)

1 R: . . . takes place this saturday from seven o clock in the morning

2   'til about ten thirty

3   (0.8)

4 S: i i i i i live here in residence now but i live in squamish really

5   (.) and i'm going home this weekend

6 R: i see

7 S: but thank you anyway (.) what was it for↑

In each of the above three examples, S responded to R's request with utterances that, conventionally, are excuses. However, R and S manifestly oriented to those excuses as refusals. It is also possible that R and S also treated those utterances as excuses. Since the talk was initiated by a request, it can be expected that at some point that request will be granted, refused or deferred in some way. Thus, for participants, treating the utterance as a refusal may be primary to treating it as an excuse. Regardless of this complication, one important point illustrated by these examples is that participants did the act of refusing a request without the use of negative declaratives.

Mapping problem 3

The third mapping problem concerns the assignment of utterance units to action, and vice-versa. In order for the proposed form–function mapping to occur, it must be the case that utterance units can be identified, the production of each of which accomplishes one action. However, examples from natural talk demonstrate that one utterance unit can do more than one action and, further, that actions are sometimes accomplished over a sequence of turns at talk. Both of these observations undermine the one utterance unit–one action assumption.

Consider, again, Examples 3:26, 3:27 and 3:28. In each of these examples, a speaker used what conventionally is an excuse in order to carry out a refusal. According to Speech Act Theory, if two speech acts are accomplished by an utterance, then there must be some way of splitting the utterance into two units, each of which corresponds to a speech act. But it is not clear how this could be done. How, for example, can 'i'm working on saturday' (3:26), 'i have a soccer tournament this weekend' (3:27), or 'i i i i i live here in residence now but i live in squamish really (.) and i'm going home this weekend' (3:28) be split into two pieces, one that carries out the refusal and one that carries out the excuse? In examples of this type, it is the upshot of the production of an utterance with the conventional structure of an excuse at a specific point in a specific sequence of turns that accomplishes the action of refusing the request. In other words, the linguistic structure of the refusal is not a separable from the total speech situation in which that structure is produced.

The next two examples illustrate similar instances in which an utterance is used to carry out more than one action and yet the utterance cannot be divided into units, each of which corresponds to one specific action.

Example 3:29

(Overheard at a bar. S and G are part of a group of men at a table in a bar that W, the waitress, is serving)

1   W: what can i get you guys↑

2   S: why don't <u>you</u> buy a round for a change↑ ((said while looking

3   at G, one of the guys at the table))

4   G: oh yeah (.) yeah (.) sorry (.) whada yuh want↑

In making his utterance, S seems to be doing three actions: questioning, complaining, and requesting. S's turn does not consist of three independent linguistic units, each encoding a specific action.

Example 3:30

(three children playing make-believe)

1 B: i'm a huntress

2 C: uh actually somebody here has to be a guard too

3 A: uh:=

4 B: =we're not [guards]

5 A: [i don't] i don't have enough time to be a guard also

6   (.) i'm very busy

In line 2, C makes a command/request, which A in lines 5–6 refuses or denies. In order to refuse, A might have said 'I am not going to be a guard'. However, what A did was make what, in our culture, is an acceptable excuse. In producing this excuse, A also refuses the request. It does not seem possible to distinguish an utterance unit corresponding to the refusal and an utterance unit corresponding to the excuse.

Actions do not necessarily get accomplished by the production of one utterance unit but may, instead, get accomplished over a sequence of turns (and utterance units). Further, the meaning of an utterance unit (i.e., the action(s) accomplished by producing it) may be negotiated and, thus, revealed over a sequence of turns. Accordingly, meaning is not tied to utterance units; rather, meaning is something that participants negotiate together across sequences of turns. Examples 3:31 and 3:32 provide illustrations.

Example 3:31

1 R: you put a <u>pic</u>ture in it↑

2   (2.0)

3 J: yeah

4   (1.5)

5 R: ummm (0.5) i don't think that's a good idea=

6 J: =((giggle)) i was joking . . .

It is not completely evident what action R is producing in line 1. However, J's response to R's line 5 indicates that J treats R's line 1 turn as an objection.

In the next example, A and B are talking about the colour scheme of A's house.

Example 3:32

1 B: you have so much off-white in in your bedroom (.) it's all over

2   the place

3 A: so which means what i should continue with off-white right↑

4 B: yea:::h

5 A: is that what you say↑

6 B: yeah

It is not clear just what action B has attempted to produce in line 1. However, the remaining turns indicate that A treats B's first turn as a command (i.e., 'don't change to a new colour'), and that B ratifies that interpretation. The example illustrates that the meaning of a turn is tied closely to how participants treat it and that it may take several turns for participants to negotiate a turn's meaning.

The conclusion to be reached from the above extended discussion of the assumed one-to-one mapping of form and function is that there is no clear mapping of linguistic form onto action nor of action onto linguistic form. What appears to be the case is that there are a potentially infinite number of linguistic forms (sentences/utterances) that will, in the appropriate situation, bring off some specific action, and there are a potentially infinite number of actions that will, in the appropriate total speech situation, be brought off by some specific linguistic forms (sentences/utterances).

Speech Act theorists would object to this conclusion about mapping deficiences on the grounds that Speech Act Theory does not actually post a direct one-to-one mapping of literal meaning onto action for all speech acts. In developing this counter-claim, the Speech Act theorist is likely to appeal to the notion of indirect speech acts, a topic briefly discussed in the next section.

Speech Act Theory and indirect speech acts

Consider an example of an 'indirect' request, a typical member of the set of indirect speech acts.

Example 3:33

(father, F, and his young daughter, D, are playing a game neither have played before)

1 F: there's five different ways to play this game

2 D: kay which okay can i s- okay can you read out the ways↑

3 F: one of the simplest ways is just like a maze (.) you just have to . . .

In line 2, D says 'can you read out the ways↑', which F treats as a request, as is evident by F reading out one of the simplest ways to play the game. Since D asks a question (literal meaning) to make a request (indirect meaning), the issue for Speech Act Theory becomes one of accounting for how D and F (and analysts) get from a question about someone's ability to a request to do some specific act. The answer of Speech Act Theory is that the literal meaning of the relevant sentence is first determined, and then inferential processes based on contextual features of the sentence are applied to that literal meaning, resulting in a determination of the indirect meaning. Applied to Example 3:33, D produces an interrogative sentence that is used to ask a question about F's ability to read. However, F is an educated adult and D's father, and thus it is extremely unlikely that D does not know that F can read. It probably is the case, then, that D is indirectly doing some act other than questioning. D and F are playing an unfamiliar game and they need to learn the rules of that game. F has already said that the rules state 'there's five different ways to play this game'. Thus, it is likely that D wants to know the five ways to play and that her question is a way of producing an 'indirect' request for D to read out the rules. F's response in line 3 confirms this interpretation.

Based on examples of the above sort, it might appear that requests and other speech acts can be 'indirect' in the way conceptualized in Speech Act Theory. Before reaching that conclusion it is important to first describe in some detail the Speech Act Theory model of indirect speech acts. The model is based on the assumption that literal (direct) meanings are encoded into words and syntactic forms. Accordingly, the first step in understanding an utterance is the decoding of the literal meaning of the sentence underlying the utterance. If those decodings seem to match the meaning of the sentence in its total speech situation (i.e., match the meaning of the utterance), utterance meaning is equivalent to the literal meaning of the sentence, in which case meaning is 'direct'. If, on the other hand, the literal meaning of the sentence is in conflict with the context or total speech situation in which the sentence occurs, interpretations are made in an attempt to find a fit between meaning built into the sentence and meanings built into the total speech situation. When such a fit is found, an indirect meaning is recognized. Importantly, finding a consistent fit between sentence and context is aided by the assumption that there are constraints on the type of sentences that can be used to do a specific type of indirect speech act. An example of such a constraint is the assumption that sentences with the form 'Can you do X?', 'Could you do X?', 'Would you mind doing X?', and 'May I ask you to do X?' among others (i.e., the linguistic form of conventionally indirect requests; see Clark, 1996, pp. 304–317) can be literal questions but they can also be used to do indirect requests.

This model runs into several problems. One problem, as has been amply illustrated throughout this and the previous chapter with examples from natural talk, is that there is no necessary relationship between the so-called literal meaning of a turn at talk 'encoded' into linguistic structures and contents and the action or actions being performed by a speaker who takes that turn at that point in the specific interaction (Levinson, 1983; Sacks, 1992). Rather, what seems to be the case is that any sentence form can be used to do a wide variety of acts. There is as yet no complete model of how this is possible, but however it occurs it certainly must involve interpretation as a major component. A second problem is that indirect meaning can be recognized without the necessity of first decoding literal meaning (Gibbs, 1983); that is, interpretation can occur without decoding. And, finally, even if decoding is the first step in the understanding process, which is doubtful, to simply say that the rest of the process is one of interpretation is not to explain much. What needs to be specified is what interpretive processes take place and how they do so; that is, a model of interpretation is required.

To summarize. Speech Act Theory fails to account for situated action, is based on an inappropriate conception of the role of mental states in the production and interpretation of talk, and fails to account for the bi-directional mapping of utterances onto speech acts. These failures stem from the mechanistic (i.e., encoding/decoding) and formalistic (i.e., sets of necessary and sufficient conditions for the production and recognition of speech acts that apply across situations) tenets of Speech Act Theory. In contrast to these basic assumptions of Speech Act Theory, observation of natural talk reveals its essentially indexical and interpretative nature.

The problems with Speech Act Theory are, perhaps, most evident in its treatment of so-called 'direct' and 'indirect' meaning; briefly, that all utterances have literal ('direct') meaning and that, for some utterances, inference is applied to literal meaning to produce 'indirect' meaning. What has been seen, however, is that *all* meaning is 'indirect' in that meaning is based on inference in context, not on a contextual encoding/decoding. Literal meaning, just like all meaning in talk, is indexical. In spite of its importance within the Speech Act Theory model of indirect meaning, interpretation is taken for granted and underspecified in that theory. What Speech Act Theory and any other theory of talk need is a model of the interpretive processes that are centrally involved in understanding. Once an interpretive model of talk is available, it is not clear what Speech Act Theory will have to offer in addition. As Levinson (1983, p. 278) puts it, 'the contextual resources that give rise to the assignment of function or purpose are of such complexity and of such interest in their own right, that little will be left to the theory of speech acts.'

4

The Inferential Model

Introduction and Chapter Overview

As has been seen repeatedly, the production and recognition of action in natural talk is an interpretive process. Any model that claims to account for talk must, therefore, be based on principles of interpretation. The present chapter examines two important claims about the interpretive or inferential nature of meaning in talk proposed by the philosopher Paul Grice. Grice's views are fundamental to models of talk which, following Schiffrin (1994), are referred to as inferential models.

The inferential nature of understanding is introduced through an examination of an ordinary episode of interaction of going to the post office to buy a stamp. This leads into a discussion of Grice's (1957) distinction between non-natural and natural meaning. According to Grice, non-natural meaning is the type of meaning central to talk. Whereas there are a number of positive implications of the concept of non-natural meaning for a model of talk, one problematic implication is that the connection between the natural meaning of words and the non-natural meaning of talk is (partially) broken. To 'get the genie back in the bottle', to retain a connection between what is said and what is done by so saying, the chapter then turns to a discussion of Grice's other major contribution, his views on the cooperative nature of interaction (Grice, 1975).

After describing Grice's Cooperative Principle and its various Maxims, examples of talk that proceed in accordance with the Cooperative Principle are presented. The chapter then turns to a discussion of conversational implicature, which refers both to an inferential process and the outcome of that process. In particular, the issue is how addressees use the assumption that the speaker is following the Cooperative Principle to fill in or revise sentence meaning, thereby determining speaker meaning. The chapter concludes with a summary of the positive attributes of Grice's views, followed by a summary of the problematic aspects.

NON-NATURAL AND NATURAL MEANING

Non-natural Meaning

Talk is action and the actions pursued in talk are part of practical activities. Consider, in this regard, a recent, unexceptional, everyday episode of practical activity in which I went to the post office to buy stamps. The episode went something like the following: I wanted to send my son, who lives in Toronto, a birthday present. I put the present in a large envelope and drove to the nearest post office. I entered the post office and went to the service counter. After an exchange of greetings with the woman at the counter who was dressed in the uniform of a post office employee, I said I wanted to mail this envelope, indicating the envelope I was carrying, to Toronto. She asked whether I wanted to send it by first or second class mail, and I said first class. She took the envelope from me, weighed it, and said that the cost was nine dollars and sixty-five cents. I handed her a twenty dollar bill, and she gave me some stamps and change. I attached the stamps to the envelope. She asked if I wanted her to post it. I said I did, handed over the envelope, thanked her, and left.

Throughout this interaction, what I and the postal clerk were doing was intentionally producing and responding to actions that both carried forward our interaction and contributed to getting things accomplished. I wanted to mail something and needed to buy some stamps. This person wanted to sell me stamps, or at least her job required that she do so. I did certain things to get the stamps purchased. She did certain things that allowed her to sell me the stamps. Together, practical activities were accomplished. Some of our joint actions were accomplished with words, but there were also many other actions that were accomplished non-verbally – I handed the clerk money, she handed me back stamps and some change, I affixed the stamps to the envelope and handed it back to her, etc. These actions contributed to and were an integral part of the interaction, and they were interwoven with the words; that is, verbal and non-verbal actions were integrated. Further, each person's actions were dovetailed with the other's actions, as when my asking for stamps was responded to with her telling me the price, or when my handing over money was dovetailed with her extending her hand to take it.

The episode of buying a postage stamp reveals three important points about talk. First, the situation was one of cooperative and coordinated interaction in which each participant dovetailed his/her own actions with the actions of the other. Put differently, S tailored his/her utterance to the specific A on the specific occasion of their talk; and A, in turn, interpreted and responded to that utterance on the basis of the assumption that the utterance was tailored by S for A on that specific occasion. Second, talk was embedded in and constitutive of the activities of achieving *transactional* goals (G. Brown & Yule, 1983) of exchanging specific factual information and producing particular actions that changed the world in some way. In other words, talk was a major component of the cooperative and coordinated activity by which transactional goals were achieved, and talk also partially constituted what it means to carry out the specific transactional activity of 'buying a postage stamp from the postal clerk'.

The final point to stress is that, over the course of the episode of buying a stamp, both participants intentionally produced overt behaviours that were intended to be recognized by the other as having been intended. For example, when I said I wanted to mail the envelope to Toronto, probably I said something like 'I'd like to mail this (indicating the envelope that I was holding) to Toronto'. By uttering those words and doing other non-verbal acts like gesturing, I intended that the clerk recognize that my intention was to mail the envelope to Toronto. Put differently, I acted as I did in order to get the clerk to recognize that I wanted to mail my envelope to Toronto. Once the clerk recognized why I did what I did, she then understood the action I was trying to accomplish. Of course, in order for our interaction to proceed to its practical end, she also had to act on that understanding; that is, she had to then act in a way that advanced my goal of mailing the envelope.

The importance in social interaction of the production of behaviour that is intended to be recognized as having been intended can be expressed in technical terms introduced by Grice. What the clerk and I were doing was communicating with one another. For Grice, communication involves an agent's intention to carry out actions and to have those actions recognized. According to this view, communication is to be distinguished from the incidental transfer of information. For example, if I get embarrassed and blush, you probably would recognize that I am embarrassed. However, on the assumption that I cannot control my blushing, the information 'he is embarrassed' that you pick up in this way is not communicated information. By contrast, imagine that I say to you 'I'm really embarrassed'. If my intention in saying this is to get you to recognize that I am embarrassed, and if you do recognize that intention, this is a case of successful communication.

In sum, communication involves the situation in which S intends to get A to recognize that S has done some specific act just by getting the A to recognize that S is trying to bring about that recognition in A. (Note that this is a much more restrictive view of communication than is normal. Thus, for example, on Grice's view the dancing bees (Ch. 2) do not communicate, though they do convey information.) The intention to have one's intention recognized is referred to as a communicative intention, and the type of meaning that is involved when someone intends to mean something by trying to get another person to recognize that intention is referred to as *non-natural meaning* (Grice, 1957).

Grice provided a technical definition of non-natural meaning; namely, for S to $mean_{nn}$ (i.e, non-naturally mean) something by uttering U to an A, S must intend:

a) S's utterance U to produce a certain response r in A
b) A to recognize S's intention in (a)
c) A's recognition of S's intention (a) to function as at least part of A's reason for A's response r

In order to clarify just what this complicated definition amounts to, consider again the situation of me at the post office talking to the clerk. According to Grice, in order to non-naturally mean something by producing an utterance, I must have intended that my utterance would produce a certain response in the clerk, my addressee. Accordingly, I intentionally said (and did) something with the intent that she would recognize that I wanted to buy a stamp. My intention was to get her to recognize that I wanted to buy a stamp. Her recognition of my intention functioned as at least part of the reason for her selling me the stamp.

It should be noted that the clerk may have understood that my intention in intentionally doing what I did was to get her to recognize that I wanted to buy a stamp, but she may, for whatever reason, nevertheless have decided not to sell me a stamp. In other words, it is important to distinguish between an addressee A's recognition of a speaker's communicative intention and A's acting in the ways that the speaker S desired. Only the former, recognition of the illocutionary act, is actually part of what is meant by a 'communicative intention'. The latter are intended perlocutionary effects.

This view of how actions in talk are produced and recognized can be summarized as follows. The action S intends to accomplish by producing an utterance is successfully achieved if A understands the intention behind the utterance. Thus, regardless of what S does, as long as A recognizes the intention of S in doing what she does, then A recognizes the action S attempted to achieve. What this means is that S needs to produce utterances in such a way that the intention behind those utterances is transparent to A. Communicative intentions and their recognition are, thus, at the heart of understanding talk.

Natural Meaning

Grice proposed that there is another kind of meaning, which he referred to as *natural meaning*, characterized by 'things' that have meaning regardless of whether there is any communicative intention on anyone's part. For example, I have learned that dynamite means danger. Thus, if I find a box of dynamite in my garage, dynamite is/means danger to me and I am going to be frightened. To recognize the danger, it is not necessary for me to recognize that someone intentionally placed the dynamite there with the intention of getting me to recognize that dynamite is dangerous; that is, it not necessary that I recognize any communicative intention behind the box being there to recognize danger. If it had been put there by accident, I would still recognize danger. And, further, even if the dynamite had been put there with the intention of getting me to recognize I was in danger, it would not be necessary for me to recognize that in order to feel in danger. Simply put, the word 'dynamite' on a box means danger whether or not anyone intended to have me recognize that meaning.

In order to clarify the distinction between natural and non-natural meaning, imagine the case of a battered wife who has been undergoing counselling. One day she goes to her counsellor and says, 'He did it again last night.' What is the connection between the uttering of those words in that situation and the actions of complaining/accusing her husband of beating her? Presumably the woman intended to say those words and she intended to have the counsellor recognize that, by saying them, she was accusing and complaining about her spouse's violent actions. Given that these words were uttered to a counsellor in a counselling setting, it is likely that the counsellor would recognize what the woman was trying to communicate. How important are the words? There are innumerable things the woman could have said and done to convey that meaning, including 'Look, I really got hurt', 'He was a real bastard last night, again!', and so on.

Natural meanings might also be present in the above situation. Thus, imagine that the woman, with bruises all over her face and two black eyes, walked into the counsellor's office. The bruises are a natural sign that something like a beating had happened, and the counsellor might well understand that meaning whether or not the woman intended to convey it. Indeed, the woman may have attempted to cover up the bruises so the counsellor could not see them and, therefore, could not come to the conclusion that she had been beaten again. But the woman's intention to convey or try to hide the fact that she has been beaten is not relevant because, in this situation, there is the natural connection between bruises and the meaning they carry – that she has been beaten.

Why is the concept of non-natural meaning necessary?

A critic of Grice's notion of non-natural meaning might object that such a complicated concept is not needed to explain how communication occurs. After all, the critic continues, words have meaning and, therefore, S can convey a meaning to A simply by uttering a grammatical string of words. Put differently, words (sentences) have literal meaning and there is no need to guess at the intention behind an intentional behaviour. Instead, A determines S's meaning merely by determining the literal meaning of the words in combination that S used. Thus, given that S's intended meaning could be decoded from her words, the issue of inferring communicative intentions would not be germane.

At this point in the book, it is not possible to present a full rejoinder to this criticism. For the purposes at hand, however, all that is necessary is to point to the many examples presented in the previous chapters that illustrate that the literal meaning of sentences (i.e., the natural meaning of words in combination/sentences) is not equivalent to the actions performed by uttering those sentences. Further, many of those examples also provide support for the view that participants seem to orient primarily to one another's actions rather than to one another's words. On the basis of this evidence, it seems that natural meanings are not sufficient to account for the understandings that occur in talk. It is, therefore, necessary to look for some alternative account of meaning in talk. Grice's notion of non-natural meaning is a likely candidate.

In spite of the above argument, there is nevertheless something compelling about the view that sentences have literal meaning and that sentence meaning is basic to what speakers convey and addressees recognize. To help dispel that view, it is useful to examine an example in which natural meaning is opposite to or in conflict with non-natural meaning.

The gift of worms

Imagine a family with the following birthday custom. On the birthday of each of their parents, the children go into their parent's bedroom first thing in the morning with a gift and a birthday card. When one of the children was three years old, the birthday ritual was carried out on his mother's birthday. The youngster collected a jar of worms, which he liked a great deal, wrapped the jar up, presented this to his mother, and said 'Happy Birthday'. After a brief pause, his mother thanked him profusely for the gift. On one level, this was an odd response because his mother found worms to be repugnant and yet she seemed genuinely pleased to receive them. What needs to be accounted for is how she could be so pleased to receive something the natural meaning of which was 'disgust'.

The explanation lies in the notions of non-natural meaning and communicative intention. Note, that the young son intentionally carried out a number of actions that in that situation were ways of doing the action of giving a gift; for example, he wrapped the worms up in a 'gift' way, he presented the worms at an appropriate gift-giving moment, he said certain kinds of words associated with gift-giving, etc. Those intentional and observable actions were intentionally and observably directed to his mother. Thus, even though his mother did not like *receiving* worms (which is consequence of the natural meaning of worms for mother), under those specific circumstances the giving of worms displayed to mother that the intention behind giving the worms to her was to show love for her (i.e., mother recognized that the worms were meant as a birthday gift).

Note that, to some degree at least, it did not matter that mother detested worms. What did matter is that she believed that her son's intention in giving worms in the way he did was to tell her that he loved her. From the perspective of the gift-giver it is also not necessary that he like worms for his intention to be conveyed (e.g., he might have disliked worms but believed erroneously that his mother liked them). All that was necessary to convey liking, and congratulations, was that the son act in a way such that mother could discern that his reason for acting in that way was to convey his liking for his mother.

Here, then, is a case of non-natural meaning in which what was conveyed by acting in a certain way clashed with the natural meaning of a central component of that action. The connection between worms and mother's natural reaction to them is equivalent to the assumed connection between words and literal meaning. By contrast, the connection between the uttering of those words (and the performing of other actions) in that specific situation is equivalent to the connection between utterances and non-natural meaning. Certainly, adults are better at giving gifts that the receiver likes (natural meaning). But even for adults this is not necessary to show one's affection for someone. All that is required is that one acts in a way that the other can recognize that the intention in so acting is to show affection. How that is accomplished is of secondary importance as long as the intention behind what was done can be recognized for what it is.

The relevance of the gift of worms for the issue of meaning in talk (and social interaction generally) can be summarized as follows. The gift of worms occurred in a sub-cultural or family ceremony of birthday gift-giving. The way in which the worms were given and the circumstances of that giving displayed to mother that the worms were meant as a gift. Thus, although mother did not like the way in which her son constructed his act of giving her a birthday gift (i.e., the act was constructed by giving her worms), mother did recognize her son's intention in doing this. And when mother recognized that intention, her son's communicative attempt was successful. The important conclusion to be reached about talk is that the literal meaning of the actions and words a speaker produces is not equivalent to what the speaker intended to convey by producing those words.

A potential problem with non-natural meaning as an account of speaker meaning

The distinction between natural and non-natural meaning allows for an account of how sentence meaning differs from speaker meaning. Specifically, as long as S acts to have her intention recognized in a manner that does, indeed, allow A to recognize that intention, it does not matter what utterances (sentences) S produces. The important point to note is that the concept of non-natural meaning seriously weakens the assumed connection between word meaning and speaker meaning. This accords with observation of spontaneous talk – what is said often differs from what is meant There is, however, a problem. If there is no necessary relation between what S utters and the meaning S conveys by making an utterance, it is not clear how it is possible for A to understand what S meant.

Constraints on Interaction and Talk

It has been argued above that, for any specific sentence there is a wide range of possible meanings that can be accomplished by uttering that sentence in talk. However, when an utterance is produced in talk, typically it is taken to mean something reasonably specific in a 'for-all-practical-purposes' sort of way. Further, addressees typically recognize the specific meaning, and the issue of how they do so thus becomes a central issue in a model of talk. One approach to this issue is to argue that the addressee must have some way of eliminating most of the possible meanings of what the speaker has said to arrive at one likely candidate. But this would be possible only if there are restrictions or constraints on the inferential processes addressees use to arrive at a candidate speaker meaning. A related view is that there must be constraints on what addressees consider to be a likely speaker meaning. (The difference in these two positions turns on whether a set of possible meanings is first constructed and then inferential processes and constraints are applied to choose one meaning from the set; or whether the constraints on inference apply directly to the choice of a likely candidate meaning. In the former type of model, many possible meanings are first constructed and then most are rejected, but in the latter type of model only one meaning is constructed.) In either case, the nature of the assumed constraints is significant.

In order to identify just what kinds of constraints might be involved, consider two examples in which what was said differs greatly from what was conveyed. With each example the goal is to try to discern what addressees must assume and what restrictions they must be applying, in deriving the conveyed meaning from the sentence meaning.

The first example is a story about a captain and his first mate. On the first week of a voyage at sea, the ship's captain is always drunk while on duty. The first mate, a responsible ship's officer who never drinks, fears for the safety of the ship and crew. In an attempt to change the situation, the first mate warns the captain that if he is ever drunk again while on duty, at the end of the voyage the first mate will report the captain to the ship's owners. This would result in the captain losing his job. Two days later the captain is again drunk on duty, and the first mate vows to carry out his threat to report the captain. The captain is really angry and wants to get back at the first mate. But how can he do this? The captain devises a plan. The captain keeps the ship's log and he writes in the log 'Today the first mate was not drunk'.

What the captain wrote differs from what the captain conveyed, which is that the first mate usually is drunk. How does the reader arrive at the conveyed meaning? One thing to note is that there are an infinite number of things that are not the case, so the issue arises as to why this *particular* thing that is not the case is mentioned. Perhaps this particular thing that is not the case is something to be noticed, that it is informative in some way. If the first mate were usually drunk, then 'not being drunk today' would be informative; that is, today would stand out from other days and would, therefore, be noticeable. Thus, on the assumption that what the captain wrote was informative, the conveyed meaning can be determined. Thus, one possible constraint on the construction of meaning is that contributions to talk (written story) are assumed to be informative.

The second example is drawn from a letter by the evolutionary biologists/psychologists J. Tooby and L. Cosmides that was printed in the New York Review of Books (July 7, 1997). These authors were responding to an attack on their work by the famous American evolutionist, Stephen J. Gould. Tooby and Cosmides argue, among other points, that Gould often uses the rhetorical strategy of saying/writing one thing while implying another. An example is Gould's statement 'I do not believe that members of my gender are willing to rear babies only because clever females beguile us'. Clearly, Gould is implying that most other evolutionary biologists *do* believe that. What constraints on what Gould has written allow us to recognize what he is implying?

Just as with the story of the captain and the first mate, Gould has written a sentence about something that is not the case, and the implied meaning is partly determined on the assumption that what was written is informative. There seems, however, to be another assumption that is made in order to understand Gould's conveyed meaning. His statement, as is true of all statements and utterances, occurs in a specific context (total speech situation), in this case the specific context of a discussion of competing scientific views about evolutionary biology. Readers are likely to assume that what Gould has written is a response to a claim that his opponents have made. It can therefore be assumed that what Gould states is somehow relevant to a criticism of his opponents' position. Thus, another possible constraint on the construction of meaning is that contributions to talk (written story) are assumed to be relevant.

On the basis of the above examples, there is reason to believe that when trying to determine speaker meaning, participants in talk assume that the speaker's contribution is informative and relevant to the issue at hand. Analysis of further examples may reveal additional constraints. The point of the examples was to illustrate what assumptions participants in talk might make and how making those assumptions is required to determine speaker/writer meaning. The illustrations, however, do not provide a general argument for the existence in talk of these or other assumptions on the basis of which speaker meaning is recognized. Fortunately, in his second major contribution to an inferential model of talk, Grice (1975) presented a careful and considered argument about constraints on meaning in interaction.

THE COOPERATIVE PRINCIPLE AND ITS MAXIMS

Grice (1975) proposed a set of constraints on interaction that he referred to as the Cooperative Principle, henceforth the CP, defined as follows: 'Make your conversational contribution such as is required, at the stage at which it occurs, by the accepted purpose or direction of the talk-exchange in which you are engaged (Grice, 1975, p. 5)'. The CP can be simply restated as cooperate and do what is needed to be said or done at that particular moment in the interaction. Grice went on to propose that the CP consists of the following four maxims:

QUALITY   Say what's true
            Don't say what's false
QUANTITY: Say enough and no more
RELATION: Be relevant
MANNER: Be clear, concise, and to the point

Grice's central claim is that producing and understanding/interpreting talk are accomplished through general principles of rationality and through cooperative conduct as specified by the CP. Further, the CP and its maxims have both a regulative and a constitutive aspect. Grice argued first of all that this is how persons should act, that it is rational to act in this way, and that if people do not act this way the coordination required for human interaction is difficult, if not impossible, to achieve. Thus, we ought to act and have the mutual assumption that people act in accordance with the CP. This is the regulative aspect of the CP. But it is also the case that acting in accordance with the CP is what it is to cooperate with others. This is the constitutive aspect of the CP. In other words, Grice's claim is that it is rational to so act/interpret, and thus we should act that way; and that acting in that way is what it means to cooperate with others.

The point of exploring the assumptions that participants in talk may make was to help explain how communicative intentions are recognized. The Gricean account is that participants in social interaction use the CP and its maxims to arrive at speaker meaning. Grice created the term '(conversational) *implicature*' to refer both to the inferential processes that participants use and the outcome of those processes (i.e., the meaning arrived at). Implicature, which implies inference or a process of reasonable 'guessing' and the resulting outcome, is to be distinguished from a term such as 'deduction' which implies a logical and determinate process with a necessary outcome. The recognition of speaker meaning is, accordingly, viewed as a reasonable process that typically, but not always, leads to a correct outcome.

Conversational Implicature

As noted, Grice (1975) argued that participants in talk make implicatures about what is said to determine what is meant. In particular, participants make implicatures to fill in, amplify, or revise the literal meaning of the words uttered (sentence meaning) in order to arrive at the intended meaning of the words uttered (speaker meaning). A critical aspect of Grice's account is his claim that participants make the implicatures they do in order to preserve the assumption that the CP is being followed. Restricting implicatures in this way allows addressees to determine speaker meaning from sentence meaning; in particular, in any specific occasion of talk A assumes that the possible meanings being created by S are restricted to just those that are consistent with the CP and its maxims.

There are two types of occasion on which implicatures are drawn. Implicatures are drawn when what S says seems consistent with the CP, in which case implicatures amplify or fill in the communicated meaning in a restricted way. In this case, S is *observing* the *CP*. The second type of occasion on which implicatures are drawn is one in which the literal meaning of what S has said is a blatant violation of the CP; it seems to A that S clearly is aware of this and, yet, S seems to be attempting to communicate. Accordingly, A tries to work out what S intended to convey, a meaning that is consistent with the CP as it applies to the total speech situation. In this case S is, on the surface, *exploiting or flouting* the *CP*. Working out an implicature in this type of situation requires that A recognize that S has produced a blatant violation, an ostentatious flouting of the CP. Thus, if A fails to recognize the violation as blatant, A may assume erroneously that S is being uncooperative.

The next two extended sections of the chapter present examples of implicatures that involve observing the CP, followed by implicatures that involve the exploitation or flouting of the CP.

Observing the CP

Example 4:1

(A motorist (M) standing by an obviously immobilized car, to a passerby, (P); example created from Grice)

1   M: i am out of petrol

2   P: there is a garage round the corner

As Grice interprets this example, P would be violating the Relevance maxim unless he believes that the garage is open and has gasoline (petrol) to sell. Thus, P's utterance is interpreted as indicating where M can get gas for his car. Although Grice did not analyse what M said, similar kinds of inferential work are at play. Given the assumptions that what M says is somehow relevant to the situation and that M has said something that clearly conveys M's intentions, P can then work out that M is asking for help. Note, however, that there are a number of possible ways to help (e.g., giving information about the nearest place to buy gasoline; offering to call a towing company for M; driving M to the garage, etc.). Further, there are a number of possible reasons for M's breakdown (e.g., the car is out of gas; the battery is dead; the engine has seized up due to lack of oil; the engine has overheated due to the radiator being out of water, etc.). Thus, additional information (e.g., the radiator is hissing steam) would be needed to arrive at the correct implicature.

The next two examples are similar to the above. For simplicity, in each case, an analysis is given only of what the second speaker implicates.

Example 4:2

(Overheard at a plaza)

1   A: pardon me (.) doyuh know where the closest bank machine is↑

2   B: there's one in the superstore

The meaning of B's utterance will violate the CP unless it is assumed that B believes there is an operating bank machine in the superstore in the plaza that A can use and, further, that 'the' superstore and 'the' plaza can be identified by A. Thus, B is most likely implicating that A can use a bank machine located in the superstore that is located in the plaza where their talk is taking place.

Example 4:3

(Overheard at a friend's house)

1   B: we got any coffee cream↑

2   N: it's in the downstairs fridge

N's intended meaning will violate the CP unless it is assumed that useable coffee cream is to be found in the refrigerator which is in some location known to B downstairs in the house where B and N are talking. Thus, this is what N means by her line 2 utterance.

In the next example, the interpretation of B's response to L's question centrally involves both the Quantity and Quality maxims.

Example 4:4

(Telephone call)

1   L: when's joanne's birthday↑

2   B: it's in december

In the local culture in which this example occurred, L is asking B to tell her the day and month of Joanne's birthday, possibly so L can wish Joanne good fortune on her birthday(e.g., send her a birthday card, call her on her birthday). On the assumption that this is what L is implicating, B's response fails to meet the maxim of Quantity – it does not provide sufficient information. If, however, it is assumed that B's response does follow the CP, then it must be concluded that B is unable to be any more specific without violating the Quality maxim; that is, B does not know exactly when Joanne's birthday is and, therefore, gives as much information as he can do so truthfully. Thus, B is implicating that he knows only that Joanne's birthday is sometime in December.

Example 4:5

(Telephone call)

1 H: wanna go to the game saturday↑

2 D: sounds grea:::t but i gotta work saturday

3 H: too bad (.) maybe yuh can make the next home game

Given some interpretive work, it appears that H was inviting D to some sort of sporting event (given the culture, probably a professional hockey or football game). On the assumption that D is following the maxim of Relevance, his response should be either an acceptance, rejection or deferral of the invitation. D's response, however, looks like an excuse. If H is being relevant and is giving sufficient information, then D may be implicating that he cannot accept the invitation due to a prior commitment that conflicts with the game. H's response, line 3, to D's utterance displays that H treats D as declining the invitation.

Example 4:6

(telephone talk)

1 B: hey, we got a letter from the lawyer (.) lisen tuh what he wrote

2   (0.2) i cannot say that this is not an unreasonable offer

3 A: say that again

In response to 'say that again', B did not say 'hey, we got a letter from the lawyer (.)lisen tuh what he wrote (0.2) i cannot say that this is not an unreasonable offer' (i.e., B did not repeat himself), nor did he say 'that' (as in, 'say that again'). Instead, B repeated only part of his initial utterance. How was B able to recognize what A meant by 'that' (in 'say that again')? On the assumption that A was following the CP, B can recognize that A needs to have B repeat something so A can understand it (otherwise, A's request would not be cooperative), and that A assumes B will understand the request. There are a number of reasons A might ask B to repeat something, including A's failure to hear what B had said and A's failure to understand what B had said. The triple negative in the lawyer's letter (i.e., 'cannot', 'not', 'unreasonable') is difficult to understand. Because of this, a likely inference is that A did not understand the triple negative statement and that this is what A wanted B to read again.

Flouting or Exploiting the CP

In spite of Grice's persuasive arguments about the regulative and constitutive aspects of the CP, observation of talk reveals that what people say often seems to blatantly violate the CP and its maxims. A trivial example is when someone makes a facetious remark. Imagine that A and B know one another, that they both know that A hates rain in the summer and longs for sun, and that A says 'it's been wonderful weather' in a summer of constant rain. What A means, and what B would recognize A means, is that the weather has been terrible. It, thus, appears that what A has said contradicts what A means; that is, A seems to be violating the maxim of Quality.

How might A respond to the accusation that she is not following the CP? Quite likely A would insist that her intended meaning was consistent with the CP, even if her words were not. Further, A might argue that she expected B to be able to work out her intended meaning as follows: I (B) believe A is cooperating, and yet she has said something that both she and I know is not true. However, I am sure A meant to convey something that is true. Both A and I know that she hates rainy summers. So, A must have meant that she hates the summer, and her remark was facetious or ironic.

It is important to distinguish flouting the CP from failing to follow the CP. As noted, flouting the CP is a cooperative activity since the CP is, in actual fact, being followed. By contrast, there are occasions in which persons hold such diverse opinions and are so highly antagonistic that each fails to orient to the CP in interpreting the other's contribution. In situations of this sort, there may be a kind of turn-taking, but unless turn-taking is cooperative (i.e., proceeds according to the CP in which a present turn is responsive to the prior turn), social interaction does not take place. Under these conditions, the CP and its maxims cannot be used to determine speaker meaning because participants have 'opted out' of the CP.

Another point to note is that following the CP and being 'cooperative' does not imply that participants have a positive orientation to one another; rather, what is implied is that each participant coordinates his/her actions with those of another participant. Thus, the notion of 'cooperation' as conceptualized by the CP applies to all forms of social interaction, including antagonistic interactions. Consider, for example, arguing. For A and B to argue requires at least that A makes a claim, that B then disagrees with that claim, and that A in his/her next turn either directly supports his/her initial claim or attacks B's criticism of A's initial claim (Muntigl & Turnbull, 1998). Arguing, then, is possible only if contributions to an argument are assumed to follow the CP.

The following set of examples contains illustrations of floutings of the maxims of the CP, followed by an example in which a participant opts out of the CP.

Flouting the maxim of Quality by not saying what is true or
by saying what is false

Example 4:7

  1 B: ooh oh ya know heh heh me and my friends (0.8) went ta go

  2   watch spice world today=

  3 A: =o:h

  4 B: ((laughs)) we heh we didn't mean to it was like a spur of [the

  5   moment thing]

  6 A: [yeah

  7   sure] (0.5) that's why i heard you on the phone planning it out

  8   right↑

  9 B: i wasn't onna phone we were at school today ya [punk]

10 A: [no: no] i heard

11   you n you were like (0.6) hey man (.) let's go see spice world (.)

12   that movie's a:wesome

13 B: ((laughs)) we were sitting in the back of the movie theatre just

14   heckling the whole movie ((A and B laugh))

In line 7, A claims that B had made plans to go see Spice World, but B denies this in his next turn. In spite of B's denial, in lines 10 through 12 A expands on his original claim and also claims that B said the movie was awesome. In response, B laughs and displays his negative assessment of the movie. At that point, both A and B laugh. From the laughter and general tone of the interaction, it can be assumed that A and B are friends and that A did not believe what he claimed about B. Thus, both A and B likely recognize that A has violated the Quality maxim by saying something he does not believe is true. On the assumption that A really is, in fact, following the CP, A's intended meaning must be consistent with his friendship with B. Friends often engage in good-natured banter or teasing, and so this must be what A intended. B's contributions, including his laughter, indicate that B did, indeed, recognize what A was up to. Note also that B refers to A as a punk, but again B's contributions indicate that he does not believe A is a punk; that is, B also flouts the Quality maxim and does so to create a joking relationship.

Example 4:8

1   A: i got a ticket from the parking bastards

2   (0.8)

3   B: i am <u>so</u> surprised

4   A: i'm not (.) i wouldn't put anything past them

5   B: ((laughs))

6   A: they murder little babies in their spare time

7   B: ((laughs))

Presumably, neither A nor B believe that parking attendants 'murder little babies in their spare time'. Thus, A has violated the Quality maxim by saying something that both A and B are likely to treat as not true. On the assumption that A really is following the CP, one interpretation is that A is being facetious and funny. This interpretation is supported both by B laughing in response to A's line 6 assertion, and by the turns prior to line 6 that consist of a joking exchange.

Flouting the maxim of Quantity by not being sufficiently informative.

Example 4:9

1   C: so how was work t'day↑

2   B: ((laughs)) it was it was work (.) what can i say↑

3   C: what hour how many hours didya work

         ((six turns missing))

12   ((laughs)) no i mean it's one of those jobs that there isn't a whole

13   lot t'tell people about because it's y'know it's being a cashier (.) i

14   put people's [gro]ceries through an i=

In line 2 B says something that is uninformative (i.e., work was work), thereby violating the Quantity maxim. In line 3, C continues to pursue the topic of B's work, and B eventually provides the information that his/her work is not that interesting. Thus, it appears that B's tautology in line 2 implicates that B is asserting that his job/work is not interesting enough to be a topic of discussion.

Example 4:10

(exchange on CB radio)

1 A: mi:ster woods (.) how's it going↑

2 B: o:hh (.) pretty good alright

3 A: how's the road between here and bellingham today↑

4 B: paved

5 A: ((laughs))

Since the road that trucks travel between 'here' (the Vancouver border crossing to the USA and Bellingham) is a major highway, both truckers obviously know the road is paved. Accordingly, B in line 4 has blatantly violated the Quantity maxim by saying something that is uninformative. In line 5 A responds to B's assertion with laughter, which is evidence that A is orienting to the flouting of the CP. In effect, A treats B's turn as a joke, which is a contribution to their talk that is consistent with the CP.

Flouting the maxim of Relevance

Example 4:11

1 B: how long can you leave oven cleaner on for↑

2 A: uh

3 B: it won't go (.) do anything will it if i leave the cleaner on there a

4   little while↑

5 A: i dunno if it would corrode it or not ((opens oven door))

6 B: it says overnight (.) it could be alaska (.) the nights are six

7   months long

8   (3.0)

9 A: wha:t↑ ((laughing))

10 B: ((laughs)) you never know

The talk does not take place in Alaska and, thus, B's turn, lines 6–7, is not relevant to A's question. The three second pause in line 8, the turn initial 'what' and the subsequent laughter in line 9 display A's uncertainty about how to treat the apparent lack of relevance of B's remark. In line 10, B displays that he/she was making a joke and, thus, that his/her remark was relevant to the talk.

Failure to Make Appropriate Implicatures

From a Gricean perspective, understanding talk requires participants to make reasonable implicatures. Since implicature is an inferential process, it is a fallible process. It can therefore be expected that participants will on occasion fail to make the appropriate implicatures in determining speaker meaning. The next two examples illustrate interactions in which one participant's contribution is consistent with the CP but the other participant fails to make appropriate implicatures in determining speaker meaning.

Example 4:12

1 A: today the constable was in our school and he was cleaning his

2 gun in the metalworks shop

3 B: ((laughs)) why:↑

4 A: i dunno (0.5) it was dirty i guess

5 B: ((laughs)) hoka:y

There are a number of possible interpretations of B's line 3 question including, why *the constable* was cleaning his gun (i.e., why that particular person), why the constable was *cleaning* his gun (i.e., why that particular activity), why the constable was cleaning *his gun* (i.e., why that particular object), or why the constable was cleaning his gun *in the school metalworks shop* (i.e., why in that particular location). It is normal in the culture for a policeman (constable) to have a gun and to take good care of his gun, but not to take care of the guns of other police. Asking any of the first three questions is, therefore, to ask for information that is obvious, and so would be inconsistent with the CP. It is, however, extremely unusual for police to clean their guns in a children's school. Accordingly, on the assumption that B is following the CP, it can be assumed that B is asking 'why in that particular location?' However, A gives an answer to the question 'why was the constable *cleaning* his gun?', thereby displaying a failure to make the appropriate implicature.

Failure to make appropriate implicatures can also occur when the CP is flouted. In order for A to work out the appropriate implicature(s) when S *has* flouted the

CP, A must first recognize that S has flouted the CP. If A interprets S's contribution as inconsistent with the CP but not as a deliberate flouting of the CP, A may be uncertain about what S intends. For example, A may assume that S has made some sort of error or that S is not being cooperative. The following example illustrates a flouting of the CP that is not recognized as such by the addressee.

Example 4:13

1 B: maybe it's just a waste of time (.) no i'm not i'm not doin for like

2   a (1.0) i'm not doin to enhance my memory i just do it because i

3   do it (.) or maybe i am *enhancing my memory*=

4 A: =cuz ya get bored

5   (1.0)

6 B: wh[at are we talkin about again↑]

7 A: [reading the same thing] (1.7) <u>what</u>↑

8 B: i'm jus kiddin (2.0) i said what are we talkin about

9 A: you're the one who's talking about your books

10 B: i was (.) that was a joke i was pretending to say [enhancing my

11   memory then i said]

12 A: [o:h (.) O::H (.)

13   that's right]

14 B: you're <u>slee</u>ping

15 A: i am

The example begins with A and B involved in a discussion of whether or not B is doing some unstated activity in order to enhance her memory. At the end of her first turn, B asserts in a quiet voice that she may well be enhancing her memory. This is ignored by A, and in the next line, line 6, B indicates that she has forgotten what they have been talking about, a surprising claim since B has just barely finished talking about enhancing her memory. In line 7, A initially ignores B's question, following which she displays confusion over B's claim (her confusion is displayed by emphasis and a questioning intonation on 'what'). B then indicates that she was making a joke and eventually, lines 12–13, A displays recognition of the joke. In sum, B's 'what are we talkin about again↑' did not display a genuine memory failure on B's part and, thus, violated the Quality maxim. Given that B's statement followed so soon after B was talking about the topic that she now claims to have forgotten, B had good reason to believe that A would recognize that B was deliberately flouting the CP. This, then, is a clear case of an attempted flouting of the CP that was not, at first, recognized as such.

In the next example, one participant makes a contribution that is not consistent with the CP, but in the next turn corrects his contribution so that it is cooperative.

Example 4:14

(student, S, and professor, P)

1   S: do you respond to email?

(1.5)

2   P: sometimes

3   S: ((laughs)) [i guess uh]

4   P: [i uh] don't have email at home so that i <u>don't</u> respond

5   to it but when i come in i mean i always do when i come in but i

6   (.) i refuse to be the slave to email

P in line 2 produces a response to S's question that is not sufficiently informative, thereby violating the CP. S orients to the violation and begins to say something when he/she is interrupted by P. At that point, P displays recognition that he had violated the Quantity maxim by providing considerable detail that renders his answer sufficiently informative.

Many of the previous examples illustrate how a speaker who flouts the CP is, nevertheless, engaging in cooperative interaction and producing contributions that are intelligible. It is, however, possible that one or more participants may actually opt out of the CP and fail to be cooperative. If S opts out of the CP yet A believes S is following the CP, A will make an incorrect interpretation of S's contribution. The next example provides an illustration.

Example 4:15

(Inspector Clouseau in the movie *The Pink Panther*. Clouseau, C, enters a store where there is a dog and a shopkeeper, S).

1   C: does your dog bite↑

2   S: no

3 C: ((pats dog and gets bitten)) i thought

4   you said your dog doesn't bite

5 S: that isn't my dog monsieur

If C is following the CP then 'your dog' in line 1 refers to the dog in the store. When S answers 'no', C is therefore justified in believing that the dog is S's dog and that it does not bite. If the dog is not S's dog, in order to follow the maxim of Manner, S should have been clear that the dog he is referring to is not the dog in the store. Thus, S's line 5 justification is not acceptable because S has not followed the CP. Although bad things always happen to Clouseau typically due to his own foolishness, in this case Clouseau is a cooperative participant and it is the shopkeeper who is not.

The Positive Aspects of Grice's Views of Non-natural Meaning, the CP, and Implicature

The major strength of Grice's views of non-natural meaning and the CP is that a major role is assigned to inferential processes and outcomes. As has been repeatedly documented, this accords well with the observation that inference is central both to the production and interpretation of talk. In any reasonable model of talk, processes of encoding–decoding, if they exist at all, must take a back seat to processes of inference. As Levinson (1995, pp. 232–233) notes in this context, '. . . we think specifically; we talk generally. I can't say what I mean in some absolute sense; I have to take into account what you will think I mean by it. One can't *encode* a proposition; all one can do is sketch the outlines, hoping the recipient will know how to turn the sketch into something more precise (if something more precise was intended)' (emphasis in original).

A second positive aspect of the Gricean perspective is that talk is conceptualized as one particular form, but not the only form, of coordinated and cooperative *social interaction*. Indeed, Grice gives examples of following the maxims of the CP that involve physical rather than verbal actions, such as passing a hammer rather than a saw (maxim of Quality) at the appropriate moment when it is needed (maxims of Quantity and Relevance) in the appropriate way to pass a hammer at that point (maxim of Manner). The view that talk is embedded in and constitutive of social activity has many important implications, two of which may be noted in the present context. One implication is that an emphasis on the practical nature of talk highlights the for-all-practical-purposes nature of actions and shared understandings (intersubjectivity) in talk. The view that talk is social interaction also carries the implication that, in order to coordinate their talk, participants must share certain assumptions, certain common ground, about the nature of their interaction. This common ground includes the mutual assumption that the CP and its maxims are being followed, that each participant has the ability to work out implicatures when required, and that each participant can recognize when a flouting has occurred. This alerts us to the possibility of other types of common ground, such as mutual assumptions about personal, social and cultural knowledge, that may need to be included in a model of talk.

A third major contribution of the Gricean perspective is that a distinction needs to be made between *laws* of action and *principles* of action. Typically, laws of action/behaviour are cause–effect statements of how one factor, often a mental state, causes behaviour. Principles of behaviour, by contrast, are templates for the interpretation of action. In other words, principles of action are used to justify action, not to causally bring it about (Garfinkel, 1967; Suchman, 1987). A further difference is that laws cannot be violated but principles can be violated. Indeed, by exploiting a principle of social interaction, participants can produce meanings they would not be able to produce otherwise, as for example, certain forms of verbal humour, irony and metaphor, all of which often involve exploitation of the maxims of the CP.

PROBLEMS FOR GRICE

There are two main problematic aspects of Grice's approach. Briefly, these are (1) the major role played by literal or sentence meaning in the determination of speaker meaning, and (2) the emphasis on the transactional orientation of talk (i.e., that people talk in order to accomplish practical activities) to the exclusion of social orientations. Each of these deficiencies is discussed in the final section of the chapter.

Role of Literal or Sentence Meaning

Central to the Gricean account of meaning is the distinction between sentence meaning and utterance meaning, where sentence meaning is equivalent to literal, linguistic meaning and utterance meaning is equivalent to speaker meaning. According to Grice, in coming to understand an utterance, sentence meaning is first determined from principles of semantics, and then the sentence meaning is transformed via the CP to yield speaker meaning. As can be seen in all the examples of this section, at the very least literal meaning is partially determined by the CP, rather than being computed before inferencing via the CP occurs (Levinson, 2000; D. Wilson & Sperber, 1981).

Example 4:16

1 T: i remember my friend she worked there (.) or i became friends

2   with one o the waitresses=

3 L: =yeah

4 T: a:nd (3.0) she accepted a cheque from one group it was like a

5   hundred an sixty five bucks a:nd (1.0) because the cheque bounced

6   they took it out of her paycheck (1.5) and that's against the law

7   (1.0) and then they fired her

8   (1.0)

9 L: oh

10   (2.0)

11 T: that was lovely

12 L: ((laughs))

In lines 6 and 7 T says 'they took it out of her paycheck' and 'then they fired her'. How do L and we understand that 'they' refers to the management of the restaurant T is talking about? The only entity that T has mentioned explicitly in her turn that could be referred to as 'they' is the group who paid with a cheque that bounced. However, members of the culture know that only an employer could have the power to deduct losses incurred by the employee from an employee's paycheck. Thus, on the assumption that T is following the CP, it can be inferred that 'they' refers to the management of the restaurant. Note that this interpretation is not based on the literal meaning of T's utterance but rather is derived by inference from the assumption that T is following the CP. Recognition that T is doing complaining occurs by inference using the CP, but that recognition relies, among other things, on understanding to whom 'they' refers. Thus, the CP enters into the determination of sentence meaning.

In the next example, a speaker makes a joke based on a potential word meaning that is excluded by the CP.

Example 4:17

(B, a research assistant, has just telephoned S to request S's participation in a psychology study. S had previously stated his willingness to volunteer. When B calls, unknown to B it is S's father F who answers the phone).

1 B: . . . ah w- doing some research for the psyc department

2 F: oh yeah

3 B: so i'm trying to get subjects

4   F: i see (.) okay ((laughs))

5   B: ((laughs))

6   F: well i don't know if i'll give ya a subject or a verb [(1.5)] just a sec

7   B: [((laughs))]

8   F: yeah

The word 'subject' can be used to refer to a participant in a research study or to a grammatical category. However, if the CP is being followed, 'subject' in this case would refer to a research participant. Thus, F in line 6 is either opting out of the CP or flouting the CP. Since both B and F treat line 6 as a joke, F is treated as having flouted the CP. In this example the CP is used to perform two functions; namely, to specify the meaning of 'subject' and to create an implicature. In other words, the CP is used both to assign a situationally-relevant meaning to a word (and to a sentence) and to create an implicature based on that situationally-relevant meaning.

The next example is similar to Example 4:17, except that it is not clear whether the speaker is producing a joke or an insult.

Example 4:18

(overheard on a bus: bus number 148 shares a route with 147, which goes to Coquitlam Centre; bus 148 pulled over and stopped for a passenger)

1   P: do you go to coquitlam centre↑

2   D: no

3   P: how long's the 147↑

4   D: forty feet just like this one ((at which point driver closed the

5   doors and drove off))

From the standpoint of literal meaning, 'long' can refer to time or to length. It is on the assumption that the CP is being followed that 'long' in line 3 is interpreted as referring to time. D's lines 4–5 turn is, accordingly, seen to flout the CP, and some interpretation is made (e.g., D is joking around; D is a jerk).

The next three examples all contain the verb 'to get'. The meaning of the verb, however, is different in each case.

Example 4:19

(previous talk about how useful a video card would be for the computer)

1 F: it'd be nice to get a video card (.) a real one

Example 4:20

1 F: so that every part of you is reflected in that one atom *actually

2   every part of you is reflected in all the atoms*

3 S: huh ( ) i d- i don't really get it at all [eh]

Example 4:21

(S and F are playing a game of pool and are arguing about the rules that apply to what S can now do)

1 S: i CAN too i can put it down right now=

2 F: =no you can't you have to put it back up there on the line=

3 S: =well i also get to put one down'n pull one up right↑

In 4:19, 'to get' is interpreted as 'to buy', in 4:20 as 'to understand', and in 4:21 as 'to be allowed to'. Whatever implicatures are made in each of these examples, those implicatures must be based on a specification of what 'to get' means in that instance. And, it seems, that the way in which 'to get' is specified is by application of the CP and its maxims.

The same point is illustrated in the next two examples of the use of the expression 'mhm'. It should be noted that it is not evident that 'mhm' even has a literal, sentence meaning. Whatever meaning 'mhm' accomplishes seems, therefore, to derive from the application of the CP to the specific context in which 'mhm' occurs.

Example 4:22

1 S: i have a question for you i don't know if i'm allow to ask you (.)

2   but i'm sort of confused

3 P: mhm

4 S: i'm doing uh (.) my project on repairs i just need to ask you . . .

In his/her initial turn, S produces a pre-question, a request to ask a question. In response, P utters 'mhm', thereby giving S the go-ahead to produce the projected question, and in the next line S does so. In the next example, 'mhm' is used to do the act of agreeing or confirming.

Example 4:23

(mother and her young child playing with blocks)

1 M: well you have to find a blue thing like that see↑

2 C: hunh (.) there's one [in the]

3 M: [and you] can push it on (.) you can push it

4   on

5 C: there's a blue

6 M: mhm (.) you could put it on that one couldn't you↑

7 C: put it on here↑

8   (2.4)

9 M: yeah

10 C: like (i did)↑

11 M: mhm

In line 6, M's 'mhm' seems to do the action of agreeing with C's claim or encouraging C to 'find a blue thing like that'. In line 11, M's 'mhm' is used to confirm that C has correctly put 'it on that one'.

What all the examples in the above section illustrate is that, contrary to the Gricean position, the CP is not something that is applied only to the output of a linguistic, semantic analysis of the literal meaning of words combined with a syntactic analysis of those words in combination. Rather, the CP is involved in the determination of both sentence meaning and speaker meaning.

There is a related complexity to the use of the CP in determining speaker meaning. Both sentence meaning and speaker meaning are tied to specific occasions of practical use; that is, they are indexical and they are of a for-all-practical-purposes type of meaning. These attributes of the application of the CP in the determination of meaning are critical in any model of talk. To illustrate their importance, consider Example 4:24.

Example 4:24

(Overheard at a store selling alcoholic beverages. T is a teenager trying to buy alcohol and C is the clerk. The legal age of drinking in this culture is nineteen)

1 T: i'd like to get a case of blue

2 C: are yuh over nineteen↑ duh yuh have any id↑

3 T: no

4 C: then i can't sell yuh any beer

Given the location (in a liquor store) and the roles of buyer and seller, T's line 1 turn is a request to buy something. In the culture in which the interaction occurred, 'blue' is a type of beer. On the assumption that the CP is being followed, T is asking to buy a case of beer. In another location, such as a cheese store, 'blue' is more likely to refer to a type of cheese (as in 'i'd like to get a case of blue, but my wife wants me to buy the cheddar'). Thus, the literal meaning of 'blue' must be determined in part by some sort of inferential process that is sensitive to the context, that is indexical. However, in this and every specific instance, there is a very large set of implicatures of an utterance. For example, when T says 'i'd like to get a case of blue', T may be implicating that the beer is in standard containers, such as bottles or aluminum cans; that the case contains full, rather than empty, bottles or cans; that the beer is fresh and has not gone off; that the case is a standard 6 pack in British Columbia (but a 24 pack in Ontario); that T intends to pay for the beer with money, a credit card or a debit card; and so on. It seems that implicatures of this sort are not part of what Grice intended to cover by the term 'implicature'. What, then, prevents the potentially enormous set of implicatures from being made?

One possibility is that the CP and its maxims can be used to rule out some of the possible implicatures (e.g., through use of the relevance maxim; Sperber & Wilson, 1986). Another possibility is that there are additional principles used to constrain interpretation, such as the assumption that everything is normal or typical unless explicitly indicated otherwise. So, for example, if T wants stale beer, he should explicitly ask for it, otherwise it will be assumed that he wants fresh beer. By including additional taken-for-granteds of this sort, most potential implicatures would not need to be drawn. Regardless of the solution to this problem, inferences must be made in a way that is relative to the total speech situation. Of course, if S's contribution to talk is not understood, A can initiate a repair in his next turn. In sum, given indexicality, a for-all-practical-purposes orientation, various sets of mutual assumptions, plus the opportunity to initiate and achieve repair, the theoretical possibility of a potentially infinite number of implicatures may not arise as a practical concern.

Grice's views of the importance of inference and indexicality have both positive and negative aspects. On the positive side, Grice recognized the central role of inference and the total speech situation in the production and interpretation of talk. In particular, Grice argued that the implicatures that must be drawn in order to interpret speaker meaning are relative to the talk-exchange in which participants are engaged. Additional principles of interpretation that are sensitive to the total speech situation seem to be needed in a complete model of talk. On the negative side, Grice did not go far enough in recognizing the role of inference and indexicality in social interaction. For Grice, sentence meaning is determinate, not inferential, and it is context-invariant, not indexical. It is only after sentence meaning is determined that context-sensitive (indexical), inferential processes are applied in the determination of speaker meaning. However, as has been seen in this chapter, all meanings in talk are determined inferentially and indexically. In other words, contrary to Grice's model, context-sensitive inference occurs at all levels in the determination of meaning.

Overemphasis on the Transactional Goals of Talk

For those occasions on which participants want to create verbal humour, irony or metaphor, there is a justification for talk that does not directly follow the CP and its maxims. However, for virtually all other types of talk, it should be expected that participants are being truthful, giving precisely enough and no more information, are relevant, and clear; that is, talk should be 'short, sweet, and to the point'. There is a type of communication that fits this characterization; namely, that of written telegrams. Because there is a charge for each word used in a telegram, a cost-conscious telegram writer will try to get the message across (typical messages involve the announcement of the persons, places and dates of births, deaths and marriages) as clearly as possible while using as few words as possible. However, observation of actual talk reveals that it is not at all like a telegram. Everyday talk is full of components that have no clear connection to the 'message' being conveyed.

Consider a typical example of a request refusal (i.e., the Gricean 'message' is the action of refusing the request). B has telephoned to ask S, whose name is on a list of people willing to volunteer for research, to participate in a psychology study. The example begins after B has identified himself and is now speaking to S.

Example 4:25

1   B: hi (.) ah i'm just calling to see if you'd be interested in ah

2   participating in a study this week

(Eight turns and 13 lines deleted during which S asked for and received clarification about the study)

16 S: well, let's see tuesday at two (.) it's up on campus eh↑

17 B: yeah

18 S: thursday well unfortunately i'm not at school either of those days

19   i go to harbour centre those nights

20 B: yeah

21 S: so um y'know i don't know if i'd want to go up

22 B: yeah i understand (.) okay well thanks anyways

23 S: thanks for calling

24 B: okay

25 S: alright

26 B: bye-bye

27 S: bye

After a series of questions and answers that clarify and confirm B's initial request, S in line 18 finally responds to that request. S's response, which if Gricean should be a granting (e.g., 'Yeah'; 'I'll do it') or a refusal (e.g., 'No';'I will not do it'), instead begins with 'well', followed by an apology ('unfortunately') and an excuse ('i'm not at school either of those days'). Perhaps a refusal is implicated by this turn, but B's response of 'yeah' in line 20 does not commit him (or us) to this interpretation. In line 21 S expresses his lack of desire to comply with the request, and B in line 22 manifestly confirms S's statement of lack of desire as the doing of a refusal. Throughout this sequence, S seems to be non-Gricean in many places. He does more than is necessary and yet performs the critical act of refusing in a round-about and vague manner.

The end of the interaction also evidences many departures from Gricean talk. Once S indicates that he is not going to grant the request, there is no Gricean need for the talk to continue. At that point either or both of the participants could end the interaction simply by hanging up. Thus, what happens after line 21 is unnecessary for a request–refusal interaction. Nevertheless, an exchange of thanks occurs in the sequences in lines 22 and 23 ('okay well thanks anyway'. 'Thanks for calling') and in lines 24 and 25 ('Okay' 'Alright'). Similarly, although the exchange of 'Bye's' in lines 26 and 27 may help B and S to coordinate the termination of their interaction, termination can proceed without coordination and coordinated termination is not required by the Gricean maxims.

There is a much simpler and more straightforward (i.e., Gricean) way for S to refuse. Consider an invented example.

Example 4:26

(invented example)

1 B: hi (.) ah i'm just calling to see if you'd be interested in ah
2   participating in a study this week
3 S: no ((connection terminated))

Unlike the actual refusal, the invented refusal is right to the point and contains no excuses, apologies, offers to help in the future, expressions of understanding ('okay') and appreciation ('thanks'), and goodbyes. Indeed, if people talked in a Gricean fashion, most of the structure present in actual talk would be missing. Why, then, is the 'extra detail' present? Consideration of Example 4:26 suggests an answer. Although S's action of refusing was produced in a way that makes it easily recognizable as a refusal, it is also likely that S would be perceived as a rude and inconsiderate person. By contrast, the person who refused in Example 4:25 is likely to be perceived as polite and considerate. It is therefore possible that the non-Gricean attributes of talk orient to interpersonal function(s).

Grice himself noted that other sorts of maxims are normally observed in talk, and he included 'Be polite' as one of them. However, Grice conceptualized the CP and its maxims as the essential bedrock of talk. Any additional maxims are viewed as secondary to the CP; that is, since additional maxims do not serve the assumed primary function of talk (achievement of transactional goals), such maxims put no more than a cosmetic gloss on talk. In contrast to this position, the discussion of Examples 4:25 and 4:26 leaves open the possibility that interpersonal concerns are as deeply implicated in talk as are the CP and its maxims. In sum, the observation that talk is rarely 'short and to the point' may be a consequence of participants' orientation both to interpersonal concerns, such as being polite, as well as to the transactional concern of getting one's actions accomplished. If so, these interpersonal orientations need to be accommodated in a model of talk. The interpersonal dimension of talk is taken up in the next chapter.

5

The Interpersonal Dimension

Introduction and Chapter Overview

It was noted in the previous chapter that much of the detailed structure of actual talk would not be produced if participants strictly followed the CP. One possible explanation for non-Gricean aspects of talk is that they arise as a consequence of participants' interpersonal orientations. The present chapter takes up the issue of the interpersonal dimension of talk, for the most part building the discussion around a critical examination of P. Brown and Levinson's (1987) politeness model.

Following a discussion of the distinction between transactional and interpersonal dimensions of talk, an argument is made for why participants in talk should take into account the interpersonal consequences of their actions and the ways in which they perform those actions. The chapter then moves to a detailed description of the most prominent model of the tradeoff between transactional and interpersonal orientations in talk, the politeness model of P. Brown and Levinson (henceforth, B&L). Examples from natural talk are used to illustrate the structures of 'politeness' identified in B&L's model. The chapter concludes with a consideration of the positive attributes and the deficiencies of B&L's model. Unlike the previous three chapters, the chapter does not present a model of talk but rather a critical discussion of the interpersonal dimension of talk, an aspect that must be incorporated into any appropriate model of talk.

Transactional and Interpersonal Orientations in Talk

The co-construction of meaning involves S who behaves in a way that allows A to recognize why S intentionally behaved that way, in which case A then recognizes what action S is performing. But S typically does not want A only to recognize her action. Importantly, S carries out her actions in order to get A to respond in some specific way. The intended effects of A recognizing S's action, which are intended perlocutionary effects, are a critical part of social interaction. If addressees typically did not carry out the intended perlocutionary effects of action, there would be no point in interacting. In other words, talk involves both the recognition by A of what action S is performing and the carrying out of an action by A that will satisfy the intended perlocutionary effects of S's action.

Grice provides a description of the most efficient way for S to get A to recognize what action S is producing. Further, once A recognizes what action S is performing, it should be simple for A to work out S's intended perlocutionary effects. For example, if S asks for directions to the closest bank machine, A can recognize that giving directions will satisfy S's intended perlocutionary effects. And A can best satisfy S's intended perlocutionary effects by responding to S in a cooperative, Gricean fashion.

An important, yet unstated, assumption of the above analysis is that the intended perlocutionary effects of talk are transactional goals (see Chapter 4). However, it is not apparent what factual information is exchanged nor how the objective world is changed by actions such as apologizing, appealing, complimenting, emoting, empathizing, esteeming, excusing, expressing affection, greeting, hedging, justi-fying, prefacing, stalling, showing support, sympathizing, and thanking. To examine what such actions accomplish, consider the action of apologizing. When S apolo-gizes, S displays concern for the other and for the offence S has visited on A by S's actions, and S also displays the self to be a considerate person who accepts responsibility for her actions. By accepting the apology, A displays himself to be a forgiving person who values S as a moral, considerate human being. The action sequence of apology–acceptance is, thus, a remedial exchange (Goffman, 1967, 1971) oriented to resolving the state of interpersonal imbalance resulting from the offence and its consequences (Owen, 1983). Accordingly, apologies, among many other actions, have an *interpersonal* orientation, which G. Brown & Yule (1983) define as 'the use of language to establish and maintain social relationships' (p. 3).

It is now possible to sketch an answer to the question of why talk is typically non-Gricean. The Gricean approach is based on the view that participants in talk adopt only a transactional orientation. However, there is an interpersonal orientation in talk; namely, in every turn at talk, S and A display, create and/or challenge identities of self, other, and their relationship. Participants' interpersonal orien-tations are likely to influence both what actions they perform and how those actions are structured. Many of the non-Gricean structures of talk reflect participants' orientation to the interpersonal dimension. In sum, in every turn at talk, participants orient to both transactional and interpersonal dimensions. Grice has provided a model based on a transactional orientation. A model is needed also that incorporates the interpersonal dimension.

Relevance of the interpersonal dimension for models of talk

Malinowski (1923) introduced the view that talk has interpersonal or phatic aspects. Malinowski held conflicting views of the nature and relevance of these interpersonal aspects. On the one hand, he characterized the interpersonal aspects, which he associated with women, as small talk or gossip, as talk that is aimless, idle, and insincere, and that fails to communicate ideas. On the other hand, Malinowski claimed that the interpersonal aspects of talk satisfy the need for social connection and recognition, the need to be in social relationships, and the need to have one's identity affirmed, created, and re-affirmed by others. From that perspective, the interpersonal aspect of talk is central to social life.

These contradictory views of the interpersonal orientation in talk continue to influence present-day models of talk and interaction. In many conceptions, talk is viewed as essentially transactional, as a vehicle for the transmission of information. The interpersonal aspects of talk are viewed as nothing more than a surface gloss that acts as a social lubricant. By contrast, the present chapter demonstrates that interpersonal considerations are built into talk from the ground up, so to speak and, further, that unless participants pay attention to the interpersonal implications of their talk, transactional functions will not be realized.

Tradeoff between the transactional and interpersonal orientations

Given evolutionary processes, participants in talk can be expected to act efficiently. Efficiency is always relative to some standard, and in talk there are efficiencies with respect to transactional and interpersonal orientations. Often, acting efficiently with a transactional orientation interferes with the ability to act efficiently with an interpersonal orientation, and vice-versa. For example, suppose S makes a request of A. Transactional efficiency requires brevity, in accordance with a least effort principle, and clarity. The result is a very blunt and direct request, such as 'put this box in my car', a request that might well offend A and leave A with the impression that S is an inconsiderate person. By contrast, interpersonal efficiency requires attributes such as indirectness, vagueness, excuses, apologies, offers to reciprocate and thanks. The result is a non-Gricean request, such as 'I'm sorry to have to bother you but I have to get this box into my car but it is too heavy for me to lift alone and I'd be really grateful if it wouldn't be too much trouble↑'. As is evident from these examples, the two sorts of efficiency are in direct opposition.

One way to deal with the conflicting efficiencies is to ignore one dimension at the expense of the other. This, however, may not be feasible. Unless participants can exchange information and bring about changes in the world through their actions, there would be little point in talking. Thus, satisfaction of transactional concerns is critical. But satisfaction of interpersonal concerns is also critical, and for two main reasons. One reason derives from the self-referential nature of a turn at talk; as Malone (1997) puts it 'Because talk is always self-referential and, as such, is metonymic, hearers interpret utterances as signs which stand for a larger self' (p. 4). Since a turn at talk displays a self identity as well as the self's view of other and the self–other relationship, when participants in talk negotiate meaning they also and at the same time negotiate identity (Rawls, 1989). Given the centrality of identity in social life, speakers are motivated to display and create certain selves while suppressing the display and creation of others. Participants in talk are also motivated to convey particular information and to produce particular effects on the world by their actions. Thus, the transactional and interpersonal dimensions are inextricably connected in talk.

The second reason for the importance of an interpersonal orientation in talk is that transactional goals will get accomplished only if interpersonal goals are attended to. Whereas A may recognize the action S has accomplished and recognize also S's intended perlocutionary effects, A must be willing (and able) to carry out the actions necessary for the satisfaction of those intended effects. There are reasons to suppose that A may not be willing to do so, one being that virtually any action S may want A to perform will interfere in some way with A's own desires. Suppose, for example, S asks A to check who is ringing the front door bell. It is likely that if A does go and check who is at the door, this will interfere with some of his own ongoing activities, and at the very least A's freedom to do as he wishes is being infringed by S. Further, A may consider himself an autonomous person who 'does not like to be told what to do'; that is, A's identity is threatened by S's request. Considerations of this sort suggest that, in general, the satisfaction of S's goals is likely to be in conflict with some of A's goals, and vice-versa. Thus, for A to satisfy S's goals A must forgo his own in the short term, at least.

The issue, then, is why A would forgo own goals in favour of other's goals. One answer is considered self-interest, the notion that it is in the best interest for A to forgo own goals in the short term and satisfy S's goals since by doing so S is more likely to satisfy A's goals in the long term; and, similarly, it is in the best interest of S to forgo own goals in the short term and satisfy A's goals since in doing so A is more likely to satisfy S's goals in the long term. Both S and A achieve greater benefits from such a strategy in the long run than they can receive from the strategy of satisfying own goals in the short term.

To summarize. Transactional goals need to be accomplished in order for social interaction to bring about changes in the world. But it is also the case that every act of meaning-making displays participants' identities. Thus, meaning-making necessarily involves participants' orientation to both transactional and interpersonal dimensions. Further, S's attainment of her transactional and interpersonal goals will often conflict with A's attainment of his transactional and interpersonal goals, and vice-versa. The strategy of considered self-interest provides the best way to maximize the attainment of both types of goals for all parties in the long run. In the next section of the chapter a specific model of this type of tradeoff is presented; namely, P. Brown and Levinson's (1987) model of universal principles of politeness in social interaction.

POLITENESS THEORY

B&L base their model on the postulates that individuals (1) can engage in and carry out means–ends reasoning (i.e., individuals are rational), and (2) have a desire to protect their identities. B&L then argue that to do 1, interacting persons must do 2; that is, in order to achieve transactional goals, individuals must achieve interpersonal goals. The rational person must somehow manage a tradeoff between transactional goals while protecting identity. According to B&L, the major inter-personal goal is identity which, following Goffman (1967), they refer to as *face*. Although there are a vast number of identities or face that persons can claim, B&L suggest that face can be conceptualized as consisting of two desires, referred to as *negative face* and *positive face*. Negative face is the desire to be unimpeded, to not have one's freedom restricted. Positive face is the desire to be approved of by particular others. Many, if not all, interactions involve face-threatening actions or FTAs. Thus, on the mutual assumption that face will be protected, participants in interaction need to carry out actions that will protect threatened face or repair damaged face. The actions that participants carry out that are oriented to face are referred to as *facework*.

Both transactional and interpersonal goals are important in interaction. However, actions oriented to face are often in conflict with those oriented to transactional goals. Thus, the rational person should do only as much facework as is required and no more. But how much facework is required in a specific situation? B&L propose that the higher the threat to face of an FTA, the more facework that needs to be done. Further, they propose that the extent to which an FTA threatens face, which they refer to as the weightiness of a face-threatening act (W_{FTA}), is determined by the following equation:

$$W_{FTA} = P(A/S) + D(S \& A) + r_x$$

In this equation, P(A/S) refers to the power of A over S; D(S & A) refers to the social distance between S and A, which varies from intimates (close) to strangers (distant); and r_x refers to the degree of imposition of the action at issue, which varies from low to high (e.g., asking for help to open a door versus move a piano).

Increasing the power of A over S, the social distance between S and A, and the imposition of the action at issue all increase the amount of face-threat, W_{FTA}. The equation captures intuitions about 'politeness'. Consider an invented example (many examples from natural talk are presented later in the chapter). Imagine an undergraduate student who, after an evening class, goes to start her car in the university parking lot, only to find that her battery is dead. There is no garage on campus. The only other person in the parking lot is either the university president or a cook at one of the campus food services. Most observers would predict that it would be more difficult (i.e., more embarrassing, harder to be assertive) for the student to ask for help from the president than the cook. Since the only factor that differs in the two cases is power or status, B&L predict that it should be more difficult to ask the president. Overall, the B&L model captures intuitions about the factors that determine degree of face-threat.

The equation for the amount of face-threat, the claim that rational persons should do only as much facework as is required and no more, and the claim that the required amount of facework is directly proportional to the amount of face-threat constitute the bases for a model of face and facework. Two additional pieces need to be added to the model; namely, a description of how participants can do facework and a measure of amount of facework. To introduce B&L's discussion of those issues, consider again the undergraduate student, S, who needs help in jump-starting her car. If S were to ask the university president for help she might say something like 'I hate to bother you but there's no one else around right now and I can't find a garage that's open so I was wondering if it isn't too much trouble if you mightn't . . .'. By contrast, if she were to ask the cook for help she might say something like 'I was wondering if you could help me . . .'. The first request contains actions such as apology, explanation, and justification and is constructed in a roundabout, hedged, hesitant, and pessimistic manner, all of which are facework strategies. By contrast, the second request is briefer and more directly to the point. The example illustrates what B&L mean by facework. It also illustrates that more facework is done by using more structures of a certain sort (e.g., apology, excuse, hedging, minimization), and that the more face-threatening the act, the more facework is produced. These aspects of facework, based on intuitions about talk, are reflected in B&L's model.

B&L relate the extent to which an act threatens face, as expressed by the FTA equation, to a set of facework superstrategies appropriate to that level of face-threat. Table 5.1 (adapted from P. Brown & Levinson, 1987, p. 60) presents this relation.

TABLE 5.1 *Degree of face-threat and the associated facework superstrategies*

Degree of face-threat	Facework superstategy
Low	Bald on record
Medium	On record with Positive politeness and/or
	On record with Negative politeness
Medium high to high	Off record
High	Do not do the FTA

In order to clarify Table 5.1, it is necessary to clarify B&L's conceptualization of facework superstrategies and the strategies that constitute each superstrategy.

Bald on record

To be 'on record' is to produce an action such that it is easily recognized and unambiguous. The strategy of being *bald on record* is to talk in a Gricean manner, which defines the way in which S should talk in order for A to most easily infer S's communicative intention. Since Gricean talk is not oriented to face, B&L are proposing that it is not necessary to pay attention to face for low FTAs.

Positive politeness

For medium level FTAs, S should go on record but should redress threats to face through the use of strategies of *positive politeness*. Use of positive politeness strategies conveys that S cares about A's desire to be approved of (i.e., A's positive face) even though S seems to be threatening A's positive face. Doing positive politeness is displaying caring, approving and valuing the other person. Positive politeness is, therefore, the politeness of intimacy and solidarity. To give a clear sense of what is meant by positive politeness strategies, the following describes some of the strategies and gives examples (interested readers should consult B&L for a comprehensive list).

The superstrategy of positive politeness consists of three main strategies: namely, claim common ground, convey S and A are cooperators and fulfil A's wants. When S claims common ground with A, S displays that she and A are members of some group (e.g., culture, school, family) who, therefore, share values and beliefs. A claim of common ground might be made by conveying that A is a valued person (e.g., by noticing A or exaggerating interest in A), by using in-group markers (e.g., by using terms of endearment or terms in a foreign language that S and A speak), and by emphasizing shared values and beliefs (e.g., by seeking agreement and avoiding disagreement). A claim that S and A are cooperators might be made by S asserting that S does consider A's wants important, and by S indicating that S and A are 'in this together' (e.g., by using pronouns such as 'we' that include both S and A rather than pronouns that separate S and A, such as 'you and I'). When S fulfils A's wants, S can do so by giving sympathy, understanding, or gifts.

Negative politeness

For medium level FTA's that are somewhat higher in face-threat than those that call for positive politeness, S should go on-record but should redress threats to face through the use of strategies of *negative politeness*. Use of negative politeness strategies conveys that S does not want or intend to interfere with A's freedom to do as A wishes; that is, S conveys her concern for the protection of A's negative face. Negative politeness is, thus, the politeness of respect/deference.

The negative politeness superstrategy consists of five major strategies: namely, don't presume/assume, but instead question and hedge; don't coerce A, but instead be conventionally indirect, be pessimistic, minimize, and give deference; communicate S's want to not impinge by apologizing, giving overwhelming reasons, begging forgiveness, impersonalizing, and avoiding 'I' and 'You'; state the FTA as a general rule by nominalizing; and redress A's other wants by going on record as incurring a debt.

Off-record politeness

As the name implies, when S goes off-record, S forms her action in such a way that there is more than one possible and likely interpretation of what action S is performing. Use of the off-record superstrategy conveys that S is giving A some freedom as to how to interpret S's action. The superstrategy consists of the strategies of inviting conversational implicature by flouting the maxims of Quantity, Quality, and Manner, and the strategy of being vague or ambiguous by flouting the maxim of Manner. In general, off-record talk will involve actions such as hinting, understating and overstating, being ironic, using metaphors, using rhetorical questions, and being vague, ambiguous and incomplete.

As can be seen in Table 5.1, B&L rank strategies according to how much facework each accomplishes: from lowest to highest amount of facework, the ranking is bald on record, positive politeness, negative politeness, and off-record. It is not clear, however, that the use of positive politeness strategies does less facework than the use of negative politeness strategies. Nor are the three superstrategies and their associated strategies mutually exclusive; that is, talk may and usually does contain a mixture of types of politeness and types of strategy. Thus, participants can do more or less facework by their choice of type of facework and by the number of strategies they use, such that the more strategies S produces, the more facework is accomplished. In addition, whereas whole actions can be used to do facework (e.g., the actions of apologizing, excusing, thanking), facework can be accomplished by elements internal to acts (e.g., 'I'm sorry' versus 'I'm terribly, terribly sorry'; 'I want to ask you a question' versus 'I wonder if it would be OK if I were to ask you a question?'; see Turnbull & Saxton (1997) for a discussion of doing facework by using modal expressions in request refusals).

Experimental evidence tends, in general, to support B&L's claims of more facework given more face-threat and their measures of amount of facework. Much of that evidence needs to be interpreted with caution, however, since it is evidence of what people write or say they would do and not evidence of what they actually would do in a face-threatening situation. In spite of this reservation, the influence of relative power and of degree of imposition, r_x, is generally as predicted by the equation for W_{FTA} (for a review of studies up until 1986, see B&L, 1987, pp. 1–50). However, the distance dimension has fared less well (Baxter, 1984; Slugoski & Turnbull, 1988; R. Brown & Gilman, 1989). Slugoski & Turnbull (1988) proposed that interpersonal distance needs to be distinguished from interpersonal affect in the W_{FTA} equation, a revision that improves the fit of data to the model.

The following section of the chapter illustrates positive and negative facework strategies present in examples of natural talk.

Facework Oriented to Positive Face (Solidarity)

Agreeing

The next three examples illustrate positive politeness strategies of agreeing, seeking agreement, and claiming common ground. In all examples participants display involvement and solidarity.

Example 5:1

1 G: i love going to the <u>movies</u>

2 J: i do too↑ (0.5) i think once i move out here (0.6) this area (0.5) i'll

3   be going to mo[ore]=

4 G: [yeah]

5 J: =movies cos especially now i live in new west

6   (0.6)

7 G: being in that [area]

8 J: [yeah] uh:: [and it's just not convenient]

9 G: [(you got it)] the bad news is downtown

10 J: yeah

11 G: it's jus right around the corner

12 J: yeah

Repeated use of direct agreement 'yeah' and other forms that display agreement (e.g., lines 1 and 2; lines 8 and 9), many instances of overlap that display involvement, uptake of G's topic by J and the continuation and expansion of that topic by both participants all function to create an atmosphere of agreement, involvement, and solidarity.

The next example illustrates a request for confirmation–confirmation sequence that displays participants' agreement.

Example 5:2

1 A: yea:h i remember they mentioned about the prototype right a

2   while back

3 B: yeah [yeah i don't see how]

4 A: [and they were] interviewing people [right↑]

5 B: [yeah]=

6 A: =yeah=

In line 4 A asks for confirmation 'right↑' and B confirms immediately in overlap. In response, A echoes B's confirmation, thereby acknowledging it, and A's acknowledgement is latched onto B's confirmation. Overall, the example displays a tight turn-by-turn structure that displays agreement and involvement.

Another way to do positive facework is through appeals to common ground, as is illustrated in Example 5:3.

Example 5:3

1 G: and the:en (0.6) the housing all around it is very city like↑

2 J: yeah

3 G: you know what i mean like it is like city

4 J: ye[ah]

In line 3 'you know what i mean' is used to accomplish positive facework in at least two ways. It functions both as an appeal to common ground (i.e., only those with shared experience will 'know what I mean') and as a request for confirmation.

Joking

Solidarity can be created through joking exchanges. For a joke to come off, it is necessary that participants share some common ground, such as knowledge of current events and attitudes. Further, in sharing a joke, participants share in a display of humour and positive emotion. Examples 5:4 through 5:8 provide illustrations.

Example 5:4

1 B: oh yesterday (0.8) i had road rage

2 A: ((laughs)) did you↑

3 B: yes (.) this gu:y (.) this old man (.) this old little fart was only

4   going forty (1.0) the who:le (.) all the way to rumble=

5 A: =i hate that

6 B: and i couldn't do anything about it (0.7) so i had road rage

7   (1.4)

8 A: did you (.) act on your road rage↑

 9 B: [no]

10 A: [you] didn't like pull out a pistol or

11 B: no (.) though i was quite tempted

12   (1.3)

13 A: i hate that that's so frustrating eh↑

14 B: yup (1.0) and i was late enough as it was cause i was coming

15   home from voice lessons and that [sucker was]

16 A: [it's <u>always</u>] when you're late

17 B: oh i <u>know</u> it's always when you're late you get all the red lights

18   (.) you always get that forty person in fronna ya

19 A: yup (.) yup yup yup

The positive facework strategies employed in this example include the use of laughter and emotional displays (using stress and repetition), exaggeration, strong agreement, facetious remarks, rhetorical questions and requests for confirmation ('eh↑'), and latching. Use of these strategies creates and displays a relationship of involvement, intimacy, solidarity and good humour.

A similar style of interaction is evident in the next example.

Example 5:5

(Father, F, ten year old daughter, D, and eight year old son, S)

1 D: what's the smallest kind of phone↑ this is a joke

        (2.0)

2 F: i don't know

3 D: a cell phone ((laughs))

4 F: ((laughs))

5 D: cell (.) phone

6 F: ahunh

7 D: and a bacterial phone ((laughs)) and a virus phone

8 S: no an atom phone

9 D: and a quark phone

(1.5)

10 S: yeah a bork phone ((laughs))

11 D: a <u>bork</u> phone↑

12 S: no a ray phone

The next example illustrates how joking can be used not only to enhance positive face but also to avoid potential threats to positive face.

Example 5:6

(Two 20 year old female friends)

1 A: and there was this one house that was for sale it was right near

2 the edge (.) and (.) it was a:ll (.) it looked kinda like a bunker↑

3 B: a what↑

4 A: like a <u>bunker</u>

5 B: o:h a bunker

6 A: yeah

7 B: i thought you said a bunkcart

8 A: [no]

9 B: [i'm like] what the hell is that↑ ((laughing))

10 A: ((laughs)) yeah i don't know what a bunkcart is either (0.8) ah (.)

11 and it looked like a perfect place to kill somebody and kinda <u>sock</u>

12 <u>away</u> the body

13 B: [e:w]

14 A: [so i'm] not gonna tell my parents about that [one]

In line 3 B initiates a repair, thereby treating A's contributions as problematic in some way (i.e., as a repairable). In line 4, A carries out the repair. Given that both B and A have oriented to an error of some sort on A's part (e.g., perhaps A has not spoken loudly or clearly enough), B's initiation of the repair and A's making of the repair are threats to A's positive face. Following the potential insult to A's positive face, B and A do a lot of positive facework. In lines 7 and 9, B makes a joke of the repairable and laughs about it, thereby diminishing its seriousness and the extent to which it threatens A's positive face. In line 10, A displays agreement with B by echoing B's laughter and following up on B's joke, thereby further diminishing the threat to his/her face. At that point, A initiates a change in topic (actually a return to the topic under discussion prior to line 1), and B in line 13 displays acceptance of the topic change and emotional involvement with it. Overall, A and B work together to repair damage to A's positive face (and to A and B's relationship) occasioned by A's production of a repairable.

Minimizing and avoiding disagreements

Because A's opinions are valued by A, if S devalues or disagrees with A's actions or opinions, S threatens A's positive face. Joking is one strategy that can be used to diminish such threats. As illustrated next, two additional strategies used for dealing with disagreements include minimizing disagreements that do arise and avoiding projected disagreements.

Example 5:7

(Young children playing Spirograph)

1 J: i don't like this one

2   (4.0)

3 J: d'ya like this one↑

4   (1.0)

5 R: i like <u>this</u> one=

6 J: =d'ya like <u>this</u> one↑

7   (1.5)

8 R: sorduv

In line 3, J asks R a direct yes/no question. After a one second pause, a marker of reluctance, R in line 5 produces an utterance that does not directly address the question (i.e., a direct response would be 'yes' or 'no'). Perhaps R is both disagreeing with J and is trying to find something that they can agree on. In line 6 J orients to R's failure to answer the question by repeating his/her question and stressing '<u>this</u>', which contrasts with the 'one' that R asserts he/she likes. In line 8 it becomes manifest that R does not like the 'one' J likes, and that R's answer in line 5 was 'no'. However, R again weakens the disagreement by hedging 'sorduv'. Silence, attempts to avoid disagreement, to find 'safe' topics (i.e., agree), and hedging are all used to minimize and avoid disagreement.

Actions such as refusing a request or turning down an invitation are similar to disagreements in that they display that what S desires is not desired by A. Example 5:8 illustrates how positive facework strategies are used to construct a rejection of an invitation.

Example 5:8

(telephone talk)

1 H: interested in goin' to a wine tasting october twelvth↑

2 D: love to but we're away that weekend

D begins the rejection with 'love to' which displays D's desire to satisfy H's positive face (i.e., H's desire to have the invitation accepted). Following this, D produces an excuse that presents a prior commitment as the reason why D cannot accept the invitation. The excuse displays D's concern for H's positive face. Further, because the action of rejecting the invitation is not made bald-on-record but rather must be inferred by H from D's excuse, D has avoided a direct attack on H's positive face (i.e., similar to the strategy of avoiding disagreements).

Negative Facework (Respect and Deference)

Negative face is the desire to be unimpeded, to not be imposed upon by others. Negative facework, accordingly, is facework directed towards minimizing and avoiding threats to freedom. It is the 'politeness' of respect and of deference. The following illustrate some common negative facework strategies.

Conventionally indirect requests

One general means of protecting negative face is to be indirect. Among the Romance languages, there is a set of conventionalized means of being indirect, the so-called 'conventionally indirect requests'. Briefly, a conventionally indirect request is an utterance for which sentence meaning is a question about A's ability or willingness to perform some action X but, in context, speaker meaning is a request for A to perform the action. Sentences of the form 'can/could you X?', 'will/would you X?', and 'might you X?' are typical conventional indirect requests in English (as are their counterparts in all the Romance languages). By being indirect in this way, S goes on-record and performs the face-threatening act of request but at the same time S conveys her desire to allow A freedom to interpret S's utterance (i.e., S conveys her desire to go off-record).

Conventionally indirect requests are very common in natural talk. Examples 5:9 through 5:11 provide illustration.

Example 5:9

(playing Scrabble)

1   M: iih::: maybe that's not a real word(2.8) can you look up for me↑

2   K: [yup]

Example 5:10

(kids drawing with coloured pencils)

1   J: may i use that one after↑

2   R: sure

Example 5:11

(Therapy session)

1   T: can we (.) go back to that for just <u>one</u> sec↑

2   C: yeah↑

In line 1 T does negative facework by using a conventionally indirect request and also by minimizing the extent of the imposition of the request with 'for just <u>one</u> sec'.

In addition to conventionally indirect requests, many utterances that do not consist of imperatives can, in sequence, be used to do a request (as was seen in Chapter 3). Example 5:12 illustrates how S uses an assertion to do a request that protects A's negative face.

Example 5:12

(Therapy session)

1   T: i must not be understanding [something]

2   C: [yeah well she] it's her boyfriend

In line 1 T's action is a request to get C to clarify some point. By framing the request in a way that places responsibility on T for the need to clarify and by leaving it up to C to interpret the utterance as a request, T minimizes the imposition on C.

Pre-sequences

The first turn of a pre-sequence projects some specific type of upcoming action but does not produce that action. For example, in turn 1 S might produce a pre-question (e.g., 'Can I ask you something?') that projects the subsequent production of a question. If A in turn 2 gives the go-ahead, S in turn 3 then proceeds to ask the question. The initial turn of such a sequence is referred to as a 'pre' and the full sequence of three turns is referred to as a 'pre-sequence'. Pre-sequences include pre-announcements, pre-jokes, pre-invitations, pre-questions, and pre-requests (Drew, 1995; Terasaki, 1976). Production by S of a pre allows A to choose whether to give S the go-ahead to produce the projected action or to turn down the projected action before it actually occurs. Further, pre-sequences can also protect S's positive face. If A responds to a pre in a way that implicates a turn-down, S can withdraw the pre. Thus, S is saved from actually producing an action that will be rejected by A.

Example 5:13

(Student, S, to professor, P. Overheard)

1   S: oh (.) a quick question

2   P: mmhh

3   S: would it be okay to show your nurseryclips in my tutorial↑

4   P: sure go ahead

In line 1 S produces what is framed as a pre-question, and in line 2 P gives S the go-ahead to produce the question. Production of the pre-question accomplishes negative facework by giving A freedom to choose to hear the question or not. In line 3, S does not produce a question but rather produces a request (i.e., S's line 1 action was a pre-request). S does this by means of a conventional indirect request, which is another way of accomplishing negative facework.

The extent to which pre's can be used to protect S's positive face is vividly illustrated in the next example.

Example 5:14

(Student, S, and professor, P)

1 S: i just need to ask you (.) um (.) a question about the midterm

2 P: m[hm↑]

3 S: [i] i uh i have to go to lethbridge (.) that weekend like we leave

4   on the wednesday

5 P: mhm

6 S: i wonder if it would be possible if (.) i could take the exam early

In line 1 S seems to produce a pre-question that both minimizes the threat to P's freedom ('just') and displays that S is 'forced' to ask the question ('need to ask you'). P responds with an unenthusiastic go-ahead. In lines 3 and 4, S does not produce a question but rather produces an excuse, which is framed as something S 'has to do' and, thus, as something over which S has no control. Again, P responds with a noncommittal 'mhm'. Finally, in line 6 S produces a request (i.e., the pre in line 1 was actually a pre-request), which is framed in a way that displays S's lack of desire to impinge – it is hesitant, does not presume anything of P ('i wonder', 'would be possible', 'if i could take'), and has been delayed over several turns. Further, the request was preceded by an explanation or excuse, All these structures protect P's negative face and some of them (e.g., excuse) also protect S's positive face (it is also likely that they influence the chance of S's request being granted).

A pre can delay an upcoming threat to the addressee's negative face, as is illustrated in the next example where an apparent pre-question leads to the eventual production of a question.

Example 5:15

1 A: i have a question i don't know if i'm allowed to ask you (.) but

2   i'm sort of confused

3 B: m[hm]

4 A: [i'm] doing uh (.) my project on repairs

5 B: yeah

6 A: and i was wondering if disagreement and repair are are the same

7   or

Not only does A in lines 1 and 2 use a pre-question that protects B's negative face, but A also frames the pre in a hesitant way that does not presume and that contains an excuse. After getting the go-ahead to produce the question, A in line 4 instead provides further rationale for the upcoming question. Again, B gives the go-ahead and A finally produces the projected question. That question is produced in a way that does not presume much of B. Overall, A protects B's negative face by projecting an upcoming question and by justifying and delaying that question, all of which give B options on how to respond.

Give justifications or excuses, hedge, be pessimistic, and diminish responsibility for the FTA

Some of these strategies were packaged with other negative facework strategies described above. It is useful, however, to present examples in which these strategies are highlighted.

Example 5:16

(Therapy session; C, client and T, therapist)

1 C: yeah (1.5) so you're gonna have to kind of guide me today or

2   something ((laughing)) i just feel like I don't have anything to

3   say you know↑ one of those times↑

4 T: mm

C gives T permission to perform the negative face-threatening act 'you're gonna have to kind of guide me today or something'. Further, C gives a reason or excuse for why C cannot guide him/herself ('i just feel like i don't have anything to say'), appeals to T for understanding and acceptance of the excuse ('you know↑'), and minimizes the extent of his/her imposition with hedges and restrictors ('kind of guide me'; 'today'; 'just feel'; 'one of those times').

Example 5:17

(Therapy session; C, client and T, therapist)

1   C: nice weather

2   T: mhm (0.8) very nice weather

3   C: i know (.) i've been golfin' all week

4   T: mm

5   C: can't complain that's for sure (6.0) so↑

6   T: so was there anything you would like to talk about↑

In the context of therapy, C is expected to talk. Thus, T's line 6 utterance is a request for C to initiate a topic and begin talking about it. T begins the turn with 'so↑', thereby positioning his/her turn as the upshot of C's prior turns. In this way, T provides justification for her upcoming face-threatening action. Next, T frames the request in a way that shifts responsibility for making the request from T to C ('anything you would like to talk about'). In effect, T conveys 'it's up to you whether you talk or not, and if you wish to talk, you can talk about anything you want'.

Example 5:18

1   A: um (.) thanks for doing <u>this</u> (.) if you could just (1.4) also do the

2   following (.) um i actually (.) need this for one thirty so if it's

3   [possible]

4   B: [o:h]

5   A: unless you're um:

6   B: oh no

In making a request of B, A accomplishes negative facework by asserting that the request is something he/she needs to do rather than wants to do or does freely. The implication is that although A is impinging on B's negative face, A does not want to do so. Further, A protects B's negative face by introducing a degree of pessimism about B granting the request ('if it's possible'). This pessimism displays that A is giving B the option of rejecting the request. In line 5, A makes another pessimistic claim that also gives B the option of rejecting the request.

Complicated facework situations

Some social actions pose facework dilemmas. Consider, for example, the difficulties A encounters when he has to respond to S's self-deprecation (i.e., to S's negative self-assessment). Since S has made the assessment, in order to protect S's positive face A should agree. However, S has made a negative assessment of herself and, thus, in order to protect S's positive face A should disagree. There is also a potential threat to A's negative face; namely, S has backed A into a corner, so to speak. Further, there is also threat to A's positive face since the way in which A responds to the self-deprecation displays A's social skills, and thus leaves A open to potential negative evaluation.

The following three examples illustrate strategies for dealing with self-deprecations (see Pomerantz, 1984, for an in-depth discussion).

Example 5:19

1 B: i don't know i d- i don't really want to talk about it i feel like (.) i

2   dunno i feel like i'm being (0.8) stupid and i feel like

3 A: honey it's not being stupid

Starting with a term of endearment (i.e., using common ground to display solidarity), A then disagrees with B's self-deprecation and does so by using a partial repeat of what B said.

Example 5:20

1 C: was cause mine's pretty straightforward ((laughs)) that's what i

2   wanted it t'be ((laughs))

3 B: well (.) no it's good i mean you know you're doing so much

4   work on it (.) can you imagine how much more it would be if

5   you actually had t'go an collect you y'know

In line 3, B prefaces the disagree component 'no' with the reluctance marker 'well'. Thus, B both threatens and protects face. Following this, B produces a compliment and offers a justification for what C has done (i.e., that for C to do anything less straightforward would be far too much to ask), both of which enhance C's positive face.

Example 5:21

1 B: god our curtains are ugly ( ) they ['re just]

2 A: [yah ours] are (.) like (.) the

3   same only they're bigger ((both laugh)) well cause they go

4   straight to the ceiling ( ) an they cover that whole

In line 2 A begins his/her response with agreement, which threatens B's positive face. But then A follows this by making his/her own self-deprecation that is more extreme than the one B made. Perhaps this is a way of finding some common ground, and it is also possible that by lowering self, other (B) is elevated (i.e., gains positive face).

EXTENSIONS OF THE B&L MODEL

In this section, two aspects of the social nature of talk that require some extension to the B&L model are described. Briefly, it is argued: (1) that a model of talk must incorporate antagonistic social relationships as well as positive social relationships of the sort described by B&L; and (2) that the social aspects of talk (including, centrally, face, face-threat, and facework) must be conceptualized as indexical accomplishments. Examples are presented to clarify and illustrate these claims.

Undermining and Attacking Face

The B&L model focuses on positive social interaction involving protecting and saving face, on 'politeness' as the term is generally used. Protecting face and repairing damage to face are not, however, the only orientations participants can take. On occasion, persons can attempt to undermine, attack and damage face (Penman, 1990; Tracy, 1990; Wood & Kroger, 1994). A model of talk needs to incorporate the antagonistic aspect of social interaction. This can be accomplished by building on the B&L model. In particular, participants in talk can attack face by failing to produce appropriate amounts of facework as measured by B&L's weighting of an FTA. Face can also be attacked by actions that display that S does *not* value A (i.e., attacks on positive face) and by actions that display that S does *not* allow A to be free (i.e., attacks on negative face). Although there are many ways to attack face, the following types of strategies are some of the more common in everyday talk.

Bald-on-record insults and accusations

When S insults A or accuses A of something, A's positive face is attacked because S has ascribed negative attributes to A and his behaviour. In addition, A's negative face is threatened because A is placed in a position where there is pressure to defend himself since failure to do so may be interpreted as acceptance of the insult or accusation.

Example 5:22

1 T: you're a real asshole

2 D: get lost moron

T insults D, thereby attacking D's positive face, and D responds in kind, thereby attacking T's positive face. In the next example, face is attacked by claiming that a person's contributions to talk are not relevant.

Example 5:23

1 C: yes it should be such a big deal

2   because i'm moving in a week

3 D: so what

The next example illustrates how disagreements and accusations can be used to attack face.

Example 5:24

(Children H and M, with Father, F; playing a game)

1 H: if you did (.) actually you <u>did</u> do three suggestions max (.) you did

2   four now

3 F: all right okay uh

4 M: no (.) <u>YOU</u> made up the <u>UDDER ONE</u> [i]

```
5  H:                                    [oh] well [don't yell at me

6        (.) it's not very nice you know]

7  F:                                    [one (.) two (.) three four

8        five]

9  H:    it's very mean max
```

H in line 1 attacks M's negative face by disagreeing with and accusing M. Although use of 'if you did' and 'actually' are face-saving, the emphasis on '<u>did</u>' and the repetition of the accusation are both face-attacking strategies. After F tries to intervene, M responds to the attack with a bald-on-record disagreement 'no', followed by the bald-on-record accusation that H ('<u>YOU</u>') is the guilty party. In line 5, H begins her turn with some face-saving talk 'oh well', but then changes to a bald-on-record command that functions as a reprimand. H finishes her turn with an attack on M and his behaviour. After F's attempt to get back to the game, H in line 9 continues with her attack on M's positive face.

Attack by recycled contradictions

When face is attacked by S, a common response is for A to attack in turn. Reciprocal face-attacking is vividly illustrated in sequences of 'recycled contradictions' (Muntigl & Turnbull, 1998).

Example 5:25

(Father, F, and 14 year old daughter, D)

```
1  F:    it wasn't much to ask for you to come in early (0.7) just one

2        night (0.7) nine thirty ten o'clock is not that out of line

3        (0.5)

4  D:    yeah it is out of line

5  F:    no it's not
```

In line 4, D produces a bald-on-record contradiction of F's prior assessment, to which F responds in kind. Both actions attack the positive face of the addressee.

Sequences of recycled contradictions occur throughout the next example.

Example 5:26

1 B: [but didn't i tell you] didn't i tell you that you didn't <u>need</u> your

2   masters=

3 L: =<u>no</u> [you did not tell me i didn't need my undergraduate]

4 B: [(you can do your] masters

5   or anything

6 L: <u>no you did not</u>

7   (0.6)

8 B: yes <u>i did</u>=

9 L: =<u>NO you DIDN'T</u>

10 B: why don't you you don't believe me (once you're an

11   undergraduate) you can do your masters in anything=

12 L: <u>no you can't no you can't</u>

13 B: *yes you can*=

Not only do B and L produce bald-on-record contradictions, but they also attempt to cut each other off. Further, L emphasizes the attack on B's face through displays of negative emotion, accomplished by speaking in a loud voice and by placing vocal stress on his/her contradictions of B. Overall, this is a very aggressive, face-damaging interaction.

The Indexicality of Face, Face-threat, and Face-work

A second complication to the B&L model is the indexical nature of face, face-threat, and facework. There has been a tendency among researchers to treat the facework strategies listed by B&L as encoding particular aspects and degrees of facework. However, analysis of facework in natural talk reveals that what participants are doing does not always match the nature of the strategy as identified by the lists provided by B&L. Such a matching problem occurs when a strategy used on one occasion to do positive facework is used on another occasion to do negative facework. For example, the strategy of 'apologize' can be used to display S's reluctance to impose on A (e.g., 'I'm sorry to bother you (but) . . .' B &L, 1987, p. 189), and is therefore listed as a negative facework strategy. However, when S gives an apology for not granting a request (e.g., 'i'm sorry but i'm busy then', from Turnbull & Saxton, 1997), the apology seems to be used to protect the positive face of both A and S (i.e., A's positive face is protected for S displays distress over not granting A's request; and S's positive face is protected for she displays herself to be a considerate person).

Although many researchers have taken an encoding view of the B&L strategies, this is an incorrect reading of B&L who conceptualize facework (and the resulting impact on face) as an indexical achievement. Recent work by P. Brown (1995) on irony in the talk of Tzeltal women offers convincing support for this claim. In Tzeltal society, irony has become a conventional means women use to display shared opinions and understandings, and to elicit sympathy; that is, women use conventional ironic utterances to display and reaffirm solidarity. However, when interaction is confrontational, conventional ironic utterances are often used to attack face. Further, conventional ironic utterances can also be used to create ambiguity about what action S is performing. In other words, although the culture provides a conventional means for being ironic, what is accomplished by using conventionally ironic utterances depends on the total speech situation in which those utterances occur. The general point to be gleaned from the case of Tzeltal irony is, as P. Brown (1995, p. 169) both concludes and cautions, that

> particular linguistic realizations are not ever intrinsically positively or negatively polite, regardless of context. Politeness inheres not in forms, but in the attribution of polite intentions, and linguistic forms are only part of the evidence interlocutors use to assess utterances and infer politeness.

Examples from natural talk illustrate the indexicality of facework.

Example 5:27

(talking about B's job as a cashier in a grocery store)

```
 1 B:   ((laughter)) no i mean it's one of those jobs that there isn't a

 2      whole lot t'tell people about because it's y'know it's being a

 3      cashier (.) i put people's [gro]ceries through an' i

 4 C:                             [yah]

 5 B:   get the occasional jerk (.) an you know

 6 C:   yah yah that's true

 7 B:   so i mean i like it (.) just 'cause it's not it's not demanding

 8 C:   that's good (.) it's nice t'have something brainless for awhile

 9 B:   oh yah

10 C:   after being in [school for so long]
```

11 B: [after being in school] (.) that's exactly the thing ( )

12   sometimes i get these people though . . .

B begins this segment with a self-deprecation, but by line 7 B has weakened the extent to which that self-deprecation threatens his/her face (i.e., a job which is 'not demanding' is assessed as a job that is not necessarily bad). In line 8, C agrees with B's assessment and then expands on it with 'it's nice t'have something brainless for awhile'. For C to claim that B is doing a job that requires no brains would seem to be an attack on B's positive face. However, in this sequence of turns, C's claim is a way to display empathy and common ground with B; that is, C displays his/her understanding of how 'being in school for so long' (line 10) can be so demanding that it is good to take some time off and do something less demanding. This interpretation is supported by B in line 11 who echoes and agrees with C's claim. In sum, if meaning were encoded into 'it's nice t'have something brainless for awhile', then C would be making a very negative assessment of B. However, in the sequence in which that utterance occurred, C used it to display concern for B.

Example 5:28 illustrates how utterances with the structure of conventional insults can be used ironically to display and reaffirm solidarity.

Example 5:28

(T and L are friends; T has just suggested that L apply for a job at a restaurant)

1 T: y'get people that tip well (.) boston pizza it's a shitty place to

2   work but

3 L: yeah (1.5) you have to be good look (.) they want like good

4   looking people if you're good look[ing and you're male]

5 T: [yeah i guess you're lack] (.)

6   yeah you're really lacking (0.8) yea::h you shouldn't ap[ply never

7   mind]

8 L: [shut up]

9   ((laughing))

10 T: you should stay at home you should just go back to u i=

11   ((laughing))

12 L: =fuck you

13 T: ((laughs))

In lines 5–7, T produces what appears to be an insult by commenting on C's lack of good looks. T and C, however, are friends and friends often engage in good-natured banter or teasing in which they say one thing but mean something else (via a flouting of the CP). Thus, the subsequent exchange of 'insults' in lines 8, 10 and 12 is likely an exchange of mock insults, an interpretation that is supported by participants' accompanying laughter.

POSITIVE ASPECTS OF THE B&L MODEL

Of the many contributions of B&L's model of politeness, three are of particular relevance for a model of talk. First, B&L demonstrate the importance of the interpersonal dimension of talk. B&L focus on one specific and ubiquitous attribute of interaction, politeness, and they stress how every interaction has both inter-personal and transactional consequences. They also argue convincingly for the necessity of some sort of tradeoff between interpersonal and transactional orientations. Politeness may not exhaust the interpersonal dimension of interaction and the particular tradeoff B&L propose may not be universal. Nevertheless, the important point remains that a model of talk must somehow incorporate both interpersonal and transactional orientations.

A second contribution of B&L for a model of talk is that they provide a conceptualization of the social attribute of face and a specification of the attributes of relative power, distance (and affect) and degree of imposition that influence face in principled ways. Given that face is central to social life, it can be expected that conventionalized strategies for attending to face would evolve in every society. B&L provide a detailed specification of some of these strategies and they demon-strate how strategies get played out in the details of interaction. Importantly, both social value, face, and strategies of facework are recognized as indexical. B&L thus provide a solid foundation for an understanding of the role of face and facework in a model of talk.

A third contribution is recognition of the reflexive nature of talk and social structure. According to B&L, degree of face-threat is a function of specified relationship factors and, given the resulting weightiness of an FTA, a certain type/amount of facework is required. Thus, in doing a certain amount of facework, in talking in a certain way, S displays or affirms a relationship with A; that is, S affirms specific values of power, social distance (and affect), plus the degree of imposition of the act. But talk is not simply a reflection of the social; rather, talk is an ongoing negotiation of social structure. Participants can attempt to negotiate a certain type of relationship by using politeness strategies that are appropriate for that type of relationship. For example, by using the positive politeness strategy of using in-group markers, S makes a claim that S and A *are* members of an in-group. In turn, A can affirm or resist that claim.

In sum, talk is influenced by social structure and talk influences social structure; that is, talk and social structure are in a reflexive relationship. There is nothing special about politeness in this respect. Both transactional and interpersonal meanings are co-constructed at every turn at talk. And at every turn at talk, A both responds to S's prior turn and projects forward to S's next turn. In this way, a turn at talk is occasioned by the total speech situation and, when produced, changes the total speech situation. Thus, the transactional and the social both influence and are influenced by ongoing sequences of turns at talk.

PROBLEMS WITH THE B&L MODEL

There are a number of problematic aspects of B&L that need to be addressed. One somewhat minor point concerns the distinction between positive and negative face. Positive face is the desire to have one's values valued and negative face is the desire to be unimpeded. Thus, if A values S's desire to be unimpeded, A values one of S's values; that is, positive face subsumes negative face. In spite of this, it is nevertheless a useful heuristic when considering facework to distinguish affiliative and intimate behaviour (i.e., positive facework) from respectful and deferent behaviour (i.e., negative facework).

A related problem concerns the distinction between speaker's face and addressee's face. Although B&L address this distinction in some detail the vast majority of examples they present focus on A's face. In practice, it is extremely difficult to decide in any specific instance whether a strategy is oriented mainly to S or to A. Consider an illustrative example.

Example 5:29

(talking about Jim Carey movies)

1 J: and i dont know↑ i've watched a couple other en i don't think

2 they're really that funny

3 (0.6)

4 G: ya: it's hard (0.5) it's hard to be into movies like that↑

5 (0.5)

6 J: cos he's so (0.5) he's so <u>repetitive</u> like it just kinda starts to get

7 tire[some]

8 G: [ya] (0.6) it's hard because uh: like my best friend craig (0.7) is

9 you know what i mean (0.5) he doesnt' really (.) he's not into

10 movies like that at [all]=

11 J: [yup]

12 G: =you know what i mean you know like i mean big thinker films

13   (0.5) but i also enjoy like mindless come[dy]=

14 J: [it's ya]

15 G: =like that kinda [thing]

In the first three turns of the interaction, J and G agree that movies of the Jim Carey sort are not funny, hard to be into, repetitive, and tiresome. In lines 8–10, G seems to be asserting that his/her best friend Craig also does not find Carey films to be funny. However, in line 12, G then seems to assert that it is 'big thinker films' that Craig does not like. G follows this in lines 13 and 15 with the claim that G him/herself likes 'mindless comedy' and thus, in this respect, is similar to Craig. By the end of the segment, G's assessment of 'mindless comedies' is in disagreement with J's assessment, but G structures the disagreement in a way that suggests both that G has not changed his/her initial assessment and that G and J still agree.

In the example, G skilfully deals with a potential disagreement by starting with initial agreement, and then following this with a smooth transition to disagreement packaged as agreement. It would therefore seem that these strategies are ways for G to avoid disagreeing with and to minimize disagreement with J; that is, the strategies are oriented to the protection of J's positive face. However, the strategies are also ways for G to display that he/she is a flexible, intelligent, and accepting person, one who does not have knee-jerk responses to the world (i.e., G can recognize the importance of big thinker films, but G can also recognize the value of the quirkiness of Jim Carey movies; and G can be friends with people who have different views). So, whose face do G (and J) orient to in this example? The answer lies in the recognition that talk is a form of co-constructed social interaction, and that face and facework are, therefore, interactional products and processes. Thus, doing facework and creating face are co-constructed activities that necessarily orient to the face of *both* participants.

Another set of problems for the B&L model involves the related issues of measuring facework and deriving predictions from the model about facework. There are several measurement models (Blum-Kulka, House, & Kaspar, 1989; Penman, 1990; Turnbull & Saxton, 1997; Wood and Kroger, 1994), all of which differ in important ways. Unfortunately, there is no standard or accepted measurement model. This leaves the door open for different researchers to detect different amounts of facework in the *same* data set. As a consequence, empirical tests of the model are likely to be inconsistent and inconclusive.

Another problem with the model is that it is potentially not falsifiable; that is, every possible outcome can be derived from the model, importantly including the prediction that some outcome, p, will occur and also that p will not occur (i.e., predicts p and not-p, which is a contradiction). A model that is not falsifiable only *seems* to be making empirical claims about reality, whereas, in fact, no empirical claims are made. One basis of the potential unfalsifiability is, again, the lack of a standard of measurement. Imagine that a set of empirical data measured by one standard seems to contradict predictions derived from B&L. These same data can be interpreted as supporting the model when a different standard of measurement is applied. Unless the measurement issue is settled, empirical tests of the model must, therefore, be inconclusive.

The issue of falsifiability also arises because the B&L model is underspecified. As has been favourably noted, the model assumes that face and facework are indexical. If, however, the model is useful for deriving predictions about talk, then it must be possible, given any particular total speech situation (or 'context') to specify how the values of the W_{FTA} equation and of face are determined, and precisely what type and amount of facework will occur. What this requires is that the B&L model must be supplemented by a model of context that includes a mapping of politeness onto context. Further, since the B&L model is reflexive, the mapping of talk onto context must be bi-directional. At present, that component is missing, and the potential unfalsifiability of the model is one consequence of this deficiency.

Consider an example. In a test of the B&L model, Cherry (1988) examined letters of protest written to a university president about the denial of promotion and tenure to a faculty member. It was predicted that the lower the power of the letter writer relative to the president, the greater the degree of face-threat and, thus, the greater the amount of facework. Letters of protest were written by graduate students and assistant, associate and full professors, a list that corresponds to a ranking of relative power from the lowest, graduate students, through to the highest, full professors. Thus, Cherry predicted that the amount of facework in the letters would map onto this ranking of relative power (i.e., most facework in letters written by graduate students and least in letters written by full professors). When Cherry coded the letters for facework and correlated amount of facework with relative power, the results did not confirm predictions. In particular, letters written by graduate students and assistant professors contained less facework than those written by associate professors. Nevertheless, Cherry interpreted this result as consistent with B&L on the view that graduate students and assistant professors were using a deliberate rhetorical strategy in which principles of politeness were flouted in order to convey the writers' outrage at the decision. This may be a valid explanation. However, unless the B&L model is supplemented by a set of principles that specify when and how face and facework are mapped onto the genre of rhetoric, there is no way to assess empirically predictions derived from the model.

Lack of an accepted standard of measurement and underspecification are also at the heart of another problem, the issue of the universality of the model. To see why this is so, consider a subcultural difference that many of my students claim to have observed; namely, that face threatening acts, such as requests and request refusals, generally contain less facework when S and A are two unacquainted French Canadians than when S and A are two unacquainted Anglo Canadians. As students point out, this result seems to undermine the claim of the universality of the equation specifying degree of face threat. Closer examination may lead to a different conclusion. One Canadian racial/ethnic stereotype seems to be that French Canadians feel a much greater sense of connection to their community (e.g., heritage, language, location) than do Anglo Canadians. If this stereotype is a correct depiction, then the social distance, D, between two unacquainted French Canadians will be closer than for two unacquainted Anglo Canadians. Thus, the average degree of face-threat for a face-threatening act would be lower for French than for Anglo Canadians and would, therefore, require less facework. On this interpretation, the difference between French and Anglo Canadians actually confirms the model.

Clearly, any cultural differences could be explained in a similar way. However, such explanations would not be convincing without independent evidence for the claimed differences in P, D, and r_x; that is, without a specification of the culturally specific factors relevant to face and facework and a way to measure these variables, the problem of the lack of falsifiability will arise: given any observation about face/facework, it will be possible to interpret it as consistent with B&L. Thus, it is necessary to specify at least (1) what facework strategies are available in a culture, how such strategies operate, and what effects on face such strategies have and (2) how people in different cultures 'measure' P, D, and r_x, and thus the weightiness of a face threatening act, and how they 'measure' the impact of a facework strategy on face. Only by making such specifications will it be possible to compare cultures and test the universality of the model.

The final problem with the B&L model is that the concept of facework is overextended. Whereas every utterance implicates identity, neither identity nor politeness exhaust the social aspects of talk. For example, if S depicts herself as having robbed a bank, there are implications about what type of person S is, but, importantly, there are also legal implications. Thus, the precise ways in which S structures her self-description may orient to those legal consequences. And if a politician's talk is replete with indirection and hedging, rather than displaying politeness these structures may be used to avoid commitment to a position that may prove unpopular. Because there are a variety of social aspects to which participants in talk may orient, the claim that a 'facework' structure is used by participants on some specific occasion to do facework cannot be assumed but must be justified (MacMartin, Wood, & Kroger, 2001). In sum, in examining social orientations in talk it will prove useful to distinguish between different categories of social concerns and consequences. It will also be necessary to provide justification for analytic claims that participants are orienting to some particular social attribute in some specific instance.

The remainder of this section illustrates social phenomena other than politeness that may be oriented to in talk. Consider, first, uses of the parenthetical modal expression 'I think', as in the request refusal 'I'm busy on Thursday, I think'. Turnbull & Saxton (1997) note that parenthetical modals qualify the degree of certainty about the proposition to which they are attached. Thus, the degree of certainty of the proposition 'I'm busy on Thursday' is relatively low when qualified by 'I think' and much higher when qualified by 'I know'. By using parenthetical modals in a face threatening act, such as a refusal, S can thereby display her uncertainty, and perhaps her hesitancy, to do the act. In other words, S can use parenthetical modals to do facework. However, since all talk is indexical, it can be expected that not all uses of parenthetical modal expressions will be used to do facework. In Example 5:30, 'I think' seems to be used to do something quite different from facework.

Example 5:30

(playing Scrabble)

1   M: so what are your points↑

2   K: nine i think (err seven eight yeah)

Whereas K utters 'i think' to display uncertainty, K does not appear to be protecting his/her own positive face by being committed to a number that may be incorrect; that is, K is not being polite. Rather, given the rules of Scrabble, including how to determine who is the winner, at every turn in the game a player's correct score needs to be recorded. The consequence of not determining the correct score is that the game is flawed in one or more ways (e.g., perhaps the wrong person is declared the winner). Thus, by expressing uncertainty and then checking his/her addition, K is performing actions that are necessary for Scrabble to be played correctly. In other words, K's 'I think' and the subsequent check of addition orient to making actions conform to the rules of Scrabble. There are social consequences to playing Scrabble correctly or incorrectly, but those consequences are unrelated to politeness.

The consequences of not playing Scrabble correctly are minor when compared with the consequences of, for example, legal and medical decisions. If a facework structure seems to be used in cross-examination in court or in a medical doctor's consultation, it might therefore be useful to check carefully that the structure really is being used to do facework rather than used to deal with legal/medical consequences, such as being found guilty, negligent or blameworthy. Consider three examples from Atkinson & Drew (1979) of talk in court (actually a tribunal of inquiry). The tribunal was investigating violent confrontations between Catholics and Protestants that occurred in Belfast in 1969. The purpose of the tribunal of inquiry was to determine what happened and why, what role the police played in those events, what the police could have and should have done and, on the basis of those findings, to allocate blame. In the examples presented a senior police officer (witness, W) who was on duty during the violence is being cross-examined about those events and his role in them by a lawyer for the crown, C. Throughout, C attempts to dispute W's version of the events and to allocate blame to W. If W is found to be blameworthy, the possible consequences include being disciplined, not getting promotions, and even losing his job.

Note that in presenting the examples, except for example number, I use the exact version of the transcript presented in Atkinson & Drew.

Example 5:31

(Atkinson & Drew, 1979, p. 166).

1 C: In any event, when you mounted that second baton charge you
2   took no steps to prevent the Protestant people following you?
3 W: I was not in a position to take any steps. If I had taken any
4   steps to prevent them I would have left more than half my party
5   and the other three or four of us would have had no effect on
6   chasing them from this fire that had been started on the Sarsfield
7   Hall.

The prior and subsequent turns in this exchange demonstrate that C is asking questions of W in way that projects an upcoming accusation. W's turn displays his recognition of the projected accusation. First, W agrees with the claim underlying C's question that W 'took no steps to prevent the Protestant people following' him by giving the excuse 'I was not in a position to take any steps'. After agreeing with C in this way, W then produces an extended rationale for his failure to act, a rationale that functions both as a disagreement with certain potential and projected implications of C's question (i.e., that W could have and should have done something he did not do) and as a defence against the projected, but not yet produced, accusation. Since W, in effect, disagrees with these implications of C's question, W's roundabout way of answering C's question and the partial agree/ disagree aspect of W's answer might be seen as facework oriented to repairing the threat to C's positive face occasioned by W's disagreement with C's claim. A more compelling interpretation, however, is that W structures his talk in these ways to deny an accusation before it is made, to justify that denial, and therefore to prevent the production of the projected accusation. All of these outcomes would have positive legal and professional consequences for W.

The next example contains two structures (i.e., 'presumably' and 'must have') used in responses that display partial agreement with a prior speaker's claim. Since failing to agree with another's claim is face threatening, these structures might be interpreted as facework strategies that display uncertainty and lessen responsibility. Analysis suggests that the strategies are used, instead, to deny a projected accusation and, thus, to avoid legal and professional negative consequences.

Example 5:32

(Atkinson & Drew, 1979, p. 108, lines 49–54)

1 C: Were those people you are referring to there Protestant people?

2 W: Presumably they were.

3 C: Were they in fact a Protestant mob that was attempting to burst

4   out into Divis Street?

5 W: Prior to sending this message I must have known that there was

6   a crowd of people there.

7 C: You know in fact now that quite a lot of devastation and damage

8   was done in Divis Street at that immediate junction?

9 W: Yes

In the complete sequence of turns from which this segment is drawn, C's question implicates that W knew or should have known that the 'people' W addressed were Protestants. W avoids directly confirming that implication by qualifying his agreement with 'Presumably', thereby displaying that he may not have known that at the time but now does. W employs a similar strategy in lines 5–6 by using 'I must have known', which conveys that W is uncertain that he was aware that he knew (i.e., 'I must have known but I'm not sure I was aware of it'). If W was not aware of certain facts, then it is difficult to hold him responsible for failing to act accordingly. In sum, both 'Presumably' and 'must have' are used by W to display that he may not have known something at the time that, if he had known it, would be grounds for finding him to be negligent; that is, they are used strategically to avoid blame. And the strategies seem to have been effective: C's line 7 'You know in fact now' is an admission that W may not have known at the time.

In the next example, 'presumably' is used strategically by C to force an admission from W.

Example 5:33

(Atkinson & Drew, 1979, p. 182, lines 49–54)

1 C: Did you see petrol bombs being thrown?

2 W: I did.

3 C: Presumably the people who threw the petrol bombs at the

4   property on the front of Divis Street must have carried them

5   down either Percy Street or Dover Street?

6 W: Correct.

At the point at which the example begins, C is leading up to the accusation that W took no steps to arrest anyone before petrol bombs were thrown. C's use of 'Presumably' in line 3 conveys that there was only one route along which the petrol bombs could possibly have been carried and, thus, anyone on the scene must have known that. Accordingly, W ought to have known that petrol bombs were carried 'down either Percy Street or Dover Street' and, by implication, W should have prevented this from happening. If the analyst were to focus only on the politeness implications of talk, then 'Presumably' might be viewed as a way not to impose an opinion on W; that is, by using 'Presumably' C weakened his claim and therefore weakened the threat to W's negative face. In context, this seems an unconvincing analysis.

It could be argued that although politeness may not be involved in these examples, face is. Someone who does not play Scrabble correctly may be accused of cheating or carelessness, both of which threaten positive face. A senior police officer who does not react appropriately in a conflict situation is someone who is not competently fulfilling his role. The argument can always be made that each and every social orientation in talk is an identity orientation. However, collapsing orientations to politeness, identity, and legal and medical consequences into the one category of identity ignores the large differences between them. For example, there are different social factors and consequences at play in a disagreement about euthanasia between acquaintances at a party, in a discussion with a medical doctor about the possible treatment of a dying relative, or in a court of law when one has been accused of murder. It is not a useful approach to reduce the social aspects of these different situations to 'identity' orientation, any more than it is useful to reduce all talk to the transactional goal of 'conveying information'.

The conclusion to be drawn from this discussion is that structures with the form of (B&L) facework strategies may be used to do politeness, identity, or some other sort of interactional work. Thus, the analytic claim that structure X is used to do politeness must be supported by evidence and argument. One type of supportive data is manifest evidence of how participants in talk treat a structure, an approach adopted by Atkinson & Drew (1979). However, there may be many occasions on which participants do not manifestly orient to a structure that the analyst believes is important. Just how the analyst should proceed in such a situation is an unresolved issue. At the very least, such analyses must be presented and treated with caution.

In conclusion, B&L's politeness model is a major contribution to an analysis of the interpersonal dimensions of talk. Politeness, however, does not exhaust the social orientations participants can adopt in talk. Models that focus on other types of social concerns, such as identity or legal consequences, are needed to fully capture the interpersonal aspects of talk. Whatever models are proposed, a major issue will be how to justify analytic claims that such-and-such a structure is used by participants on specific occasions to do specific types of interactional work.

6

Conversation Analysis

Introduction and Chapter Overview

In this chapter I consider Conversation Analysis (henceforth, CA), the approach to the study of interaction created by the sociologist Harvey Sacks (1992) and his colleagues E. Schegloff and G. Jefferson (for reviews of CA see Atkinson & Heritage, 1984; Goodwin & Heritage, 1990; ten Have, 1999; Heritage, 1984a; Hutchby & Wooffitt, 1998; Levinson, 1983, Ch.6; Psathas, 1995; Sudnow, 1972). Sacks' basic research question was how participants produce and understand social interaction. Rather than adopting the dominant approach of basing analysis on constructed instances of idealized interaction, Sacks stressed the importance of studying the details of single episodes of natural interaction. Sacks claimed no special interest in talk, but natural talk was readily available and could be audio-taped, thereby allowing the researcher to examine repeatedly and in detail single episodes of interaction. As a consequence, CA emerged as a particular sociological approach to the empirical study of natural talk. In this chapter, CA is evaluated as a psychological model of talk. Since this is not the orientation of CA, those conclusions may not reflect an evaluation of CA proper.

The chapter begins with a brief summary of the theoretical foundations and methodological approach of CA. Research in CA has discovered resources participants use to do talk, and the bulk of the chapter explores those resources. In the final section, the positive aspects of CA for a model of talk are described, followed by a discussion of deficiencies.

THEORETICAL BASES OF CA

The theoretical assumptions of CA can be divided into two sets; namely, a set based on the central assumption that there are orderly methods for doing talk consisting of manifest and sequential structures, and a set based on the central assumption that a turn at talk is both context-shaped and context-shaping. CA's theoretical bases are difficult to comprehend in the abstract. Any confusion should be cleared up in the section on the structural organizations of talk where these abstract notions are explored and illustrated with examples.

Orderly Methods for Doing Talk Are Manifest and Sequential Structures

CA conceptualizes talk as a form of social interaction that is orderly. (Recall from Chapter 1 that talk is both a set of activities (e.g., producing turns at talk) and a product of those activities.) The orderliness of talk arises from the orderly methods participants use together to create talk. Whereas orderly methods are used to produce talk, participants also use those methods as inferential mechanisms for drawing interpretations about what is being done in talk. Further, the orderly methods for doing talk are (1) social and (2) structural. The methods are social in the sense that they are tools or resources provided by a culture. A child born into a culture gradually acquires those orderly methods. Thus, even though individual persons use the methods in talk, the methods are resources of the culture. The structural nature of the orderly methods for doing talk derives from the adjacent positioning of utterances and of turns. A turn may consist of one utterance or several utterances, each of which is adjacent to a specific other utterance. Further, each turn is adjacent to a specific other turn. Thus, the major method for doing talk is the sequential location of an utterance in a turn and of a turn in a sequence of turns.

The orderly methods for doing talk inhere in the detailed structure of turns and sequences of turns. Accordingly, no detail can be dismissed *a priori* as irrelevant to how talk is accomplished. From an intuitive perspective, attributes of talk such as filled (e.g., 'um', 'ah') and unfilled (silence) pauses, repetitions, hedges, and 'well' or 'oh' at the beginning of a turn reflect only verbal disfluency and, thus, to be irrelevant to what is being accomplished. Research reveals, however, that such details are orderly structures; for example, acceptances of invitations typically do not contain such structures, whereas rejections typically do. Thus, many of the intuitively 'irrelevant' details are not 'noise' that interferes with the signal but rather are important resources by which action is accomplished and recognized, and on the basis of which inferences are made.

A final aspect of the orderly methods for doing talk is that they have moral force. Consider, in this regard, the situation in which S produces a question to which A does not respond. S can demand of A that he respond to the question or that he give some account of why he is not responding. Further, even if A does not answer the question, he may well give an explanation, justification or excuse for his failure to do so. In each case, neither participant treats A's failure to answer as incomprehensible or as violating the statistical regularity that answers follow questions. Rather, they treat A's failure as a moral issue, as something he ought not to have done.

Talk is Context-shaped and Context-shaping

For talk to occur, A must construct a turn that responds to S's prior turn and projects forward to S's next turn. Sequences of turns at talk are part of the total speech situation or context. Thus, a turn is both influenced by the context in which it occurs and, when produced, influences that context. A second aspect of the backwards- and forwards-oriented aspects of a turn is that A in a present turn manifestly displays his interpretation of S's prior turn. For example, if S says 'gee it's cold' and A responds with 'sorry but the door's jammed open and I can't close it', A has treated S as doing the action of making a request to close the door, and A has done so by refusing to grant S's request. S can accept that interpretation of her action, either overtly (e.g., 'well thanks for trying') or indirectly by continuing on with the talk. Alternatively, S can contest the interpretation, perhaps by attempting to get A to recognize that S meant something else (e.g., S claims she was not making a request but rather an assertion about the unseasonably cool summer). In either case, the backwards and forwards orientation of a turn allows intersubjectivity to be monitored and negotiated on a turn-by-turn basis.

METHODOLOGICAL BASES OF CA

The methodology of CA consists of five basic postulates.

Natural talk

Sacks was opposed to the dominant social science approach of studying idealized talk/interaction. He argued convincingly that naturally-occurring talk displays a level of order and detail that is not present in talk generated from intuition or recollection. Since a model of talk must account for the structure of actual talk, relevant data must consist of audio- or video-taped instances of naturally-occurring talk.

Transcription

Once the data have been acquired, they are transcribed according to a transcription system similar to the one used in this book. The goal of transcription is to capture the detailed structures of talk, which can then be carefully examined. The data are the tape-recordings, and the transcripts are a useful representation of the data. Analysis, thus, rests ultimately on the tapes.

Structural analysis

Analysis focuses on the orderly structures by which participants together produce and understand talk. The approach to analysis is inductive: rather than basing analysis on *a priori* theorizing about what must be the case, the analyst tries to discover what phenomena are present in the data. Analysis focuses on specific examples and, typically, no coding, quantitative or statistical analyses are done.

Participants' meanings

CA in the first place examines participants' manifest meanings. In hearing/seeing how A responded to S, all of S, A and the analyst are presented with manifest evidence of how A and S treated or interpreted S's turn. Analysis often goes beyond participants' immediately displayed meanings since what S is displaying at the moment may conflict with other evidence (e.g., S manifestly answers a factual question but other evidence is consistent with the interpretation that S is attempting to avoid providing the correct answer).

Ignore exogenous features of talk

Context refers to a large, innumerable set of competencies or knowledge assumed to be shared by members of a culture. In social science, the context of an action is critical to its interpretation. CA adopts the view that a contextual feature can be used in analysis only if that feature is manifestly displayed in the talk at issue (Schegloff, 1997). Thus, for example, if Betty has a problem understanding Bert, CA would not attribute the problem to gender differences (i.e., theories of gender shared by Betty, Bert and members of the culture) unless Betty and Bert manifestly oriented to that context. In other words, analysis includes only endogenous context and ignores exogenous context. Thus, if participants do not orient to them, CA ignores contextual features such as participants' competence with natural language, their gender, age, role, relationship, personality, culture, prior history (memory), knowledge, goals, intentions, etc.

STRUCTURAL ORGANIZATIONS AND RULES OF TALK

This section of the chapter describes the major structural organizations and rules of talk that CA research has identified.

Turn-taking

Sequential, alternating, and responsive turn-taking is the fundamental and universal aspect of talk. Accordingly, coordinated turn-taking is essential for talk. Observation reveals that in most natural talk, transitions between turns are timed so perfectly that either there is no perceptible temporal gap or the gap is no more than a tenth of a second. Smooth turn-taking occurs in face-to-face talk and in talk on the telephone where there are no visual cues; with varying numbers of participants, including two person and multi-person talk; and in talk involving participants with different relationships and levels of formality, as for example casual talk between friends or strangers and formal talk between client and therapist. The issue, thus, arises as to how speakers manage to coordinate their turns at talk under widely varying circumstances.

One possibility is that for each type of interaction there is a set of rules that preallocates turns by specifying when each participant talks and for how long. Although there are types of talk governed by such rules, as for example the rules of turn-taking in formal debates, there do not appear to be rules in everyday talk that preallocate turns to speakers. Further, given the enormous range of types of participants, settings and topics in which the turn-taking system for natural talk must operate, there would need to be a correspondingly huge set of pre-specified rules. Indeed, since it is always possible for a new situation of talk to be encountered (e.g., when I first talked to a Carmelite nun in a church about immortality), the list of rules would have to be potentially infinite. For these reasons, it is highly unlikely that turn-taking in natural talk is governed by a set(s) of rules that preallocate turns. Rather, the system must be indexical, such that turns are allocated on a turn-by-turn basis in every specific interaction.

A locally-managed or indexical system for turn-taking was proposed by Sacks, Schegloff, and Jefferson (1974). According to these authors, turns at talk are composed of turn constructional units (single words, phrases, clauses, sentences, etc. of variable duration). The turn-taking system operates across these units. At the end of each turn constructional unit is a transition relevance place (TRP), a point at which speaker change may occur. A TRP does not necessarily occur at the end of a sentence or a set of sentences. Rather, both prosodic features (pause units, tone units, discourse markers) and pragmatic factors (who is doing what with whom on what occasion) determine the position of a TRP (Ochs, Schegloff, & Thompson, 1996). Sacks et al. (1974) proposed the following rules for the selection of next speaker at a TRP, where C is current and N is next speaker:

Rule 1 applies initially at the first TRP of any turn:
a) if C selects N in current turn, then C must stop speaking, and N must speak next, transition occurring at the first TRP after N-selection.
b) if C does not select N, then any (other) party may self-select, first speaker gaining rights to the next turn.
c) if C has not selected N, and no other party self-selects under option (b), then C may (but need not) continue.
Rule 2 applies at all subsequent TRPs:
when rule 1 (c) has been applied by C, then at the next TRP rules 1 (a)–(c) apply, and recursively at the next TRP, until speaker change is effected.

The next three examples illustrate the operation of the turn-taking rules. Example 6:1, which comes from a class discussion between an instructor (I) and her students, including Susan (S), illustrates the operation of Rule 1a, C selects N.

Example 6:1

1 I: susan did you have something↑

2 S: um: no do you want me to keep reading↑

3 I: yeah sure

Although in this example the current speaker in line 1 selects the next speaker by naming her ('susan'), this is not the only means available for selecting the next speaker. In the appropriate situation, 'you,' gaze, pointing or gesturing, intonation, and the topic at issue can all be used to select the next speaker.

Rule 1b, next speaker self-selects, is illustrated in another example from the same classroom corpus as Example 6:1. Students are identified as S1, S2, S3.

Example 6:2

1 I: so grammar is in burke's and bakhtin's terms a eulogistic term

2   (.) if you put grammar beside anything then you've got a

3   positive connection so grammar and the high tech world (0.5)

4   grammar and (0.4) um: *what else could it be↑*

5 S1: the global economy

6 I: grammar and productivity (.) grammar a::nd

7 S2: toilet paper

8 I: REAsoning

9 S1: ((laughs))

10 I: an and all along grammar has been connected with logic (0.7)

11   um: and clear thinking

12 S3: orderliness

13 I: orderliness and discipline (.) respect (.) values um::

Although the instructor called for some student to respond, he did not select a particular student. Thus, one of the students had to self-select. Instances of self-selection occur in lines 5, 7, 9, and 12.

Rule 1c, C continues given that Rule 1a does not apply and no speaker self-selects, is illustrated next. Potential TRP's are noted.

Example 6:3

1 I: so the ninth (.) ((TRP)) is that a wednesday↑ ((TRP))

2 S1: yeahup it is (.) ((TRP)) the ninth is a wednesday i think because

3 you gave that as the final day of class ((TRP))

4 I: umhm (.) it can't be the sixteenth now anyway (.) ((TRP)) how

5 bout we do make it the ni::nth and (0.4) are people able to come

6 say at one-thirty↑ ((TRP)) what you do then is you hand your

7 paper in (0.5) umm two days later ((TRP))

Participants' orientation to turn-allocation rules minimizes gaps between turns, overlapping turns, and interruptions, and prevents one speaker from taking an extended series of turns. Of course, turn-taking does not always proceed in this way. On occasion, speakers overlap and interrupt, and one speaker may take an extended series of turns while the other mainly listens, as in narrative. In spite of this, these phenomena all provide evidence of participants' orientation to the turn-allocation system.

Overlap often occurs when a listener self-selects but begins too soon, or mistakenly self-selects and begins a turn when the current speaker is only pausing before continuing. Such overlaps tend to be brief as one participant quickly gives way and lets the other take the turn, thereby displaying an orientation to the turn-allocation system. Another common type of overlap occurs when, as one person is taking a turn, the other overlaps with short contributions, such as 'mhm', 'right', 'yeah', 'I see', 'oh really', or laughter. These structures, backchannels, display A's reaction to the other's turn, and are used by A to display that S should continue to hold the floor. Being given permission to hold the floor for an extended period is necessary in order to tell a story, and backchannels are common in narratives. Typically, the storyteller S displays that her next turn will be longer than usual, something that may be done through the use of metacomments (e.g., 'okay, so I have to tell you about my day at work today' or 'well, that just brings me to something I was gointa ta tell you'). Further, S may appeal to A for feedback and check that A understands by using tokens such as 'right?' or 'okay?', or by ending utterances with rising intonation. For his part, A displays both his willingness to listen and his agreement to let S hold the floor, actions mainly accomplished by backchannels. Using these actions, S and A work together to temporarily suspend the normal turn-allocation rules.

Interruptions, occurring when one or more participants compete for the turn, are violations of the turn-allocation system. However, when interruptions occur, they are noticeable and trigger inferences. For example, someone who interrupts may be seen as someone who is attempting to control talk or someone who is an aggressive or uncooperative participant. Such inferences could only arise if participants (and analysts) orient to interruptions as actions that ought not to have occurred. Thus, an interruption and reactions to it confirm participants' orientation to the very turn-allocation rules of which the interruption is a violation.

Evidence for the operation of the turn-allocation system is also found in the ways in which episodes of talk are brought to a close (i.e., closings). Closings pose an interactional problem because when S stops speaking at a TRP, this is an opportunity for A to take the next turn or, failing that, for S to continue. To close talk, however, both participants must refrain from doing this, and the issue is how they manage to do so. Observation reveals that participants produce pre-closing sequences that project the potential closing of talk. In a pre-closing S asks, in effect, 'are you ready to end the interaction?' and A gives the go-ahead to do so, or not. Speakers often manifestly display that they are doing a pre-closing by beginning their turn with discourse markers such as 'so' or 'well then', and by doing the making of arrangements for meeting or talking again. After a pre-closing sequence, participants may then proceed to an exchange of terminal elements involving the 'goodbye' sequence (e.g., 'bye'/'bye'; 'see ya'/'see ya').

Consider an example of a pre-closing sequence followed by a closing.

Example 6:4

(telephone talk)

1 B: if i don't come and find you right away (.) know by like well by

2   eleven or so you know

3 A: okay

4 B: okay so i'll see you tomorrow

5 A: all right

6 B: bye=

7 A: =bye

8   ((talk ended, presumably due to telephone disconnection))

B in line 1 makes an arrangement to meet with A. What follows is a pair of confirmations ('okay', 'okay'). B in line 4 uses the discourse marker 'so' to summarize the upshot of the previous turns, and then initiates a pre-closing ('i'll see you tomorrow'). In line 5, A agrees to the pre-closing, following which there is an exchange of 'bye's' and the termination of the talk when the telephones are hung up.

In sum, the turn-by-turn structure of talk is the fundamental way interaction is accomplished. An important attribute of the system for allocating turns is that it is locally organized or indexical. Participants treat the turn-allocation system as a set of rules that ought to be followed. An important consequence of the local organization of turn-taking is that meaning is a function of composition and location of an utterance in a turn, or a turn in a sequence of turns.

Adjacency Pairs

Talk proceeds over time, sequentially, turn-by-turn. In a turn at talk, a speaker orients to the prior turn and makes relevant some set of potential actions in the next turn. Because speakers project turns both backwards and forwards, connections are established between adjacent turns. Adjacency, the side by side placement of turns, is thus the major resource for creating talk.

Because actions follow actions in sequence, all talk contains orderly structures of adjacency. A particular type of two-turn sequence, *adjacency pairs*, is found within the overall structure of adjacency. Adjacency pairs are sequences in which a particular type of action in one turn makes relevant a restricted range of actions in the next turn. Adjacency pairs thus define a more constrained order of structure than does simple adjacency. Common examples include assertion-agree/disagree, invitation-acceptance/rejection, question-answer/no answer, and request-granting/refusal. Following Schegloff and Sacks (1973), adjacency pairs are defined as follows:

> Adjacency pairs are sequences of two utterances that are: (i) adjacent; (ii) produced by different speakers; (iii) ordered as a first pair-part and a second pair-part; (iv) typed, so that a particular first pair-part action requires a particular second or range of second pair-part action; for example, the first pair-part action 'offer' requires second pair-part actions 'acceptance' or 'rejection'.

Schegloff and Sacks also proposed a principle of adjacency pair production; namely, having produced a first pair-part of an adjacency pair, S must stop speaking, and A must produce at that point an appropriate second pair-part.

Examples 6:5, 6:6, and 6:7 illustrate, respectively, question-answer, offer-rejection, and greet-greet adjacency pairs.

Example 6:5

1   M: and who's sarah mad at↑

2   C: him

Example 6:6

1 A: perhaps you'd like to make some trades here

2 B: i don't think so

Example 6:7

1 A: hi

2 B: hi john

Expansion Sequences

The simplest adjacency pair structure, as illustrated above, is an organization of talk across two turns. The two turn structure can be complicated by expansions that involve pre-sequences occurring prior to the production of a first pair-part, insertion sequences occurring between the first and second pair-part, and post-sequences occurring immediately after a second pair-part. Expansions result in organizations of talk across three or more turns.

Pre's and pre-sequences

Pre's and presequences were described in Chapter 5 where the emphasis was on their function as a negative politeness strategy. Students should reread the relevant material in Chapter 5. To recap briefly, a pre is a turn that projects the production of the first pair-part of an adjacency pair. If S produces a pre and A responds with an uptake, S then produces the first pair-part of the projected adjacency pair. By contrast, if A responds to a pre with a turn-down, the projected first pair-part is not produced. In sum, the pre-uptake sequence is produced prior to an adjacency pair, resulting in a four turn sequence if the projected adjacency pair is produced, as illustrated in the next example.

Example 6:8

1 A: oh a couple other things [oh]   ((pre-question))

2 B: [mhm↑]   ((uptake))

3 A: first of all when do you need this for↑ is this for today's class↑

                                                      ((question))

4 B: yep   ((answer))

Insertion sequences

An insertion sequence occurs when B responds to A's first pair-part with something other than an expected second pair-part and B's response becomes the first pair-part of an embedded sequence that delays the completion of the initial adjacency pair. This shift from expected second pair-part to first pair-part of an embedded sequence is conditional on the eventual completion of the original adjacency pair; that is, the embedded first pair-part is interpreted as being relevant to the eventual completion of the original adjacency pair. Example 6:9 provides an illustration.

Example 6:9

(Customer, C, taking to service-person, S, about costs for cellphone options)

1   C: how much is it

2   S: ok depends what you want in paging (.) [cau]

3   C: [just] messages in paging

4   i guess

5   S: ok (.) do you want it to show numeric message on the screen or

6   do you want it to be able to get text messages on the screen

7   C: numeric

8   S: ok (.) numeric (0.5) i think they charge an extra four dollars a

9   month for it now

C asks a question in turn 1 that S does not answer until five turns later. The intervening turns, an insertion sequence, are oriented to checking precisely which services C wants. Without that information, S cannot answer C's question, and once S has the information S produces the second pair-part to the initial question.

Post-expansion sequences

Post-expansion occurs as an elaboration, follow-up, or ratification of a second pair-part.

Example 6:10

1 A: is there anything else that automatically rules em out↑

2 B: a:h (.) criminal record

3 A: criminal record↑ okay

In turn 2 B answers A's question, thereby completing the adjacency pair, and A in turn 3 acknowledges and ratifies that answer.

Conditional Relevance

Although Examples 6:5 through 6:7 fit the strict definition of adjacency pairs, many examples do not. In cases involving insertion sequences, the first and second pair-parts of an adjacency pair are not adjacent. On some occasions, the participant who produces the first pair-part also produces the second pair-part. And there are occasions when after production of a first pair-part, a second pair-part is never produced at all. Since each of these phenomena seems to violate one or more components of the definition of and production rule for adjacency pairs, it might appear that the adjacency pair is not an orderly structure of talk. That conclusion is not correct. To appreciate why it is not correct, CA's conceptualization of the orderly structures of talk and rules of talk needs to be clarified.

To a psychologist, on first blush CA's claims about adjacency pairs may appear to be either a statement of an empirical regularity (i.e., an empirical generalization of the type 'birds fly', which is true of most but not all birds) or a cause–effect law (of the type 'physical exertion causes an increase in heart rate'). CA, however, takes a very different view. Orders of social interaction and the rules that operate on those orders are conceptualized as templates for interpretation, as standards against which actions are made intelligible or found lacking in some way. Knowing how an action will be interpreted influences what action is done, and in this sense a rule, such as the production rule for adjacency pairs, will influence what actions participants produce. But, according to CA, the main use to which participants put such rules is the interpretation of action.

As noted in Chapter 1, in order to interact, in every turn at talk a speaker must respond to the prior turn and project forward to a next turn. An important consequence of this requirement is that production of a turn by S constrains both A's response and S and A's interpretation of A's response. This constraining aspect of adjacent turns in talk is referred to as *conditional relevance*. Participants who fail to produce and interpret turns at talk according to conditional relevance fail to produce interaction. In other words, conditional relevance is a constitutive rule of interaction that specifies what counts as interaction.

There are several important implications of conditional relevance for the structure, production, and interpretation of adjacency pairs in talk. Recall that the production rule for adjacency pairs states that after A produces a first pair-part, B must immediately produce an appropriate second pair-part. Applying the requirement of conditional relevance to adjacency pairs results in a subtle shift in the formulation of the production rule; namely, the rule is that production by A of a first pair-part makes relevant the immediate production of an appropriate second pair-part by B. In other words, the production rule is not that a second pair-part has to occur immediately or at all; rather, the rule is that a second pair-part is immediately relevant and expectable after production of a first pair-part. The latter interpretation is consistent with the fact that no one can be forced to produce a second pair-part or forced to carry out any specific action, for that matter. Failure to carry out an expected action does, however, have implications both for the interpretation of whatever action did occur and for the impressions formed about the agent of the action.

Consider the influence of conditional relevance on the interpretation of actions occurring in the slot where a second pair-part is expectable. When a second pair-part is produced immediately after the first pair-part, the interpretation of that second pair-part is strongly influenced by its status as a second pair-part to the specific first pair-part. For example, the action accomplished in a turn can be identified as an answer in part because it is a response to a question. Conversely, the interpretation of a second pair-part influences the interpretation of the prior first pair-part. For example, if the action accomplished in a second pair-part is treated as an answer, the action accomplished in the prior first pair-part is likely to be treated as a question.

Conditional relevance also influences the interpretation of sequences in which an expectable second pair-part does not occur immediately after a first pair-part. In particular, because of the expectation that a second pair-part is expectable, its absence is noticeable – it is a noticeably absent action. Given a noticeable absence, some interpretation is made. Consider, first, the case in which the slot where a second pair-part is expectable is occupied by a pause, either an unfilled pause consisting of silence or a filled pause consisting of non-lexical vocalizations such as 'um', 'ah', or 'hum'. The role of conditional relevance in interpreting an unfilled pause occupying the place of an expectable second pair-part is illustrated next.

Example 6:11

(recalled interaction of A talking to B; A and B are a married couple)

1   A: i'm getting fat

2   (3.0)

3   A: do you really think so↑

The transcript indicates three seconds of silence between A's first and second turn. That silence is attributable to B because A has produced a first pair-part, (a self-deprecation), reached a TRP, and stopped talking. It is expectable that B now take a turn and respond to the first pair-part. Because a second pair-part is not produced, B's silence is noticeable, therefore calling for some interpretation and possible inferences about B. In turn 3, B's silence is interpreted by A as the action of agreeing, which is an appropriate second pair-part. An inference that might be drawn from B's silence is that B is displaying reluctance to agree with A's self-deprecation.

Several important points are illustrated by this example. One is that 'silence' is a concept that is interactionally-defined rather than objectively defined. From an objective standpoint, when A is talking and B is not talking B is, objectively, silent. Participants in talk will not, however, treat B as being silent in this case. By contrast, when B fails to speak (or fails to make non-verbal actions, such as pointing) when it is expectable that B should speak/take a turn, failure to do so will be treated as silence. In other words, interactional silence is noticeable absence; in particular, it is the lack of an expectable bit of talk. A second point is that only if B's silence is assumed to be conditionally relevant can some interpretation be made of it (and perhaps also some inferences be drawn about B). Precisely what interpretation is given of B's silence depends on specific aspects of the total speech situation and the nature of the first pair-part. Consider another interaction in which silence is given a different interpretation.

Example 6:12

(overheard as C and D looked at a painting in an art gallery)

1   C: i really like that

2   (3.0)

3   C: well i mean i think it's the type of work that kinda grows on

4   you

In line 1 C does the action of making an assessment. Following the same rationale for Example 6:11, the three seconds of silence is attributable to D. In this case, however, D's silence is heard as the action of disagreeing. A possible inference is that D is reluctant to disagree with C. In sum, Examples 6:11 and 6:12 illustrate the role of conditional relevance both in defining a failure to speak as 'silence' and interpreting that silence.

Consider, next, the case in which the slot where a second pair-part is expectable is occupied by an action that is not an appropriate second pair-part, as for example when a question is responded to with a question. One possible interpretation is that what is produced where the second pair-part was expectable but did not occur is somehow relevant to the eventual production of the second pair-part, as with insertion sequences (see Example 6:9). Another interpretation, illustrated next, is that the speaker has violated conditional relevance.

Example 6:13

1 A: you still haven't answered my question

2 B: mm i'm not gonna answer that question

3 A: why↑

4 B: cause it's a loaded question

5 A: no it isn't

6 B: yeah it is (.) i think it is

7 A: okay why do you think it's a loaded question↑

8 B: cause i just think it is

9 A: why↑

10 B: because

11 A: all i'm tryin ta do is come to a decision that is fair to both of us

12 B: well y-

13 A: hat's all i'm tryin ta do i'm not trying to entrap you or

14   something don't be stupid

15   (2.5)

16 B: it is a loaded question

17 A: it is not

In line 1, A orients B to the fact that B has not answered A's question. In line 2, B treats A's action as that of demanding an answer, and B refuses to do so. In line 3, A again orients to the fact that B has not answered the question by asking another question (i.e., why is B refusing to answer?). B's response to this question ('cause it's a loaded question') is both an answer and a justification for why B refuses to answer the initial question. Overall, B's position is that since A asked a loaded question, B is not therefore obliged to answer it. By contrast, A argues that it is not a loaded question and, therefore, that B is obliged to answer it.

The important point illustrated in Example 6:13 is that failure to answer a question is treated by both participants as something that ought not to have occurred. By presenting a justification for why he/she will not answer the question, B implies that answers ought to be given to questions but that this case is an exception. In doing so, B also places blame on A for B's failure to answer. Further, when A continues to press the case, B continues to defend against the implied accusation that he/she is obliged to answer the specific question. In these ways, A orients to B's failure to answer as a moral violation, and B accepts that failure to answer is an accountable matter but not in this specific case. It is possible that A is using the demands of conditional relevance as a strategic device for manipulating B. Regardless, the sequence of turns at talk would not be interpretable without the assumption that failure to answer a question is a moral matter. Conditional relevance thus has a moral aspect.

In sum, conditional relevance is a morally charged template for interpretation. Interaction is not possible and talk would not be intelligible unless participants generally acted in accordance with the demands of conditional relevance. The demands of conditional relevance provide participants in talk with a motivation for listening to the other's contribution; namely, to understand that contribution in the ongoing flow of talk and to respond to it. No understanding will be possible unless each participant trusts that the other(s) will do likewise. In this way a moral component, trust or obligation, enters into the constitutive rules of interaction. As Malone (1997, p. 143) puts it, participants in social interaction have an obligation to 'demonstrate involvement by demonstrating understanding'. Violations of trust, of moral obligation, are accountable matters. It can be demanded of a person who seems to be violating the requirements of conditional relevance that he/she explain, justify, or excuse those actions, and possibly also that he/she apologize for doing so. Inferences may also be drawn about the person's character.

Given the above discussion, it is now possible to characterize conditional relevance, and orderly structures and rules of interaction generally, as conceptualized by CA. In the discussion of Grice's Cooperative Principle (Chapter 4), the distinction was made between laws and constitutive rules of behaviour. Following Bilmes (1988a), there is need also for a distinction between strongly constitutive and weakly constitutive rules. A person who violates a strongly constitutive rule, such as the rules of English grammar, does something incomprehensible (e.g., produces the meaningless non-sentence 'democracy the in in aghast greenly'). By contrast, a person who violates a weakly constitutive rule, such as the CP or conditional relevance, does something that is comprehensible, but it is also noticeable and accountable. If participants orient to a violation, that violation will typically be interpreted as somehow consistent with the very principle that it violated. However, it is always possible with a weakly constitutive rule that, even though a violation is noticeable, it may not be noticed and, even if noticed, it may be ignored.

Preference Structure

All turns at talk are adjacent, and thus ordered. Adjacency pairs constitute a more tightly ordered structure than mere adjacency because production of a first pair-part makes relevant the production of a member of a restricted set of second pair-parts. An even finer level of structure, *preference structure*, is to be found in the ordering of the restricted set of second pair-parts to a first pair-part. The potential second pair-part actions are not equivalent; in particular, one type of second pair-part is the preferred action, another the dispreferred action, and the rest neither preferred nor dispreferred actions. (In CA, preference has no psychological connotations whatsoever but rather is a technical term for a purely structural phenomenon of talk.) Preference is the constitutive rule that production of a first pair-part makes relevant the production of the preferred second pair-part. Thus, whereas conditional relevance makes relevant the production of any member of the set of second pair-parts, preference makes one of those actions, the preferred action, more relevant than all others.

Determining which is the preferred action for some specific first pair-part is based on an ordering rule that operates on three types of action – the preferred, P, dispreferred, D, and neither the P nor D actions, N. That rule is 'if N, then speaker has produced D' (Bilmes, 1988b). For example, if S makes an accusation of A to which A responds with silence or by trying to change the topic, A will be heard as agreeing with the accusation. Thus, the preferred action is denial, the dispreferred action is agreement, and all other potential second pair-parts are neither preferred nor dispreferred actions.

Preference also extends to the way in which second pair-parts are structured (Pomerantz, 1984). A second pair-part is in preferred structure when it is produced without delay (and even in overlap or latched onto the first pair-part), and is short and to the point. By contrast, a second pair-part is in dispreferred structure when it is delayed, and contains filled pauses (often a turn-initial 'well', 'umm' or 'oh') and accounts, all of which operate to weaken and push the response to the first pair-part back into the turn, thereby delaying it. There is also an order linking the nature of the second pair-part and its structure; namely, it is expectable that the preferred response is in preferred structure, and the dispreferred response in dispreferred structure. Violations of these patterns are noticeable and are a resource for drawing inferences. For example, if S responds to a request with a delayed and hedged granting, such as '(2.0) uh uh yeah i i guess i can', a preferred response in dispreferred structure, S may be perceived as displaying her lack of desire to grant the request. Perhaps also the participant who made the request may be unsure as to whether it has, indeed, been granted. And if S responds to a request with a bald on record refusal, 'no', a dispreferred response in preferred structure, S may be perceived as hostile, humorous, or creative depending on other aspects of the total speech situation.

The following examples illustrate various aspects of preference.

Preferred response in preferred structure

Example 6:14

1 M: and they know mum and daddy are coming home pretty soon

2   soon righ[t]↑

3 C: [y]eah=

4 M: =they'll be home tomorrow

5 C: yeah

The expected response to M's line 1 assessment is for C to confirm her assertion.
M manifestly appeals for agreement with the tag 'right↑'. Failure to respond would
display that C does not agree with M. Thus, agreement is the preferred response.
C produces the preferred response in overlap with M's turn, and C's response is
short and to the point; that is, it is in preferred structure. The next sequence of the
example begins with an assertion in line 4. In line 5, C responds immediately with
an agreement. This sequence also illustrates a preferred response in preferred
structure.
    Example 6:15 illustrates a similar pattern of preference.

Example 6:15

1 A: would i be able to come back some other time↑

2 B: yeah sure

Dispreferred response in dispreferred structure

Recall that the dispreferred response is the response that is not projected by the
production of the first pair-part.

Example 6:17

1 A: would you be able to support us with a membership (0.8) or any

2   other way↑

3 B: um i- is it is it like a (.) what what would it be↑

The preferred response to A's request is a granting. B's response is hesitant and drawn out, features typical of dispreferred structure. Although B has not refused outright, the dispreferred structure combined with the question ending the turn displays a potential rejection (that was eventually produced).

Example 6:18

1 C: i i think at this point in time that the university (.) that there's

2   no longer a need for uh (.) post secondary education because (.) if

3   you can get a job say in a big company (.) starting way below (.)

4   you know you learn your way up in that company how that

5   company functions (.) with that company

6 A: well the only problem with that is that you end up um (.) kind of

7   (1.0) vulnerable to (.) the market cause you're only going to have

8   training in one job

After C's assertion, A begins the turn with 'well', follows that with a hedged disagreement ('the only problem with that', 'kind of vulnerable'), and ends with an account. These features, typical of dispreferred structure, weaken, delay and justify the disagreement.

Preferred response in dispreferred structure

The combination of a preferred response in dispreferred structure can lead to problems of understanding and to inferences, as is illustrated in the next two examples.

Example 6:19

1 A: would you be interested in uh (.) i can leave you guys some

2   literature and stuff

3   (0.8)

4 B: um

5   A: to look [through]

6   B: [sure]

7   A: yeah↑

8   (1.0)

9   B: um

In response to A's request, B produces a vague filled pause 'um' that may function as a granting. The subsequent turns confirm that B has done a weak and hesitant granting (i.e., a preferred response in dispreferred structure). Perhaps B employed that structure to display his/her manifest reluctance to grant the request, and also to project an upcoming refusal. The potential ambiguity of B's response is oriented to by A (line 5) who, instead of acknowledging B's granting, expands on the original request. In line 6, B overlaps with the end of A's turn and produces a token of strong agreement. Both the overlap and strong agreement are aspects of preferred structure; that is, B has done a granting in preferred structure. However, perhaps because of the contrast between the weak and hesitant agreement that possibly projects a refusal, followed by the unhedged granting, A in line 7 seeks confirmation that his request has been granted. The example vividly illustrates how production of a preferred action in dispreferred structure can lead to confusion as to just what action has been performed.

A similar case of ambiguity and confusion is found in the next example.

Example 6:20

1 A: there are things that you know anyone of us could do if we had

2   to take someone's appendix out we probably could figure it out

3   (0.6) you know↑ it's not that hard (.) the thing would look like

4   an appendix and (.) would look like a skinny little wormy thing

5   and we'd (.) cut if off (.) you know

6   (1.0)

7 B: yeah i guess so

8 A: you know what i mean↑

9 B: yeah (.) i know what you mean

10 A: like there's (.) i mean you wouldn't want to try to perform heart

11   surgery or something

B in line 7 produces an agreement to A's prior assessment that occurs after a delay of one second and is strongly hedged ('i guess so'). Although B seems to have produced an agreement, much of the structure of his/her response projects disagreement. In line 8, A displays uncertainty over the interpretation of B's response, as is evident by A seeking confirmation that B really has done an agreement. B confirms that he/she has, indeed, agreed with A, and does so in preferred structure. However, A then clarifies and modifies his/her original assertion, thereby continuing to display doubts about B's agreement with it.

Dispreferred response in preferred structure

Dispreferred responses produced directly and without hesitation (i.e., in preferred form) can lead to interpersonal inferences.

Example 6:21 illustrates participants engaged in an aggressive argument.

Example 6:21

1 B: you'll have to do it up at school [(   )]

2 L: [I CAN'T] it won't accept my

3   DISK

4 B: yes it will=

5 L: =no it wo:n't oh my god you're not listening to me (.) the

6   COMputer will not read my file on the disk . . .

In line 2, L overlaps B's turn and loudly disagrees with B's suggestion, both of which constitute preferred structure. However, L ends her turn with an explanation, which is a dispreferred structure. In line 4 B disagrees with L in preferred structure. L latches her disagreement onto B's turn and produces an emphatic 'no', both illustrative of preferred structure, and L continues by making an accusation of A. The aggressive tone of the interaction is conveyed, in part, by the sequence of 'in your face' disagreements (i.e., disagreements in preferred structure).

Dispreferred responses produced in preferred structure do not necessarily create aggressive or negative social relations. This type of 'mismatch' can also be used in joking exchanges, thereby doing the creation of intimacy and positive personal relations, as is illustrated next.

Example 6:22

(friends playing Scrabble)

1 A: d'you pass↑ did you pass↑

2 B: no bullshit (.) i passed

3 A: ((laughs))

4 B: wake up eh↑

5 A: [((laughs))]

6 B: [((laughs))]

Repair and the On-Line Monitoring of Intersubjectivity

In order to interact meaningfully, participants in talk must maintain intersubjectivity; they must agree for all practical purposes on what is going on in their interaction. CA views that achievement as a byproduct of the turn-taking system. To explain CA's position, consider the situation in which S telephones A and says 'want to drop by for a glass of wine?', to which A responds 'sure I'll be right over. Want me to bring some beer?'. In responding to S's turn, A both produces an action and manifestly displays how he treated S's turn (Bilmes, 1992). Thus, the responsiveness of a next turn to a prior turn gives A the opportunity to display to S that A treats S's prior turn either as understandable or as a problematic mishearing or misunderstanding. In the former case, A typically displays his understanding of S's contribution indirectly; that is, A would not normally say, for example, 'I understand that you have invited me over for a glass of wine' but rather, as is illustrated in the example, would display his understanding by accepting the invitation and moving on in the talk. By contrast, A displays problems of understanding directly by orienting manifestly to S's prior turn as problematic in some way. Of course, S in the next turn also has the opportunity either to accept or contest A's manifest interpretation of her prior turn. In this way, S and A constantly monitor intersubjectivity on a turn-by-turn basis.

Example 6:23 illustrates how the operation of the turn-taking system is used by participants as a resource for reaching intersubjectivity.

Example 6:23

1 B: we went to playland all day

2 A: oh you guys did↑

3 B: yeah

4 A: oh did you phone james↑

5 B: yeah

6   (1.0)

7 A: oh did uh uh=

8 B: =he didn't go

9 A: oh

10 B: he didn't go cause he had some project or somethin he had to do

11 A: o::h

12 B: but um (0.7) yeah we went (0.4) it was uh (0.8) raining like this

13   morning and we (.) we kinda held off for a bit and then we went

14   at like two

Consider how B in line 8 was able to interpret A's 'oh did uh uh' as the question 'Did James go to playland with you today?'. In line 4, A's query as to whether B telephoned James follows B's announcement that 'we' went to Playland. Possibly A is trying to discover whether James was included in the 'we' who went to Playland. B answers A's question but not the possible implication of the question. The one second of silence that then occurs, attributable to A, displays that A is having some difficulty with B's reply. B does not take the floor during the silence, and A continues with 'oh did uh uh'. Without pause, B then supplies the missing answer to the implied question of line 4. Following this, A and B take a series of turns that confirm that A's action in line 4 was one of asking whether James went to Playland. In isolation, 'oh did uh uh' has no meaning. However, given its location in this sequence of turns and the responses of A and B to each turn in that sequence, the participants (and analysts) can recognize a question that is never actually asked and, thus, reach intersubjectivity.

Repair sequences: negotiating the correction of breakdowns in intersubjectivity

Typically, participants in talk are able to maintain intersubjectivity for all practical purposes, as evidenced by the fluid progression of most of the fragments of talk presented in this book (and of talk in general). However, talk is not always smooth and unproblematic. When something does go wrong and an interactional problem arises, perhaps a difficulty in producing, hearing, or understanding a turn or turn component, a repairable item, *repairable*, occurs. Evidence that participants orient to a repairable is provided by *repair sequences*, orderly sequences of turns manifestly oriented to restoring intersubjectivity.

Repair sequences are orderly structures describable in terms of which participant initiates the repair, which participant performs the repair, and where in sequence the repair is performed (Schegloff, Jefferson, & Sacks, 1977). The participant initiating and/or performing the repair can be either the person who produced the repairable ('self' or 'S'), or the other participant ('other' or 'O'). As such, there are four possible combinations of who initiates and who performs the repair: S/S, S/O, O/S, and O/O. There are four opportunities or locations for a repair to occur. Taking the first turn (T1) as the one containing the repairable, a repair can occur within that turn (in T1, first position), upon completion of the first turn but before the second turn (in the T1–T2 interval, second position), in the second turn (in T2, third position), or in the third turn (in T3, fourth position).

Combining the possibilities generated by who initiates and who performs the repair and where repair occurs yields four types of repair; namely, Self-Initiate/Self-Repair in first position (in T1), Self-Initiate/Self-Repair in second position (in the T1–T2 interval), Other-Initiate in third position (T2)/Self-Repair in fourth position (T3), and Other-Initiate in third position (T2)/Other-Repair in third position (T2). According to the research literature, the ranking of frequency of type of repair is, as presented above, from S/S in T1, most frequent, to O/O in T2, least frequent.

First Position Self Initiated-Self Repair

Example 6:24

1   A: did they have any of tho- that serendipity or whatever it is↑

In turn 1, A cuts off the word 'those', resulting in 'tho-', and then immediately replaces 'tho-' with 'that'. The repairable is 'tho' and 'that' the repair, and the repairable and the repair are produced by A (self-repair) in first position, T1.

A similar type of repair is illustrated in the next example.

Example 6:25

1   A: they were talkin to her (.) she was was general (.) general

2   anesthetic [oh sorry local]

3   B: [or a (.) oh local] anesthetic↑ that's (.) was it really↑

4   A: yeah

In this case, A says 'general anesthetic' and then immediately self-repairs with an apology and 'local'. In response to the repair, B checks for confirmation and A confirms.

Second Position Self Initiated-Self Repair

Example 6:26

1	A:	like they're so out of the way that (.) the average person doesn't
2		really see them except for like (.) the natives and the loggers that
3		are flown in and [it's like]
4	B:	[yeah]
5	A:	everything
6	B:	and the squatters (0.9) all the [people]
7	A:	[yeah]

B in line 6 produces the repairable 'the squatters' followed by a 0.9 second pause. The pause is a potential turn transition point, a point at which A could have taken the next turn. But A does not take the floor and, instead, B produces the repair 'all the people'. In partial overlap, A confirms the repair.

A very similar sequence occurs in Example 6:27.

Example 6:27

1	A:	but you just do a whole cross stitch instead of one stitch (0.8)
2		[one half stitch]
3	B:	[exactly]

Other Initiate in T2/Self Repair in T3

Example 6:28

| 1 | A: | i never stayed anywhere long enough to really get like that (.) i |

2   <u>hated</u> waitressing (.) i couldn't wait tables i was no good at it

3 B: a lot of people aren't nice

4   (2.4)

5 A: what (.) waiters↑=

6 B: =to waiters

7 A: mm (.) yeah i know that's why it sucks

In line 3, T1 of the repair sequence, B produces 'a lot of people aren't nice'. After a 2.4 second pause, A in T2 (position 3) initiates a repair with 'what (.) waiters↑', thereby treating 'a lot of people aren't nice' as a repairable. In the next turn, T3 (position 4), B corrects him/herself and makes the repair 'to waiters'. The repair is acknowledged by A in the next turn.

Example 6:29 illustrates a similar sequence of repair that arises from a difficulty in hearing.

Example 6:29

1 A: cards is cool cards is a good way to kill time but i think hacking

2   is a better way

3 B: cars↑

4 A: cards

5 B: oh cards

The repairable, 'cards', is produced by A in T1. In T2 (position 3), B initiates a repair by repeating A's word but with a questioning intonation, 'cars↑'. In T3 (position 4), A repeats the word that B treated as repairable. B then produces 'oh' to display a change in mental state, and by repeating 'cards' B displays that the particular change in mental state is that he/she now understands. B was displaying that he/she had some difficulty hearing what A said in T1.

Other-Initiated at T2/Other-Repair at T2

The next two examples involve a mother, M, and her young child, C.

Example 6:30

1 C: okay (.) i will count

2 M: okay

3 C: o:ne (.) two (.) thwee (.) four (.) five (.) six (.) uh eleven (.) twelve

4   (.) fourteen

5   (3.2)

6 M: o:h you counted that one all by yourself (.) let's count again

7 C: yeah

8 M: [one (.) two (.) three (.) four (.) five (.) six (.) seven]

9 C: [one (.) two (.) three (.) four (.) five (.) six (.) eleven]

10 M: seven

11 C: seven

C is learning to count and makes a mistake. In lines 5 and 6 M initiates a repair by responding to C's counting with silence, thereby displaying some problem. When C does not respond to M's silence with a self-repair, M begins an Other-repair which she completes in line 8. C, however, continues to count incorrectly, and in line 10 M makes the repair again. C confirms the correction by repeating it.

Example 6:31

1   M: what do you see↑

2   C: um (0.5) mud

3   M: MUD i think she she got them dirty from eatin all that candy . . .

In line 3 M displays the repairable by uttering it in a loud voice ('MUD'). M then completes the repair and provides evidence to support it.

Complicated repair sequences

Just as with adjacency pairs, there are various complications to the four basic types of repair sequence, including post-expansions in the form of acknowledgements and confirmations. Sometimes, rather than being confirmed the repair or the need for repair is challenged, in which case another repair sequence is initiated. This results in the stringing together of one repair sequence onto another, and so on. A simple case is illustrated in Example 6:32.

Example 6:32

1 A: went to see eraser the other night

2 B: went and saw what↑

3 A: eraser

4 B: eraser ↑

5 A: yeah with arnold

6 B: with who↑

7 A: ARNOLD (0.9) schwartzenegger

8 B: o::h how was it

The initial repairable, 'eraser', occurs in T1, is Other-Initiated in T2, and is Self-Repaired in T3. However, the repair is challenged in the next turn; that is, the T3 repair becomes a repairable. Thus, line 3 is T1 of a new repair sequence, in which case line 4 is a T2 Other-Initiation and the 'yeah' of line 5 is the T3 Self-Repair. However, the adding on of one repair sequence onto another is still not complete. In line 5 A also introduces the information that Arnold Schwartzenegger is in *Eraser*. This becomes T1 of another repair sequence in which line 6 is a T2 Other-Initiation and line 7 is a T3 Self-Repair. The whole sequence then ends with a confirmation and shift of topic.

Preference and Repair

Preference structure extends into repair. There is evidence for a preference of self-repair over other-repair. Of the four positions in which repair can be made, three are in the turn of the person who made the repairable. Further, there are two opportunities for self-repair to occur (T1 and the T1–T2 transition) before the possibility of other-repair at T2. Thus, the structure of repair provides earlier and more opportunities for self-repair than for other-repair.

There is also evidence that participants act to avoid other-repair, and if it does occur, to delay and weaken it. Consider in this regard Examples 6:30 and 6:31 of M repairing her young child, cases of Other Initiated at T2/Other Repair at T2. In

6:30 M provides two opportunities for C to self-repair and only after C's failure to do so does M produce the repair. In 6:31 M weakens her repair with 'i think'.

POSITIVE ATTRIBUTES OF CA FOR AN APPROPRIATE PSYCHOLOGICAL MODEL OF TALK

Talk is social interaction

The basic structures of talk are those of social interaction and not of language, where language is conceived of as a Chomsky-like linguistic competence. An important implication is that talk is not writing. Failure to recognize this has resulted in many confusions and many inadequate models of talk. Consider some differences between writing and talk. Writing does not require the participation of two or more persons who engage in the sequential alternation of conditionally relevant turns. Writing can occur without any response, and if there is a response, it is delayed and occurs after the conclusion of the written text. With writing there is also no opportunity for monitoring intersubjectivity on-line. Further, although it might appear that a writer writes for some audience and, thus, that writing is recipient-designed, this is really an overextension of the concept of recipient-design. Writers might have an audience in mind that can be characterized by some general demographic attributes, but that is a far cry from talking to a specific addressee. In sum, writing can be used to communicate but writing is not social interaction.

There are other major differences between writing and talk. Writing, unlike talk, is a human artefact that many cultures never developed and that some persons in literate cultures never master. Further, writing and talking are different semiotic systems that influence conceptions of reality in qualitatively different ways (Innis, 1951/1991; McLuhan, 1964; Ong, 1982). The important conclusion reached is that a model of talk must not be based on the nature of writing. A corollary is that the data for the study of talk cannot consist of samples of writing but must consist of samples of natural talk. (Recall that for CA, transcriptions are only representations of the data. The data are tape-recordings of talk.)

Sequential orders of structure

Through an analysis of natural talk, CA has discovered that talk is ordered at many levels and that these orders are, in the main, sequential structures of various sorts. The chapter focused on the use of the orderly structures of talk for the production of transactional meaning. However, CA's emphasis on structure does not eliminate an orientation to the interpersonal dimension of talk. The structures of talk are resources for the doing of interpersonal work; that is, talk constitutes an inter-action order in which identities are displayed and negotiated (Goffman, 1983). For example, Malone (1997, ch. 5) demonstrated how S in a contentious argument designed utterances (recipient design) in ways that cast A into a role that was congruent with S's claim or position (i.e., the strategy of altercasting). In a study of request refusals, Turnbull (1992) demonstrated a close relationship between facework strategies and the preference structure of refusals (for other CA work on social orientations in talk, see Greatbatch & Dingwall, 1998; Lerner, 1996; Wooffitt & Clark, 1998; Zimmerman, 1998). In sum, because every turn at talk implicates self and other, CA necessarily has an interpersonal component (Rawls, 1989, 1990).

Co-constructed negotiation of meaning

The creation of talk through the use of orders of sequential structure has important implications for a theory of meaning. In particular, because meaning is determined by both the content *and* sequential location of utterances and turns, a temporal component is introduced into a model of talk. Participants act together in the production and understanding of meaning. Models of talk must, therefore, be at least dyadic. Further, in co-constructing talk, participants negotiate meaning for all practical purposes. Taken together, it follows that a model of meaning-making in talk must be a model of how individuals together construct and negotiate meaning for all practical purposes over sequences of turns at talk (i.e., a model of an indexical, co-constructed, for all practical purposes, and sequential achievement). This type of model is in stark contrast to standard models of context-independent, individualistic and mechanistic processes of meaning.

Talk is a situated human practice

Talk is produced and interpreted in terms of weakly constitutive rules that are applied in specific moments. The violation of a strongly constitutive rule is an incomprehensible or meaningless act, whereas the violation of a weakly constitutive practice is a meaningful act. Because psychology is based on the philosophy and methods of the physical sciences, psychological models conceptualize talk in terms of deterministic and lawful cause–effect processes. A model that emphasizes weakly constitutive practices is likely to be radically different.

The practices of talk are moral practices

Participants in talk orient to a violation of a practice of talk as an accountable matter; that is, production by S of an utterance/turn that violates a practice of talk results in demands by A for justification, explanation and apology. Typically, the violator will provide such accounts, often without prompting, or provide reasons why such accounts are not necessary (e.g., by the claim that no violation in fact occurred).

In either case, the violator has oriented to the accountability of a violation of a practice of talk. Thus, the practices of talk are moral practices.

When psychologists think about morality, they tend to think of large moral issues involving life and death decisions. However, since interaction requires a commitment from participants to make their contributions conditionally relevant, morality is endemic to social interaction. Thus, it can be expected that the micro level of everyday interaction plays a key role in moral development. Turnbull & Carpendale (2001b) propose that the morality of social interaction, moral order 1, is the universal basis of morality. Moral order 1, however, does not provide a specification of the interpersonal quality of contributions to interaction. According to Goffman (1967), the construction of preferred identities necessitates that participants together display trust, respect, solidarity, and an obligation to others (see also Taylor, 1989). But this is not the only orientation participants in interaction can take – disrespectful and aggressive actions also occur. Whatever orientation is taken to self and other defines moral order 2. It can be expected that moral order 2 is built on moral order 1, but that moral order 1 does not guarantee a specific kind of moral order 2.

Psychological models are value-free. However, because social interaction is moral 'from the ground up', a moral component must be included in a model of talk. Whereas the morality of talk points to a deficiency in psychological theorizing, it also opens up some interesting research issues. Primary among these are how children develop moral order 1, and how specific moral orders 2 develop. Research on either of these questions will require close attention to the details of natural talk.

DEFICIENCIES OF CA FOR AN APPROPRIATE PSYCHOLOGICAL MODEL OF TALK

CA rejects quantitative research designs

CA insists, correctly I believe, that analyses must be based on natural talk. However, CA's rejection of quantitative data analysis and of correlational and experimental designs in psychological research on talk is unconvincing (Garfinkel & Wieder, 1992; Schegloff, 1993; but see Heritage (1999) for a more positive view of quantification in CA). As long as the corpus consists of natural talk, which can be generated in both correlational and experimental designs, data can be measured, coded, and quantified (Turnbull, 1992, 2001). Of course, the ways in which the researcher engages in these activities will differ from traditional approaches; for example, the manifest details of talk will be the starting point for analysis, indexicality will need to be taken into account when offering explanations and making predictions, and analytic techniques based on an assumption of deterministic cause–effect processes will need to be revised accordingly.

CA is a social level of analysis only

Imagine two people doing a waltz in a ballroom dancing competition. Waltzing is a joint activity of two persons that requires moment-by-moment coordination of action. There are also a set of culturally-defined movements that each individual must master in order to waltz. No matter how well a couple's motions are coordinated (i.e., in synch), the waltz will not be judged highly unless the motions of each individual dancer meet some standard, and no matter what the quality of each individual's movements, the waltz will not be judged highly unless the couple's motions are coordinated. In other words, waltzing is both a social and individual activity. Talk too is both a social and individual activity. CA has and is providing a description of the culturally-available resources out of which persons construct and interpret talk. But individual persons have to use those resources when they talk. A psychological model of talk will need to take into account both the social and individual components (Clark, 1992).

Development, not just change

CA allows for an analysis of how talk changes from moment to moment, or from one interaction to the next, but not of how talk develops. Further, since CA is non-psychological and adopts an endogenous view, the notion that talk is directed towards some ideal state would be rejected. For the psychologist, there are good reasons to insist on models of change that can be incorporated into a model of talk. First, many psychologists are interested not just in change but in development; for example, in how the relationships of married couples get better or worse, or in how children's understanding of mind progresses as a function of the quality of mother–child interaction. Second, psychologists are not committed to incorporating models of development into their research that rest on the presumption of a universal, teleological, ideal end-state or goal. Chapman (1988) distinguishes two models of development. One is a unidirectional teleological model in which progress is defined as reducing the distance between where the system is at present and some predetermined end point. Another model is multidirectional in which progress is defined as increasing the distance between where the system is at present and where it is at some future point. Depending on the total speech situation, either of these models could be appropriate. In sum, CA has no model of development and, perhaps given its focus, has no need of such a model. But many psychologists who want to apply CA to the analysis of talk will need such models. A major challenge is how to 'translate' abstract models of change into manifest, orderly and sequential structures of talk.

Importance of Exogenous Factors

CA claims to ignore all exogenous features in analysing talk; that is, CA claims that a contextual feature enters into the analysis only if it is manifestly oriented to by participants (Duranti & Goodwin, 1992; Schegloff, 1997). There are some reasons to doubt that CA really does proceed in this way (Billig, 1999) and even more reasons to believe CA's model of context is not acceptable in a psychological model of talk.

Language

One critically important type of knowledge that participants must bring to talk is knowledge of the natural language they use in talk. Although that knowledge is not specifically oriented to in most talk (i.e., only on occasion do people talk about language), it is knowledge that is required for talk to occur. The tendency to ignore knowledge of natural language as an exogenous and critically important contextual factor most likely stems from the observation that there is no necessary relationship between the linguistic structure of an utterance and the action(s) created by producing that utterance (Turnbull & Saxton, 1997). However, although there is no deterministic encoding–decoding of utterance form onto action, the relationship between form and action is not arbitrary. Thus, what is needed is a description of language, a grammar, that is not deterministic but that does relate sound-syntax-semantics-pragmatics in some principled ways. Two possibilities are functional linguistics (Budwig, 1995; Thomasello, 1998) and systemic functional linguistics, SFL, (Halliday, 1994). The following brief example illustrates how SFL can contribute to a model of talk.

Muntigl (2001) examined the grammatical and sequential resources of talk that clients and counsellors use in couples' counselling. The research focused on how clients construct their relationship problems in counselling, how the counsellor reformulates clients' problems, how clients use those reformulations to develop new meaning-making resources for constructing their problems, and how reformulations are used in the effacement of client problems. Because Muntigl's analysis is highly technical and draws extensively from systemic functional linguistics (Halliday, 1994), it will not be possible to discuss in any detail the precise grammatical resources that were used and developed in counselling. All that can be attempted here is to describe, through close examination of the detailed structure of talk in counselling, 'what gets done by what gets said' (Labov & Fanshel, 1977, p. 71) .

In a comparative study of counselling therapy, Horvath (1981) videotaped 47 couples experiencing marital distress, each of which participated in six counselling sessions with one of six counsellors. Muntigl's analyses are based on the transcriptions of all six sessions of one couple chosen at random.

At the beginning of counselling, clients described various problems that brought them to therapy. Analysis revealed that clients' initial descriptions of problematic behaviours were presented as extreme case formulations (Pomerantz, 1986), as behaviours characterized as occurring always or never. By using extreme case formulations, clients both focused attention on those behaviours and construed them as problematic. Consider an example. (In all cases, except for the example number, I use the exact transcription from Muntigl, 2001: page number is presented in parentheses following the example number.)

Example 6:33

(p. 181; W is female client)

```
7  W:   he likes to lecture? (1.2) on any: any subject
8       that he feels even mildly uh uh y'know animated abou::t
9       he likes to lecture
10      and and go on and on and on and on about it .hh
```

By characterizing her husband as someone who lectures her endlessly, W identifies lecturing as a recurrent activity that causes problems in their relationship. This construction of the problem firmly locates the problem in a disposition of the husband and, thus, places responsibility for the problem on the husband.

The counsellor reconstructs clients' extreme case formulations through the use of grammatical structures that nominalize the problem. For example, W's extreme case formulation 'he likes to lecture on any subject' is reformulated by the counsellor as the nominalization 'a man who has a lecturing style'. The next step in the counsellor's reformulation is to display the problem (i.e., the noun phrase 'a lecturing style') as something that causes clients' negative behaviour. Consider an illustration.

Example 6:34

(p. 172, C is counsellor)

```
1  C:   =awright .hh so in this therapy we talked a little bit about the
        effects
2       (1.0) that the problem has on your life .hh
3       an how it shapes you .hh
4       an how it u::h influences you .hh
```

5 an how it u::h changes your reputation in other people's eyes?

6 .hh

C constructs the problem not as some character flaw of husband or wife, but rather as an agent that affects, shapes, influences and changes the client in various negative ways. In this way, the counsellor constructs the problem itself as the problem, rather than the personal characteristics or behaviours of husband and wife. Whereas blaming one another is unlikely to lead to any solution to the couple's problems, depersonalizing problems in this way makes them objects that can be dealt with without finding fault with the other person. Over the course of counselling, clients themselves begin to construct their problems in the same way as the counsellor. Thus, one outcome of counselling is that clients acquire a new set of grammatical resources for constructing their problems that provides a better chance of problem solution.

Once the problem has been identified as an agent of clients' negative behaviour, the next stage in counselling is problem effacement. The counsellor provided a solution by making the clients, rather than the problems, agents who can believe or behave in a different way than they do at present. This construction is a solution to clients' problems because the problem is no longer in charge of what happens and, thus, the negative effects of the problem no longer occur. A first step in getting the client to construct themselves as agents is to get them to behave or think in new ways; that is, to use grammatical forms that place the client in the agentive role.

Consider an example in which W's problem was letting others down.

Example 6:35

(p. 235)

18 W: =its been really i uh interesting the last couple of weeks .hh

19 when I have simply said

20 no::: .hh I'm not going to do tha::t

W is now able to recall occasions in which she acted in a way that was contradictory to her problematic behaviour. This new thought that she can say 'no' without letting anyone down allows W to construct a relationship between behaving in a new way and having a positive day (see next example). What C does at that point is to formulate W as the cause of the positive day.

Example 6:36

(p. 247)

21 W: I have had some day::s when I've been I've been pretty (.8)

      happy? (.)

22   mhm=

23 C: =I'm rea::lly curious about how you made that made that

      happen

24   for yourself (0.8)

25   how you made that positively happen .hh

In saying 'how you made that happen' and 'how you made that positively happen', C constructs W as the agent of her positive day. At this point, then, the construal of the problem as the agent of W's negative thoughts and behaviour has been replaced by the construal of W as the agent of her own positive thoughts and behaviour.

Muntigl demonstrates in precise detail how the counsellor encourages clients to use specific resources of grammar to construct their problems and solutions to those problems. Since life is lived mainly in talk, it can be expected that the grammatical and sequential resources used in counselling are used also in the construction of personal, social and cultural realities generally.

Context

A second set of exogenous factors that needs to be included in a psychological model of talk is referred to as 'context'. I am thinking here of knowledge of such things as categories of persons, roles, and objects (e.g., domineering, dentist, cars), activity types (Levinson, 1992), genres, and interpersonal relations and orientations (e.g., politeness and impoliteness). Consider an example. (Note that the example begins at a topic shift. What immediately preceded this sequence was an unrelated topic.)

Example 6:37

1 K: how many babies have you shot

2 G: u::h about thirty now

3 K: thirty just today↑

4 G: no (.) altogether

5 K: oh wow (1.0) a lot of screaming crying ones↑

6 G: no actually they're pretty good i've had tw-two screaming ones

7   today

8 K: good (.) that's not bad (.) two out of thirty

9 G: that's not bad (1.5) still doesn't make me want one though

10 K: ((laughter))

11 G: other people's kids are fine

As the analyst proceeds through the sequence, it becomes apparent that the participants are talking about vaccinating babies. As claimed by CA, that awareness must, in part, be based on factors endogenous to the talk; that is, to some extent participants and analysts understand what is happening in talk by the nature of the talk itself. It is also important to note that there is endogenous context for the participants that we, overhearers, are not party to. Given the recipient-designed nature of talk, G and K create context for themselves, not for analysts who are overhearers. As a consequence, analysts may have to import context into their analyses of talk since for them (overhearers) the necessary context is not endogenously available. The need for exogenous context is then, to some extent, an analyst's problem and not a participants' problem.

There is, however, reason to believe that participants themselves need access to exogenous context. G and K, for example, need to know such things as what a nurse is and what he/she does; what a vaccination involves and, thus, why it might be painful; that babies in our culture are vaccinated and why; that babies, unlike adults, are likely to cry when suffering minor discomfort, etc. This knowledge *is* exogenous to G and K's talk. Similarly, in coming to understand this segment of talk, analysts too need to draw on all kinds of exogenous knowledge, including knowledge of what people typically do and do not do (e.g., people rarely shoot babies with a gun; people would not find shooting babies with a gun to be interesting nor amusing), of what nurses do, of what vaccinations consist, etc. Thus, a model of context as an endogenously-produced accomplishment of participants is an inadequate psychological model of the nature and role of context in the production and understanding of talk for both participants and analysts. A psychological model of talk must describe which factors are part of the psychological context of particular instances of talk and how those factors enter into the production and interpretation of specific instances of talk.

7

Social Pragmatics

Introduction and Chapter Overview

Building on the positive aspects of the models reviewed in previous chapters, a social pragmatic model of talk is developed. To incorporate fully the individual, cognitive component of talk, the model needs further specification. Some promising directions for future development are suggested. The next section of the chapter describes the research paradigm of social pragmatics. After emphasizing the importance of studying natural talk, the discussion focuses on ways of generating the corpus of talk that is to be analysed. Three examples of psychological research based on a social pragmatic paradigm illustrate that approach.

Next, the advantages and disadvantages of social pragmatics and the associated research paradigm are summarized. The chapter closes with an exploration of four criticisms of social pragmatics; namely, that social pragmatics ignores cultural differences, is a form of behaviourism, puts a misplaced emphasis on manifest behaviour, and contradicts what is known about cognition. Discussion of the last two criticisms is quite technical, and the general reader may wish to proceed directly to the final chapter. Readers with a professional interest in talk/social interaction should find the discussions challenging but important.

Unlike previous chapters, the present chapter does not focus on specific structures of talk but, instead, examines more abstract issues, such as models of memory that are consistent with social pragmatics. Those issues do not lend themselves readily to illustration by examples from natural talk. Accordingly, relatively few examples of natural talk are presented.

SOCIAL PRAGMATICS

Because the Code Model is unable to account for the vast majority of natural talk, nothing from it is incorporated into social pragmatics. Three aspects of the Speech Act Model are included. First, the Speech Act conception of talk as a form of human action is, in a slightly revised form, a central assumption of social pragmatics; in particular, social pragmatists conceive of talk as a form of social interaction. Second,

Speech Act theorists note that some speech acts are carried out only when the Addressee acts in some specific way. For example, when S makes a bet ('I bet you $20.00 the summer Olympic Games will be cancelled due to fear of terrorism'), the action is not complete until A takes up the bet ('You're on'). What this amounts to is that Speech Act theory assumes that some actions are constructed by both S and A. Social pragmatists argue that all actions in talk are co-constructed.

The third contribution of Speech Act theory is the relevance of perlocutionary acts/effects in talk. Recall that intended and unintended perlocutionary acts and effects include overt physical and social actions A carries out in response to S's prior action (e.g., boiling water, expressing gratitude) as well as covert psychological actions and effects (e.g., A forms an attitude about S given what S said). Perlocutionary acts and effects are the least developed concepts in Speech Act theory, but they are central to social pragmatics. In particular, social pragmatists assume that participants talk primarily to coordinate their actions and bring about perlocutionary acts and effects. An important implication is that transactional, interpersonal, and psychological orientations must be incorporated into social pragmatics.

Following Grice, social pragmatists assume that talk is embedded in and constitutive of practical activities (e.g., buying a stamp). Although not highlighted by Grice, the example of buying a stamp also illustrates talk is recipient-designed; that is, talk involves some specific Speaker who designs a turn at some specific point in a sequence for some specific Addressee. (Levinson (1988) uses the notion of 'footing' to describe other roles that participants in talk can take.) The view that weakly constitutive rules of talk/interaction, such as the Cooperative Principle, are used by participants to make their actions intelligible and accountable is also borrowed from Grice. To employ weakly constitutive rules as templates for interpretation implies that participants in talk have certain inferential abilities. Inference is, thus, central to social pragmatics. A weakness of the present version of social pragmatics is that a psychological account of those inferential abilities is not sufficiently specified.

Brown and Levinson's (B&L) insistence on the importance of interpersonal aspects of talk is shared by social pragmatists who assume that talk is the primary site of sociality in all cultures. Based on B&L's convincing arguments and illustrations, social pragmatists also assume the social interaction is strategic. However, politeness is not the sole social orientation of talk: participants may produce talk to equivocate, convince, assign blame, avoid legal consequences, etc. Further, because (a speaker in) a turn at talk has both transactional and one or more personal, interpersonal or cultural orientations, social pragmatists assume talk is multifunctional.

B&L's claim, that personal, social and cultural identities are all displayed in and created in talk (i.e., there is a reflexive relationship between talk and social relations) is incorporated into social pragmatics. Recall that talk is also assumed to be constitutive of practical (transactional) action. The upshot of these assumptions for social pragmatics is that talk is based on the total speech situation (context-dependent), but talk also partially constitutes that total speech situation (context-forming). Put differently, talk 'is not merely *about* actions, events and situations, it is also a potent and *constitutive part* of those actions, events and situations' (Potter & Wetherell, 1987, p. 21, emphasis in original).

Many of the tenets of Conversation Analysis are adopted by social pragmatics; central among these is that talk is social interaction. CA's claim that talk is a manifest, orderly and sequential activity accomplished through participants' use of orderly resources is critical for social pragmatic theory and methodology. Acceptance of that claim necessitates a model of talk with both social and psychological components. The social-structural nature of talk accords with a sociological orientation in which 'the proper study of interaction is not the individual and his psychology, but rather the syntactical relations among the acts of different persons mutually present to one another' (Goffman, 1967, p. 2). However, it is individual persons who use those resources in concert with others to create interaction. Thus, in contrast to CA, social pragmatics requires a model of language, a model of exogenous context and the processes by which context and present processing are combined, and a model of cognition, especially of memory and inference. Some directions for developing the cognitive aspects of social pragmatics are discussed later in the chapter. Social pragmatics also differs from CA in employing a research paradigm similar in many respects to experimental psychology.

The social pragmatic conception of talk can be summarized as follows. Face-to-face talk is a universal form, and probably the basic form, of social interaction. Other forms of talk, such as telephone talk and therapy talk, are variants of this basic form of social interaction. Face-to-face talk between two or more persons is the primary site of sociality in all cultures. It is the place where persons together negotiate meaning and personal, social and cultural identities. Talk is situated action: it is action occurring manifestly and locally between two or more specific persons. Further, talk cannot be achieved without the mutual assumption that each participant will respond to a prior turn with a conditionally relevant turn. Thus, talk is not possible without trust. Overall, then, social pragmatists view talk as a manifest, co-constructed, for-all-practical-purposes, indexical, moral achievement.

Because social pragmatists assume persons use the manifest resources of talk to construct meaning together across specific observable sequences of turns at talk, it follows that talk is best analysed by examining the details of its accomplishment. The resources participants use to construct and interpret talk include orderly structures of adjacency and orderly structures of language, both of which are processed in an orderly, human cognitive system. Application of these orderly structures proceeds according to weakly constitutive rules.

Research Paradigm of Social Pragmatics

Step 1: Obtaining a corpus of natural talk

The first step in the methodology of social pragmatics is to audio- and video-tape instances of natural talk relevant to the phenomena of interest. In most research on talk, it is typical for researchers to create scenarios depicting situations of talk and for research participants to complete self-report measures of what they would do or say in some situation. Thus, the social pragmatist's insistence on the study of natural talk conflicts with the reliance on researcher and research participant intuitions typical of the dominant paradigm.

Consider a specific example. A researcher may recall a situation in which she avoided a projected confrontation with her husband by telling a white lie. The researcher then hypothesizes that persons will tell the truth unless doing so will jeopardize an important relationship, in which case they will lie. To test the hypothesis, the researcher constructs two scenarios that involve a potentially threatening evaluation occurring between two people who have a positive and relatively intimate or non-intimate relationship. For example, the scenarios might be: 'Imagine S is a close friend whom you've known for many years (Intimate Relationship)/S is a neighbour with whom you're on good terms but don't know well (Non-Intimate Relationship). One day, S says to you "How do you like the colour we just painted our house?" You really think the new colour is dreadful.' Each research participant is presented with one of the two scenarios and asked 'What would you say?' and 'Why would you say that?'. Research participants' intuitions about what they would say in such a situation and why are taken to reflect what they actually would say and why they would say it.

This type of approach to the study of talk is highly problematic. Intuitions are naïve theories of action that usually deviate in many ways from situated action (Bem & McConnell, 1970; Gilovich, 1990; Nisbett & Wilson, 1977; Wilson & Brekke, 1994). Further, due to impression management, people may believe they would do one thing but, when asked, say they would do something else that puts them in a better light. Thus, intuitions about talk are unlikely to match the structure of natural talk (Turnbull, 2001).

Nevertheless, when presented with S's request for evaluation, research participants might produce the actions of positive evaluation (white lie) and negative evaluation (truth) in the expected relationship conditions. However, there are many reasons to doubt that the structure of those actions will match the structure of their natural counterparts. One reason is that the scenarios depict a sequential relationship across only two turns at talk, yet in natural talk the request for evaluation–evaluation adjacency pair is likely to be embedded in, and possibly negotiated over, longer sequences. For example, given the face-threatening potential of the depicted situations, a request for evaluation might be projected through a pre-sequence (e.g., 'Did you notice we had the house painted?'). If the addressee recognizes a request for evaluation is being projected, he can avoid making a negative evaluation by producing a turn-down (e.g., 'Oh, yeah. Anyway, on that issue about our tax rebates

. . .'). In this way, the addressee protects his relationship with the speaker without resorting to the strategy of telling a white lie. It is also likely that the person responding to the request for evaluation would display hesitancy through the use of filled or unfilled pauses at the start of the turn. Those pauses constitute a potential turn transition point, a place where S could take the turn and retract or revise his/her request for evaluation. What these considerations suggest is that *when* and *how* white lies are produced in natural talk are likely to differ in important ways from what the experimental scenario allows.

Another serious problem with the scenario approach is that S's talk is not designed for a specific recipient, but rather for a type of recipient (i.e., a close friend versus an acquaintance). Natural talk, however, is not designed for classes of persons but for specific persons in specific total speech situations. Thus, the structure of what S 'says' may not match the structure of what a specific S would say to a specific addressee. In sum, given the sequential and recipient-designed nature of natural talk, it is highly likely that both the talk research participants are asked to respond to and their response to that talk will differ in important respects from natural talk. Thus, whatever research participants say, it remains unclear what is learned about actual talk.

The above arguments support the view that analyses of talk must be based on corpora of natural talk. This may seem to pose a serious problem for research since, given ethical standards, persons must give permission to have their talk used in research. The issue, then, is whether natural talk can occur in research settings in which participants know that their interaction is being taped. Potter and Wetherell (1995) argue convincingly that natural talk should not be equated with talk that occurs in mundane, everyday settings, nor with talk that would have occurred whether or not a researcher was present or involved in its production. Turnbull (2001) proposes that natural talk is talk that occurs in situations in which speakers can talk freely and without restriction on what they say or how they say it, and without awareness that it is specifically their talk that is the object of study. Thus, Turnbull concludes that natural talk can be generated using ethical techniques that allow experimental research.

Many phenomena of social pragmatic interest (e.g., complaints, promises, refusals) do not occur frequently in everyday talk. Simply giving research participants a tape recorder and asking them, for example, to tape mealtime discussions will very probably require hundreds of hours of taping to get a useable sample size. Thus, in addition to generating natural talk ethically, another criterion of a good pragmatic elicitation technique is that it should efficiently produce many instances of the phenomena of interest; that is, pragmatic elicitation techniques should generate natural talk ethically and efficiently. There are many pragmatic elicitation techniques, including both experimental (Turnbull, 1992, 2001) and correlational approaches (Drummond & Hopper, 1993; Muntigl & Turnbull, 1998; Turnbull & Carpendale, 1999b) that meet these requirements. To give a clearer sense of what a good pragmatic elicitation technique looks like, I next present an example in some detail.

Refusing a request is universally a highly face-threatening act and, thus, is a useful phenomenon for examining Brown and Levinson's politeness model. Turnbull (2001) tested the hypothesis that refusing a request of someone of relatively higher status is more face-threatening than refusing the identical request of someone of relatively lower status. Thus, refusals made to a higher status versus lower status requester should contain more facework. To generate a corpus of refusals, a researcher telephoned students in a volunteer research pool. When the student answered, the research assistant said either 'Hi, this is Sandra Robinson. I'm a graduate student working as the senior research assistant in the social psychology lab at Simon Fraser University', or 'Hi, this is Sandi. I'm a high school student helping out in the social psychology lab at Simon Fraser University'. In this way, relative status was manipulated (High and Low Relative status, respectively).

After identifying herself, the research assistant made the identical request of all students: 'I'm phoning to see if you'd like to participate in a psychology experiment. The experiment will take place up at the university on Saturday morning from 7:00 o'clock to about 10:30.' She did not speak again until the research participant made a response. If asked, the research assistant said the study involved completing tests of logical and mathematical ability. The research assistant and student continued talking until the student began a pre-closing, at which point the research interrupted and told the student about the true nature of the call. Students were told that the call had been taped, and were asked for permission to use the data.

The hypothesis was also assessed using four other pragmatic elicitation techniques; namely, Written and Oral discourse completion, Role-Play, and refusals occurring in a situation with no experimental manipulation (i.e., Natural). In the Written discourse completion technique, students from the same university were given a written description of the research and what they were expected to do. Students read that the research concerned 'what people say, their exact words, when they talk to others'. Students were then asked to imagine receiving a telephone call in which the caller made a specific request, and they were instructed to 'write out exactly what you would say; that is, the exact words you would use' in responding to the request. The request and the manipulation of relative status were written out but identical in all other respects to the Experimental condition. The Oral discourse completion technique was identical to Written discourse completion except that all instructions were given on audio-tape, students replied orally to the request, and their responses were audio-taped.

In the Role-Play condition, students were informed that the research concerned how well people can imagine being in a certain situation and responding to something that occurs in that situation. To study this, the researcher and student sat on either side of a screen, each holding a (disconnected) telephone. After 'telephoning' the student, the researcher identified herself as either the High or Low status requester, and then made the request. Researcher and student talked until the 'telephone call' was complete. All conversations were audio-taped.

In the Natural condition, telephone calls were made from the same laboratory to students in the same volunteer pool as the Experimental condition. Compared to the other conditions, there was no manipulation of status and the request was less demanding.

All pragmatic elicitation techniques were efficient in generating refusals, though there were large differences across conditions in the percentage of refusals: Written = 77%, Oral = 60%, Role-Play = 53%, Experimental = 74%, and Natural = 28%. Comparison of refusals generated by the various techniques to Natural refusals yielded important results. In particular, refusals generated by the Written and Oral discourse completion techniques were non-representative and overly simplified, in contrast to refusals generated by the Role-Play and Experimental technique, which were highly similar to Natural refusals. Role-Play refusals tended, however, to be more rambling, repetitive, and forced relative to their Natural counterparts. Another interesting finding was that the face-work hypothesis was supported in the Role-Play condition only. The importance of studying natural talk to assess claims about talk is underlined by this result. In sum, the study illustrates that researchers can create controlled situations that ethically and efficiently generate many representative instances of the phenomenon of interest.

Step 2: Transcribing the corpus of natural talk

Taping and transcription of natural talk are required due to the speed at which talk occurs, to the tremendous amount of detail in the structure of talk, and to the importance of this detail for what participants produce and interpret in talk.

Step 3: Describing and analysing talk

The third step in the research paradigm of social pragmatics is description and analysis. A general working assumption, borne out by a large literature, is that no detail of talk can be assumed *a priori* to be irrelevant to what participants accomplish. Accordingly, even though research programmes are usually motivated by specific issues, the analyst strives to adopt an inductive approach to the data. Analysis of talk focuses in the first place on how participants treat their talk. Thus, every analysis is rooted in and backed up by reference to participants' meaning. The social pragmatist attempts to categorize and/or quantify these orderly structures. As in psychology generally, issues of (inter-rater) reliability and generalizability need to be addressed. Computation of both descriptive and inferential statistics may be warranted.

Many of the features of the social pragmatic paradigm are shared by discursive psychology (Edwards & Potter, 1992; Potter, 1996) and discourse analysis (Stubbs, 1983; Wood & Kroger, 2000). There are, however, some important differences. The latter approaches base analyses on data from written and oral texts, and statistical analyses are generally avoided. Social pragmatists, by contrast, do not study writing since it fails to share most of the characteristics of social interaction, and they do find value in statistical analyses. Thus, much of the literature in discursive psychology and discourse analysis is not relevant to social pragmatic concerns.

EXAMPLES OF SOCIAL PRAGMATIC RESEARCH

To illustrate social pragmatic research and its advantages for examination of psychological issues, three social pragmatic studies are described next.

Study: Arguing exchanges in families (Muntigl & Turnbull, 1998)

Introduction

Conflict, 'interaction between persons expressing opposing interests, views, or opinions (Cahn, 1990, p. 1)', is an important aspect of marital satisfaction and of intimate relations generally (Brehm, Miller, Perlman, & Campbell, 2001). Recent research on the determinants of marital satisfaction, including the role of conflict, typically examines actual instances of interaction and focuses on interpretations of behaviours/emotions (Bradbury, Fincham, & Beach, 2000). Conflict, then, is typically studied by observing partners discussing relationship problems and obtaining each partner's interpretations of own and other's behaviour in the discussion and other conflict situations.

Emphasis on the interpretation of behaviour stems from the view that it is not conflict behaviours *per se* but rather partners' interpretations, especially their attributions, that reflect and predict relationship satisfaction. By contrast, social pragmatists focus on providing, in the first instance, a detailed description of the resources by which partners co-construct conflict. Interpersonal conflict can be constituted by a wide variety of actions and action sequences, including accusing, arguing, blaming, criticizing, disagreeing, interfering with other's goals, and trying to control other. Thus, in order to develop an empirically-based description of how conflict is constituted, it is necessary to focus on a specific type of conflict.

Muntigl and Turnbull (1998) focused on arguing. They proposed that arguing minimally consists of a three-turn exchange beginning with a claim by S, which is responded to by A with an oppositional action (e.g., a disagreement), to which S in the third turn responds either by supporting her initial claim or opposing A's oppositional act. To explore whether such arguing exchanges did occur and, if so, what their structure was, Muntigl and Turnbull obtained audio-tapes of families, each consisting of mother (M), father (F) and teenage daughter (D), discussing in their homes an unresolved moral issue and one of Kohlberg's moral dilemmas. The researchers also obtained audio-tapes of university student discussions occurring in their homes or at the pub. All participants were free to erase any or all of their taped discussion, and anonymity was guaranteed by deleting all proper names from the transcripts.

Analysis

In the corpus, 164 arguing exchanges were identified. All examples presented are from the family discussions. Rather than line numbers, the three turns of an arguing exchange are numbered.

Example 7:1

T1 F: what were you doing in the shops then↑

T2 D: what shop↑ i wasn't even in a shop

   (2.4)

T3 F: well i thought i saw you walking into that shop at the grocery store

D in T2 challenges F's T1 turn, and F in T3 provides support for his original T1 claim, thereby opposing D's T2 action. The claim–opposition–opposition three turn structure of an arguing exchange is evident.

   Next, the researchers examined the structure and content of T2 in all arguing exchanges. Several different types of oppositional actions were identified, each constituted by particular structures and content.

Example 7:2

Irrelevancy Claim

T1 D: yes it should be such a big deal because i'm moving in a week

T2 F: so what

F's oppositional action is produced without pause or mitigation (i.e., preferred structure). F claims that D has made an irrelevant contribution. Because F opposes the relevancy but not the content of D's T1, F's action closes down further negotiation of D's T1 claim.

Example 7:3

Challenge

T1 D: on a [weekly basis

F: [ah wait

T2 F: ah wait (.) ah when when was this

F's oppositional action is first produced as an attempted interruption. When F produces the whole turn in the form of an interrogative, F implicates that D cannot provide evidence for her T1 claim. F provides no alternative to D's T1 claim, thereby failing to open up negotiation on it.

Example 7:4

Contradiction

T1 F: laura listen to what i'm saying to you (0.5) it doesn't matter who

[it was

T2 D: [yes it does

D in overlap produces a bald on record (i.e., preferred structure) contradiction. As with Irrelevancy Claims and Challenges, Contradictions fail to provide information that might facilitate negotiation.

Example 7:5

Counterclaim

T1 F: well we'd like to know where you are (0.6) in the late hours of

the night

(1.5)

T2 D: i tell you where i where i am but i don't have to tell you what

i'm doing

D's oppositional action is produced after a pause, contains repetitions and the mitigating modal 'have to', and the opposition is pushed back later into the turn (i.e., dispreferred structure). Further, D produces a claim of her own that is an alternative to F's T1 claim, thereby opening up potential negotiation.

Similar types of oppositional moves were observed in T3, as in the next example.

Example 7:6

Contradiction

T1 F: it wasn't much to ask you to come in early (0.7) just one night

 (0.7) nine-thirty ten o'clock is not out of line

T2 D: yeah it is out of line

T3 F: no it's not

Although any type of T3 is possible for any T2, analysis revealed a statistically significant T2–T3 relationship. To account for this relationship, the researchers proposed that the structural features and content of each type of oppositional act have different potential for damaging the face of the person being opposed. (The ranking of acts from most to least face-damaging is Irrelevancy Claim and Challenge, Contradiction and Counterclaim.) One possible T2–T3 pattern is aggressive 'tit-for-tat' in which the more face-damaging T2, the more face-damaging is T3. Another possible pattern orients to defusing face-damage; namely, the more face-damaging T2, the less face-damaging is the T3 response. The data supported the latter pattern, perhaps not surprisingly as these arguing exchanges occurred between persons in intimate and generally positive relationships (for a similar finding, see Margolin and Wampold, 1981).

The social pragmatic approach was useful in characterizing how arguing is co-constructed and how various co-constructions affirm positive relationships. Cognitively-oriented psychologists are likely to resist the social pragmatic approach, claiming that analysis of couples' interpretations, rather than the manifest structure of their interactions, is more revealing. The social pragmatist has two responses. First, whatever interpretations are made of behaviour, those interpretations must be based on observation of the behaviour, not idealizations of it. (Note that if a person's interpretations of behaviour seemed completely unrelated to the behaviour, one would consider the person delusional.) Behaviour is manifest, complex and orderly, and the details *do* matter to what gets done (e.g., different ways of disagreeing have different structure and different implications for relationships). Therefore, even on the assumption that interpretation is important, a description of behaviour is required for any examination of the interpretive process. Second, the assertion that researchers can best understand how conflict is related to marital satisfaction by exploring couple's interpretations is an empirical claim. It is reasonable to pursue empirically the alternative claim that it is mainly in the manifest structures of talk that couples both display and negotiate identities of self, other and relationship.

Study: Criteria and the development of an understanding of mind (Turnbull & Carpendale, 2001a)

Introduction

An important issue for social-cognitive developmentalists is how children come to understand the nature of mind and emotion. The dominant, though not the only, position (for a review see Hala & Carpendale, 1997), is that children come to understand mind by forming a theory based on a commonsense psychology of beliefs and desires. The relationship between beliefs and desires is that if person P, wants some outcome, O, and if P believes B, that doing D leads to/causes O, P will do D. On this view, a critical stage in the development of a theory of mind is the development of an understanding of belief and, particularly, of the distinction between belief and reality. A child who understands this distinction can recognize that beliefs can be false and, therefore, that someone with a false belief will act inappropriately to attain a goal. False belief understanding is, thus, a/the major milestone in understanding mind.

Researchers initially assigned a minor role to the influence of social interaction on the development of understanding mind. Recent research, however, indicates that social interaction and understanding mind are related (Jenkins & Astington, 1996; Lewis, Freeman, Kyriakidou, Maridaki-Kassotiaki, & Berridge, 1996; Perner, Ruffman, & Leekam, 1994). To explain this relationship, one common assumption is that the child's exposure to mental state terms facilitates an understanding of mind. Accordingly, it is typical to count the frequency of use by caregiver and child of mental state terms, such as 'think' and 'believe', and relate those frequencies to the child's understanding of mind (Cervantes & Callanan, 1998; Dunn, Brown, Slomkowski, Tesla, & Youngblade, 1991).

Social pragmatists identify several problems with this approach. One is the assumption that when a mental state term is used in talk, it is used to refer to a mental state. That assumption, however, is unfounded since the literal meaning of a word may not correspond to what participants use that word to do. A related problem is that talk about mind can occur without the use of any mental state terms. Consider, for example, the concept of 'hiding'. Whereas 'hiding' is not a mental state term, to understand what it means to assert that someone is hiding something does require an understanding of mind.

Both of the above problems derive from confusion about the relation between talk and understanding. The dominant view is that a child first understands some concept and then learns to use a word to represent it. By contrast, Wittgenstein (1970), argues that talk and understanding are inextricably intertwined. Wittgenstein (1953) further argues that it is not possible to learn about one's mental states entirely through introspection. Rather, persons must learn the public criteria for the appropriate ways to talk about mind (see Montgomery, 1997, for an accessible discussion of Wittgenstein's argument). Criteria for mind are likely displayed in social interaction. Thus, the development of an understanding of mind should be related to the extent to which and way in which criteria for talking about mind are displayed in caregiver–child interactions.

Research issue and overview

The objectives of the study were to examine the display of criteria for understanding mind in mother–child (M–C) talk about mind, and relate the display of criteria to C's level of understanding mind. To do this, M and C made up a story that centrally involved a false belief and attendant emotions. A list of criteria that would contribute to an understanding of these story components was created. Each M–C story was examined for the presence of these criteria. For each criterion produced, the researchers identified who elicited and who produced it. Finally, the frequency and pattern of elicitation/production of criteria were related to independent measures of C's level of false belief understanding. The research also focused on precisely how criteria were elicited and how displayed. Because of the small size of the sample, these results are not reported.

Methodology

Each of twenty-four M–C dyads was presented with a book of pictures with no words, and M was instructed to make up a story with her child based on the pictures. Children ranged in age from approximately three to five years. Each dyad was video-taped while creating the story, and the tapes were subsequently transcribed. The picture book showed two children, Billy and Sarah, getting chocolate bars from their mother. Sarah immediately gobbles hers, making a mess in the process. Billy eats some but decides to save the rest for later by hiding it under the sleeping dog. However, although Billy is unaware, Sarah sees him hide his chocolate bar and, while Billy is outside playing, Sarah takes it and puts it in her pocket. When Billy returns to get his chocolate bar he has a false belief about its location. At this point the story gets more complex than the standard false belief task because Billy's suspicions are immediately aroused when Sarah laughs. Billy gets angry, pushes Sarah, and the chocolate bar falls out of her pocket. Then Billy and Sarah's mother intervenes. The picture book was designed to encourage talk about the mental world because the story involves hiding, trickery, false beliefs, emotions, and morality yet the task does not restrict what the mothers and their children say nor how they say it.

Children's level of understanding mind was assessed on tests of false belief understanding. For illustration, consider the unexpected transfer task (Wimmer & Perner, 1983). C is shown two puppets, a toy and a blue and a red cup. One of the puppets places the toy in the blue cup, and then the other puppet, Maxi, leaves the room. While Maxi is away, the toy is moved to the red cup. C is asked where Maxi will look for the toy when he returns. To answer correctly, C must recognize that Maxi was out of the room when the toy was moved and, therefore, that Maxi does not know it was moved. C must also know that people act on the basis of what they believe, not what is the case. Thus, Maxi should act on the basis of his false belief and look for the toy in the blue cup, where it was when he left the room, not in the red cup where it now is. Typically, before the age of 3 years children fail false belief tests, but by the age of 4 years, most are passing those tests.

Analysis

As anticipated, all dyads constructed a story that included a deception-false belief-associated emotions component. The researchers identified 17 key elements critical for an understanding of this false belief situation. Key elements are criteria that should be identified and explained in teaching someone who does not understand the deception-false belief-associated emotions story. Examples of key elements include: Billy puts/hides his chocolate bar under the sleeping dog; Sarah watches while Billy hides his chocolate bar; Billy is not aware of this; while Billy is outside playing, Sarah takes the chocolate bar; Billy goes inside and looks for his chocolate bar under the sleeping dog (see Turnbull & Carpendale, 2001a, for a comprehensive list).

For the false belief section of each M–C transcript, coders identified every key element present. In addition, coders identified who produced the key element and who elicited it. A key element is produced if it is explicitly present in the transcript. A key element is elicited if M or C made an utterance, the conditionally relevant response to which is a key element. For example, M might say 'what is Sarah doing?', an utterance that elicits the key element that Sarah is taking Billy's chocolate out from under the dog. If C supplied the correct answer, the key element is elicited by M and produced by C (i.e., M-elicited/C-produced key element). In some cases a key element was both elicited and produced by the same person. For example, if C failed to answer M's question about what Sarah was doing, M might produce the answer/element herself (i.e., M-elicited/M-produced key element); alternatively, without any elicitation from M, C might say 'look, Sara's taking Billy's chocolate bar' (i.e., C-elicited/C-produced key element). In a very few instances, a key element was elicited but never produced.

It was expected that mothers whose child had a low level of false belief understanding would, perhaps unconsciously, try to teach C about false belief by talking about many of the key elements/criteria necessary for understanding the false belief situation. Because of the low level of C's understanding, M would also need to elicit key elements from C and, in many cases, might have to produce them also. By contrast, there should be less need for M to elicit key elements from C who has a high level of false belief understanding. For these children it is also more likely that key elements that were produced would be elicited and/or produced by C. Thus, the researchers predicted (1) a higher proportion of M-elicited/M-produced key elements in dyads where C had a low as compared to high level of false belief understanding; and (2) a higher proportion of C-elicited/C-produced key elements for Cs with high as compared to low false belief understanding.

Results and discussion

On the basis of performing poorly or well on the false belief tests, children were assigned to the Fail (N=14) or Pass (N=10) group. Groups showed little difference in the total number of key elements produced (scores are averages): Fail = 12.0, Pass = 13.6. On average, mothers elicited 89% of key elements, but mothers elicited more in the Fail group: M-elicited in Fail = 97%; and in Pass = 79%. Children in Fail produced fewer elements (46%) than their mothers, but children in the Pass group produced more elements (54%) than their mothers. Finally, there was a large difference between groups in the percentage of elements produced by C that were not elicited by M (i.e., C-elicited/C-produced): Fail = 4%; Pass = 38%.

These results demonstrate that whereas both Fail and Pass children were capable of producing elements elicited by their mothers, only Pass children were capable of producing elements that were not elicited by mother. What these data suggest is that as children develop their ability to understand situations of false belief, they are better able to attend to public criteria that allow them to understand what others are thinking and feeling. Given experiences of this sort, children are eventually able to talk about mind and, thus, understand mind in more and more diverse situations. In this way, the development of talk and the development of an understanding of mind are inextricably intertwined (Wootton, 1997).

A social pragmatic analysis of manifest aspects of M–C interaction revealed the role of M and C in the elicitation and production of criteria for the appropriate ways to talk about false belief. Criteria were manifestly displayed and tied to the particulars of the situation of false belief. Further, M–C talk was not simply a conduit for the expression and recognition of C's understanding, but rather M–C talk was an occasion on which criteria for understanding false belief were displayed. In other words, M–C talk was a resource for C's understanding of false belief. In sum, the research demonstrated a close interrelationship between talk and social understanding.

Study: Relationship style in M–C talk and the development of an understanding of mind (Turnbull & Carpendale, 2002)

Introduction

Social interaction is important for the display of criteria and the co-construction of understanding. Precisely *how* interaction is achieved should also be important. For example, since young children may not understand a false belief component of a story, M is largely in control of how, and whether, criteria are displayed. M could act unilaterally by simply stating the criteria, or she could act in ways that encourage and help C to display criteria him/herself (e.g., by guiding and scaffolding C's understanding). These relationship styles have been characterized by Piaget (1932/1965) as falling on a continuum from relationships of constraint and one-sided respect to relationships of equality, cooperation and mutual respect. In a constraining relationship, M ignores C's contributions or fails to build on and incorporate them into the interaction. Relations of constraint are characterized by M's control and domination. In a cooperative relationship, M takes C's contributions into account by building on and extending them and, thus, control is shared by M and C. When M and C engage in talk, constraint–cooperation is constituted by the ways in which M–C construct their talk. Thus, constraint–cooperation can be conceptualized as the relationship style of an M–C dyad.

Piaget proposed that cooperative relationships among equals facilitate moral development because it is in such relationships that children come to more fully understand other people's perspectives. Understanding others' perspectives is a major component in developing a mature understanding of mind. Thus, it can be expected that being involved in many interactions in which M takes C's perspective into account will facilitate C's development of the ability to take another's perspective into account. In this way, the quality of the M–C relationship should affect the development of children's understanding of mind.

Research methodology and data

The purpose of study was to describe the structures of M–C talk that are constitutive of constraining and cooperative relationships. Once this is accomplished, it will then be possible to examine the impact of relationship style on the development of children's understanding of mind. Data consisted of transcripts of the talk of seventy M–C dyads from the same study as used in the key elements analysis.

Analysis

The structures that constitute constraining and cooperative relationships are not attributes of M or C, but rather are attributes of co-constructed talk. It is likely, however, that when mothers and their young children talk about mind, the inter-action is determined more by M than C due to M's superior understanding of mind. Although there are many possible structures by which relationship style is displayed, the present analysis focuses on repair sequences. In the context of creating a story from the picture book, repair sequences are important because many story details are critical for understanding. How C understands the story is related to C's level of understanding of mind. But it is also the case that being helped by M to improve his/her understanding of the story should facilitate the development of C's understanding of mind. For these reasons, it can be expected that M will orient to C's errors in story understanding.

Repairs can be done unilaterally by M (e.g., M initiated-M repair) or in ways that build on the child's contributions (e.g., M initiates but allows C to repair). The relevance of how repair sequences are constructed to constraint–cooperation is that the recipient-design of utterances (i.e., S designs her utterances specifically for A at each moment in the interaction) requires some ability to take the perspective of the other into account. Thus, the ways in which M carries out her moves in repair sequences displays the extent to which M takes C's perspective into account.

Results

Every instance of repair in all the transcripts was identified (approximately 150), and a structural analysis was made of each repair. All repairables were produced by C. The structures of repair tended to fall along a continuum, from cases in which M repaired C's repairable immediately and without hedging or providing help to C, to cases in which M initiated a repair and, through a sequence of turns, gradually enabled C to make his/her own repair.

The following examples illustrate the continuum of repair structures from highly constraining through increasingly cooperative relationships.

Example 7:7

1   M: and there's sarah what is she doing↑

2   C: she's dropping it

3   M: no she's eating it look she's got chocolate everywhere

M disagrees with C's answer in preferred structure and provides the repair. There is no input from C on the repair, and M allows no place for such input. In effect, M ignores C's potential contributions to making a repair. M does, however, provide criteria for the repair by directing C's attention to the picture of Sarah all messy with chocolate. This interaction illustrates a constraining relationship.

Example 7:8

1   C: no (.) i mean those are pills

2   M: ther they're what↑

3   C: pills

4   M: no they're candies (.) sweetie

M initiates a repair in line 2, and C responds by again producing a repairable. In line 4, M disagrees in preferred structure and produces the repair. She does, however, soften the disagreement and correction with 'sweetie'. Compared to Example 7:7, M in Example 7:8 does initiate a self-repair and is, thus, more cooperative in that respect. On the other hand, unlike M in Example 7:7 who offers evidence/criteria to support her correction, M in Example 7:8 does not do this and, in this respect, is more constraining.

Constraint is evident also in the next example, though it is not as extreme.

Example 7:9

1   M: so he's very upset isn't he (0.5) and she doesn't look too upset

2   (0.9) hu:hh: *what did he do↑*

3   (1.2)

4   M: what did he do↑

5   C: i don't know

6   M: look ((pointing at the picture)) (.) he pushed her off the chair

Unlike Examples 7:7 and 7:8, before producing the repair M in line 6 first displays a criterion for the correct answer; namely, M points to the picture in the picture book that shows the answer to her question. This allows C to discover the answer and make the repair him/herself. M, however, does not wait for C to produce the repair, but instead completes it herself. Thus, M acts in a cooperative manner by displaying a criterion that would allow C to make a self-repair, but M acts in a constraining way by not allowing C to make the repair.

The next three examples illustrate, in turn, increasingly cooperative relationships.

Example 7:10

(C identified with the picture character Billy, and both M and C referred to Billy as 'you', meaning C; see 'you' in line 1, for example)

1   M: mommy (0.5) and what does she have for you↑

2   (2.0)

3   C: i don't know

4   M: is that candy↑

5   C: uh hugh (3.0) and we like to eat it

6   M: your right

After C in lines 2–3 is unable to answer her question (the repairable), M initiates a repair in the form of a polarity (yes/no) question. The question contains the repair. In this way, M both displays a potential repair without making it and focuses C's attention so that C is more able to make a self-repair. The strategy is effective, as C makes a self-repair in line 5 and even elaborates on it. M in line 6 acknowledges C's self-repair. Compared to the mothers in the prior examples, M acts in ways that help C to produce a self-repair. Acknowledging a self-repair is also a way for M to display her respect for C's contributions. Of course, an acknowledgment of C's self-repair can only occur if C makes a self-repair. Thus, self-repair by C offers more opportunities for M to convey her respect for C. Overall, this type of sequence displays a highly cooperative orientation.

Cooperation is also evident in the next example.

Example 7:11

1   M: [oh look] what is billy doin now↑

2   C: i don't know

3   M: ((pointing to picture)) what are those↑

4   C: playing with trucks=

5   M: =uh huh

M in the above example provides considerable help to her child to allow a self-repair. M first produces an identification question ('what is billy doin now↑') that C cannot answer (i.e., failure to answer is the repairable). In her next turn, M produces two actions that can help C make a self-repair; namely, she points to the relevant picture and she produces another identification question that, compared to her first identification question, more directly focuses C's attention on the correct answer ('those' in 'what are those↑'). In line 4, C is then able to make a self-repair, on to which M latches an acknowledgment. Thus, M both helps C to produce a self-repair and acknowledges that self-repair. Unlike mother in Example 7:10, M never states the repair but, instead, allows more freedom for C to recognize his/her error and make a self-repair. In other words, M treats C as a more equal participant in the interaction than does mother in Example 7:10.

Example 7:12

1 C: billy and sarah are

2   (0.9)

3 M: are what↑

4 C: are (4.0) i don't kno[w]

5 M: [figh]ting↑

6 C: fighting

7 M: accusing each other (.) is that the word you're looking for↑

8 C: they're tattling on him and sarah and billy

9 M: they're tattling on each other

10 C: yeah

The degree of cooperation is the highest in this example. C produces the repairable, an incomplete utterance, in line 1. Rather than immediately taking a turn, M waits for 0.9 seconds, an interval in which C can take the turn again and self-repair. When C fails to do that, M initiates a repair in the form of an identification question. In line 4, C is unable to make the repair. The four seconds of silence in line 4 gives M an opportunity to take the turn, but, once again, she allows C to continue to hold the floor. In line 5, M provides a possible repair in the form of a polarity question. C acknowledges that 'fighting' is the repair. Because of the way this two turn sequence unfolds, the repair can be considered to be both an other-repair and a self-repair. M in the next turn suggests a more refined repair, and C in line 8 displays remembering that the correct answer to the original line 2 question is that they are tattling on each other. C has actually rejected M's suggested repair and has replaced it with a repair of his/her own. M in line 9 echoes C's repair, thereby acknowledging it, and C acknowledges M's acknowledgment in return. This is a highly cooperative interaction. Both participants build on the other's contributions and the final repair is very much a collaborative achievement.

The social pragmatic approach has several advantages here. A common way to measure 'parental style' is through self-report questionnaires about how one treats one's child. The perils of treating what people report they do as a valid measure of what they actually do were discussed previously. It is much better to observe what people actually do. The social pragmatic paradigm was used to generate natural talk containing a lot of talk about mind. Further, social pragmatics, borrowing from CA, was used to characterize the detailed structure of repair sequences and, thus, to make distinctions among various types of repair. Differences in repair were conceptualized as displaying and creating different M–C relationships. Having characterized relationship styles in terms of repair structure, a next step is to examine how different relationship styles are related to present and future levels of the child's understanding of mind.

POSITIVE ASPECTS OF SOCIAL PRAGMATICS AND THE ASSOCIATED RESEARCH PARADIGM

Social pragmatics incorporates the positive features of all other models reviewed and accounts for all the examples of natural talk presented. Although highly similar to Conversation Analysis, social pragmatics has a different methodology than CA, one that is useful for psychologists. Of particular importance are pragmatic elicitation techniques that generate natural talk/social interaction yet allow researcher control. There is an overwhelming tendency in psychology to study imagined or constructed social interaction. On those rare occasions when actual social interaction is examined, the interaction typically occurs in odd situations with considerable reactivity. For example, two strangers in a psychology laboratory may be asked to get to know one another. The resulting interaction is likely to be awkward and self-conscious, and probably not representative of interaction that occurs when people get to know one another. Pragmatic elicitation techniques can be used to generate natural talk/social interaction. These interactions are likely to contain the full range of culturally-available resources participants use to co-construct interaction.

DEFICIENCIES OF SOCIAL PRAGMATICS AND THE ASSOCIATED RESEARCH PARADIGM

No model of language, interpersonal relations, or context

Several deficiencies of social pragmatics were identified also as deficiencies of CA. In particular, social pragmatics needs a model of language, of interpersonal orientations, and of context (but see the discussion of unitary models of memory which contain a model of context, pp. 205–210). For a fuller explication, the reader should consult the relevant material in Chapter 6.

Ignores cultural differences

Social pragmatics was developed from examples of natural talk, the vast majority of which involves middle-class Canadian speakers of English. The question arises as to whether the assumptions of social pragmatics apply to other cultures and other languages. It would take a book to do justice to this extremely complicated issue. All I attempt here is to present a brief synopsis of competing positions.

Both Grice's CP and B&L's politeness model have come under attack for being ethnocentric. Ochs Keenan (1975), for example, argues that the Cooperative Principle, and in particular the informativeness maxim, is not universal. The Madagaskar villagers Ochs Keenan studied typically gave less information than they could have and less than would have been useful to their interlocutor. Further these villagers did not make the implicatures Canadians do given insufficient information. For example, if S were to say 'I want to send JoAnne a birthday card. When's her birthday?' (to use a Canadian example), and A replied 'In December', the implicature would be drawn that A does not know the day of JoAnne's birthday, only the month. By contrast, a Madagaskar villager would only assume that her interlocutor knew more than he was conveying. There is, then, some reason to doubt the universality of the CP.

In the introduction to the reissue of their original 1975 paper, Brown and Levinson (1987) address the claimed universality of the politeness model. B&L conclude that face, power, distance, and imposition are all culturally determined, and that language/culture affords different facework strategies. Thus, for example, languages with highly-articulated systems of honorifics, such as Japanese, provide different ways of displaying and creating social relations than does English (see, e.g., Ide, 1982). In spite of these differences, B&L argue that the 'bare bones' notion of face, the equation for the degree of face threat, and the ranking of facework strategies is more or less universal.

Not everyone agrees (e.g., Scollon & Scollon, 1983). Consider two examples viewed as evidence of cultural variability in 'politeness'. Schiffrin (1984; but see the criticisms of Lee & Peck, 1995) reports that, in Jewish arguing, what would be characterized by B&L as face-damaging acts are actually ways of affirming and creating solidarity and positive relations. Blum-Kulka (1992) demonstrates cultural variability in whether indirectness or directness is viewed as more polite. Based on examples of this sort, many researchers conclude that language reflects culture (Wierzbicka, 1986), and that cultures differ both in terms of how face-threatening an act is and how much facework is done by a 'politeness' strategy.

Arguments in favour of the universal position tend to focus on features that define what it is for behaviour to constitute interaction. For example, in all cultures each participant must coordinate his/her actions with the other's actions. This seems to require that participants take turns on a sequentially alternating basis (i.e., concurrent turn-taking does not allow A to respond to S's prior action) and dovetail their turns with the other participant's turns (i.e., coordination only occurs if A responds in a conditionally relevant manner to the prior turn of S). Also, to engage in social interaction requires means of moving into and out of interaction, of introducing and changing topics, and of initiating and carrying out repair. If, indeed, such features must be present in order for social interaction to occur, they must be culturally universal.

The above view of the universality of certain resources of talk/social interaction does not rule out the possibility that the ways in which those resources are structured may be culture-specific. Possible culturally-variable structures include what constitutes a turn construction unit, a transition relevant place, a repair initiator, a preferred or dispreferred response, and markers of preferred and dispreferred structure. For example, Fox, Hayashi, and Jasperson (1996) demonstrate that differences in the syntax of English and Japanese are reflected in associated differences in same-turn self repair in those two languages. Fox et al. also report another important finding; namely, that repair influences syntax: 'Speakers can thus use repair to create utterances whose interactive achievement would not be possible within the limits of "normal" syntax in a given language at a given moment in time' (p. 226). Given these results, what is the answer to the question of whether the structure of talk is universal or culturally variable? On the one hand, repair is influenced by language and thus is culturally variable, but on the other hand repair occurs in and affects the structure of all languages, and thus is universal. Hopefully, this very brief review is sufficient to demonstrate that the issue of cultural universality or variability in the nature of talk is highly complicated and contentious.

Social pragmatics is a form of behaviourism

Because of the social pragmatic emphasis on manifest details of talk, cognitively-oriented psychologists may conclude that social pragmatics is a brand of behaviourism, a seriously flawed conception of human action (Fodor, 1968, 1983). The social pragmatist responds to this criticism by arguing that lay person and professional psychologist alike use a common, everyday vocabulary to describe and explain human action. At bottom, there is no other way to describe human action except by using that common, everyday vocabulary. And, critically, that vocabulary is loaded with mentalistic concepts. The social pragmatist concludes that the description of human action necessarily contains mentalistic concepts and, thus, social pragmatics cannot be a form of behaviourism.

To clarify the social pragmatic position, consider the following example.

Example 7:13

1   A: i'm just checking i was gonna ask you i think i did though (0.5)

2   did i ever get casablanca back from you↑

((14 lines of talk deleted))

17 B: yeah i know i totally forgot about that

18 A: oh that's okay [yeah]

19 B   [yeah]

B in line 17 produces the action of 'excuse' for not having returned the movie *Casablanca*, A responds with the action of 'accept' the excuse, and B produces the action of 'confirm' A has accepted the excuse. The identification of these actions is based on the manifest and sequential structure of the two turns in the total sequence, including the way in which the participants treated those turns. Suppose a critic were to ask what I meant by A 'accepted' B's excuse. I would assume the critic was asking why A accepted B's excuse, rather than rejected, challenged, or failed to recognize it; that is, I would assume that whatever is puzzling about A accepting B's excuse, it is not that the critic is puzzled about what 'accept' means in this situation. If, however, the critic insisted she wanted to know precisely and in detail what I meant by 'accept', I might become suspicious or exasperated. If I really believed she was not playing the fool, about all I could say would be 'You know, accepted it, believed it, regarded it as a good reason for not having returned the movie'. I would assume that we had experienced similar situations, spoke the same language, and that competent speakers know what it is to accept an excuse.

Suppose, however, the critic persisted and asked what I meant by 'believed'. Again, though suspicious about the critic's claim of ignorance, about all I could do would be to give a paraphrase, such as 'persuaded of the truth' of the excuse. This definition contains another everyday word, 'persuaded', about which the critic could seek clarification. If the critic continued to seek clarification for every common term I used, I probably would eventually get back to the term I used initially – 'persuaded' as in 'accepted the truth of it'! Whether or not that happens, the point is that I have no other way of describing the action other than by using the everyday, common vocabulary.

It is highly unlikely that a competent member of the culture would have any problem with understanding what 'accepted' the excuse meant. Both the critic and I have a shared, everyday vocabulary that members of our culture use for describing human action. What is important in this context is that when that common vocabulary is used, for example, to describe behaviour as 'accepting' an excuse, that description characterizes the action in part as intentional, unless it was an odd sort of accepting, such as accepting under the influence of a drug. In a similar vein, describing an action as 'believed' versus 'pretended' categorizes it in part in terms of different mental states. What this means is that the description of manifest action is necessarily a mentalistic description. There is no other way to describe human action and interaction than to use that common vocabulary. As a consequence, descriptions of human behaviour cannot be reduced to descriptions of mere physical movements or occurrences (Stroud, 1996). Thus, a social pragmatic description of manifest human action and interaction is not a behaviourist description.

Manifest action or mental states?

Social pragmatists claim the best way to understand action is to describe the manifest and sequential structures by which it is accomplished. Cognitively-oriented psychologists, by contrast, view mental states as the causes of action and, thus, claim that identifying causal mental states is the best approach to understanding action. The relative merits of these two views are discussed next.

To understand why cognitive psychologists emphasize the importance of mental states, consider as an example the distinction between premeditated murder and accidental killing. Imagine that Joe feeds Harry a poisoned sandwich, and Harry dies as a consequence. Suppose Joe's action was either premeditated murder or accidental killing. How do these actions differ? If each action is described as 'Joe feeds Harry a poisoned sandwich', they would seem behaviourally identical. The actions, however, are not the same. What seems to differentiate them is Joe's state of mind that caused him to feed Harry a poisoned sandwich. In particular, either Joe intended to poison Harry (premeditated) or he did not intend to do so (accidental). Generalizing from the particular case, it would appear that an action is recognized through the identification of the causal mental states that produced it.

A critical assumption of this argument is that the two actions were behaviourally identical. That view is compelling only if the complexity of behaviour is ignored. Note that 'Joe feeds Harry a poisoned sandwich' is an idealization of Joe's behaviour. There are good reasons to reject idealized data for the study of talk, and those reasons apply equally to the study of other sorts of human action. The idealized description of Joe's behaviour also discounts the sequential structure of Joe's behaviour. Because sequential location is a major resource for constructing and interpreting actions in talk, it is probably important for action generally.

The upshot of these remarks is that an idealization of Joe's behaviour that ignores sequential relationships is an inadequate description. A better description is obtained from an examination of tape-recorded instances of behaviour. Such observation would reveal large differences in the behavioural sequences constituting different actions, including the actions of intentional and unintentional poisoning. Obviously, ethical and legal considerations prevent the taping of instances of intentional and accidental poisoning. However, in order to give a flavour of what such an approach might yield, consider scenarios of actual cases of premeditated and accidental poisoning.

The following scenario of intentional poisoning is based loosely on the movie *The Young Poisoner's Handbook*, which is based on a real life crime: On many occasions, A is physically assaulted by B; A neither provokes nor reacts to these assaults; A reads about poisons, their effects, and effective masking agents; A buys several poisons; A observes the effects of each poison on some cats and dogs; thallium was 100 per cent effective in leading to a long and painful death; A puts a dose of thallium in a roast beef sandwich (A had read that mustard and meat mask the taste of thallium); A serves the sandwich to B; B eats the sandwich, gets sick but doesn't die; sometime later, A puts a larger dose of thallium in a ham sandwich and serves it to B; B eats it and dies; the autopsy reveals B's gut contains the remains of a ham sandwich, mustard and thallium; the coroner concludes B died from ingesting thallium; A initially denies poisoning B, but eventually admits to it.

Consider, next, a temporally-organized scenario of an instance of accidental poisoning that is based on media accounts of an actual incident: A and B have a long history of cooperative, friendly interactions; A and B often eat lunch together; while eating lunch, B asks A to bring him something to drink; A takes a bottle labelled 'Cola' out of the refrigerator and gives it to B; yesterday, unknown to A and B, another person, C, needed a bottle in which to store a toxic pesticide; C filled an empty cola bottle and screwed on the cap; because the pesticide needed to be stored at a cool temperature to retain its toxicity, C put it in the refrigerator (C is, of course, an idiot but C did commit this act of stupidity); B takes a drink of the 'cola', is unable to breathe, and dies before the ambulance arrives; the autopsy reveals B died from paralysis of the autonomic nervous system caused by the ingestion of toxic pesticide; the police find pesticide in the cola bottle; A admits to giving B the cola; when told that the cola contained poison, A claims he had no knowledge of that; C finally admits to putting pesticide in the cola bottle.

Several important points can be drawn from a comparison of these scenarios. The actions of intentional and accidental poisoning are constituted by different sequences of observable behaviours and events, including avowals of mental states (in talk or in writing) by the agent and others. Further, those behaviours and events occur in a specific temporal, and sometimes causal, order and in specific physical, social, and cultural settings (i.e., they are sequential and indexical), and persons in addition to the agent are part of such behavioural sequences (i.e., the behaviour and event sequences that constitute action are co-constructed). These behaviour and event sequences are *criteria* for the appropriate description of an action as some specific action, such as intentional poisoning. Criteria are the sorts of things people would point to in teaching a child on some particular occasion what some particular act is, or how some particular act is constituted (Chapman, 1987).

Regardless of the relevance of manifest behaviour for understanding others' actions, it may appear that the manifest details of behaviour are irrelevant when it comes to recognizing one's own actions. Presumably, when I recognize and explain own behaviour, I have privileged access to my own inner mental states. Therefore, I have no need to rely on overt behaviour when interpreting my own actions. Instead, all I have to do is examine my mental states to determine the cause of my manifest behaviour. Furthermore, since only I have direct access to my mental life, I am the ultimate judge of the correctness of the categorization of my behaviour. Thus, regardless of the role that overt behaviour may play in how observers recognize my own action, manifest behaviour plays no role in how I recognize my action. This conclusion follows for every ego. It therefore follows that any model of human action based on publicly available criteria must be seriously flawed.

Consider an example of how the distinction between ego and observer seems to undermine the social pragmatic view. Recall the intentional poisoning scenario, but imagine that as the poisoner A prepares to serve the poisoned sandwich to B, A has a change of mind. It occurs to A that poisoning is unconscionable, and so A decides not to carry out the murder. Just then the telephone rings and A goes to answer it. Unbeknownst to A, B finds the poisoned sandwich, eats it, and dies. Clearly, A did not intend to poison B (B's death was an accident), and A can determine that by observing his mental state. However, an observer cannot see that mental state, and if an observer relied on A's behaviour in making a judgment, the observer would reach the erroneous conclusion that A intended to poison B. Thus, A is the only person who really understands the nature of his or her own actions, and this is so because only A has direct access to the mental states causing A's actions.

In response, the social pragmatist emphasizes the richness of behaviour by calling attention to the criteria that constitute 'changing one's mind about murdering someone, but being prevented from undoing harm', as is captured in the following scenario: A was searching for a sealed container he could put the poisoned sandwich in when the telephone rang; while A was on the telephone, B started eating the sandwich; A got off the telephone, saw B eating the sandwich, grabbed the sandwich from B, and tossed it in the garbage; A told B that the sandwich was poisoned; B passed out and A called the emergency services; an ambulance was dispatched and B was rushed to hospital; A told the paramedics that the sandwich was laced with thallium; B died and A confessed to the police that he had laced the sandwich with poison, that he had changed his mind about poisoning B, that he had been in the process of disposing of the sandwich when he had been distracted, and that this had allowed B to eat the sandwich; A grieves for B and falls into a severe depression; A commits suicide and leaves a note in which A indicates that he cannot bear the guilt he feels over killing B. This scenario constitutes one particular behavioural sequence of changing one's mind about poisoning someone but being prevented from doing so.

Consider, next, a scenario in which an observer would not believe A's claim that he had changed his mind about poisoning B but was unable to prevent B from eating the poisoned sandwich: A carried out all the actions of an intentional poisoning up to the point at which the sandwich was prepared; A left the sandwich in the refrigerator; A then left and went to work; B got hungry, looked in the refrigerator, took out and ate the sandwich; B died and A was indicted for the murder; A claims he had intended to poison B, but changed his mind at the last minute, and that is why A did not serve the sandwich to B but put it in the refrigerator; the prosecutor argues that A would have done a lot more to prevent the poisoning if A really had changed his mind; A admits that, with hindsight, he should have done more, but says he was under such stress that he was not thinking clearly; A continues to profess his innocence. In this scenario, A did not do what a reasonable person could be expected to do to prevent B from eating the poisoned sandwich. The only criterion in support of A's claim is his own avowal. Accordingly, there would be great doubt about A's innocence.

These scenarios illustrate, as is true of any human action, that every instance of the actions of 'changing one's mind but being prevented from reversing the course of an intended action' and of 'not changing one's mind but pretending to do so' is constituted, for both agents and observers by a specific sequence of behaviours, including avowals of mental states, occurring in a specific setting and on a specific occasion and involving specific persons. If many of the relevant criteria are present, agents and observers will feel confident about what action is being accomplished. If few of the relevant criteria are present, agents and observers will be unsure as to what action is being accomplished. In sum, although the agent may have access to private mental states, nevertheless the agent's recognition of his/her own action relies critically on manifest sequences of the behaviour of the agent and others.

The point of this extended discussion is that public (i.e., manifest) criteria play a critical role in the recognition and categorization of both own and others' action. Describing action requires talk of the mental. This does not imply, however, that manifest behaviour provides only indirect evidence of covert, causal cognitions. Put differently, the fact that a mentalistic vocabulary must be used to describe human action does not mean that those who use that vocabulary must necessarily be drawing inferences about inner (non-observable mental states) from observation of outer (observable, manifest behaviour). Rather, the conclusion to be reached is that talk about mental state terms is part of the identification and categorization of sequences of manifest behaviour. For example, the intention to turn left while driving consists of a set of manifest behaviours, such as slowing down, looking in the rear-view mirror, checking the intersection, signalling, starting to turn the wheel, etc. (Button, Coulter, Lee, & Sharrock, 1995). Thus, there is no need to postulate hidden mental causal states that constitute having an intention.

Several recommendations for an approach to the analysis of talk and social interaction follow. Examination of public criteria as they are displayed in manifest and orderly sequences of behaviour is a necessary step in developing models of talk and action. Further, claims about the causal role of mental states should be treated with caution. [Note that the relation between mental state and action is conceptual, not causal]. Thus, for example, although a mental state, such as a motive, may be invoked as a causal explanation of behaviour, talk about motives is often employed as an after-the-fact justification for behaviour, not as a prior cause of the behaviour (Peters, 1958). A psychological model of talk will need to be clear about the status of mental states on particular occasions of use. Finally, it is important to recognize that talk is a skilled human performance. The richness of human behaviour is apparent in skilled performances such as cooking risotto, building a house, playing the piano, or ballroom dancing. The complexity of behaviour is so evident in such cases that there is little appeal to the view that manifest behaviour is epiphenomenal, nothing more than the effects of causal mental states. But asserting, blaming, disagreeing, informing, requesting, etc. are also skilled, orderly performances worth studying in their own right. In sum, an adequate model of talk/social interaction must be based on a conception of talk as a manifest accomplishment and on a methodology for the examination of the manifest details of that accomplishment. Social pragmatics provides both a relevant model and methodology.

Social pragmatics is inconsistent with cognitive psychology

Many psychologists would argue that social pragmatics cannot be a viable *psychological* conception of talk because what is known about human memory contradicts the view that meaning and understanding are (co)-constructed and indexical achievements. The criticism rests on the claim that memory is composed of different subsystems, each of which is used to carry out qualitatively different functions (Tulving, 1995). One broad distinction is that of the subsystems of episodic and semantic memory. The episodic memory system stores representations of specific experiences (i.e., episodes) of objects and events. These copies of specific past experiences are used in remembering (e.g., recalling what one did last New Year's Eve). By contrast, on the basis of repeated experiences with specific objects and events in many different contexts, the cognitive system abstracts what is common, typical or generic about those objects and events. Generic knowledge includes knowledge of categories of types of persons (e.g., introverts, lawyers, people in love), objects and concepts (e.g., cats, trees, books, nouns, democracy), events and activities (e.g., going to a restaurant, attending a lecture) and, of special importance for a model of talk, knowledge of words (i.e., the general meaning of each word in a person's vocabulary) and the rules of grammar that operate on those words. Knowledge abstracted from specific experiences is assumed to be stored in a semantic memory system. That knowledge is retrieved from semantic memory in tasks requiring knowledge of what is common or generic, such as determining what a word means or recognizing into which category an action fits.

If the episodic–semantic memory distinction is a valid account of human memory, three implications follow for any model of talk. First, given that the cognitive system automatically abstracts what is common from the various occasions on which a word is used, the system would abstract the literal meaning of words. Second, the semantic memory system would be a storehouse for the literal meanings of words. Third, when semantic memory was accessed in order to use a word, the stored, literal meaning would be decoded from the representation of the word.

The above three implications contradict the social pragmatic conception of meaning-making. In particular, if producing and understanding words were based on representations that encode the literal meaning, meaning-making would be an encoding–decoding process, not a constructive process. Further, if word meaning were based on abstracting what is common about a word across a set of situations in which the word is used, word meaning would be independent of context (i.e., *not* indexical). Thus, if the human memory system has a semantic memory component that automatically stores representations encoding context-independent, literal meanings, and if that type of knowledge is used in producing (encoding) and understanding (decoding) talk, such a system would contradict the social pragmatic assumptions that talk is a constructed and indexical achievement

The social pragmatist's response to this criticism is, briefly, that unitary models of memory are consistent with social pragmatics. Thus, there is no in-principle reason to reject social pragmatics on the grounds that it is non-psychological. In the following section I describe a particular unitary model of memory and show how it is consistent with the assumptions of social pragmatics.

Unitary models of memory: the example of SCAPE

Multiple memory system models are not the only memory models in cognitive psychology. There are also unitary models of memory with which social pragmatics is consistent. To clearly characterize such models, I discuss a specific model of memory that fits nicely with the social pragmatic model. Whittlesea (1997) put forth a model of memory referred to as SCAPE, the Selective Construction And Preservation of Experiences. SCAPE theory posits a single memory system, the functions of which are the production and subsequent preservation of psychological experiences (i.e., performance) and the evaluation of the act of production (i.e., the subjective experience that accompanies performance). The production of experience consists of the construction of a covert (mental) or overt (manifest behaviour) response to a stimulus complex. Memory stores the actions that are performed in constructing experience. Stimuli are never encountered in isolation. Rather, persons encounter a stimulus complex consisting of the stimulus, tasks (i.e., the purpose(s) of the encounter, the person's intentions), context and representations in memory of similar prior experience.

A critical assumption of SCAPE is that the same principles are used in production regardless of how experience is used (e.g., regardless of whether constructed experience is used in recall or categorization). The production of every experience is guided by the details of the stimulus complex in interaction with one another. For example, if the task is to verify that 'dog' rhymes with 'fog', a different experience will be constructed than if the task is to decide whether each is a noun. These different experiences arise in part because current processing of a stimulus is guided by representations of the actions performed in constructing prior similar experiences with the stimulus. The more similar the current purpose and context in which the stimulus is encountered to past experiences with the stimulus, the more the current experience is influenced by past experiences.

Differences in the similarity of present and past experiences pave the way for two general types of subjective experience. If there is little similarity between a present stimulus and past purposes and contexts in which that stimulus was encountered, current processing will be guided mainly by the present, unique stimulus. For example, imagine that you see a cat with no tail. Given that most cats have tails, your current processing is unlikely to cue many past experiences because you have had very few similar experiences. If, in spite of this, a past experience is cued and comes to mind, you will have the experience of remembering a unique past occasion on which you saw a Manx cat. Alternatively, if a person encounters a stimulus that he/she has encountered many times in the past, and if the present task and context present no distinctive cues, the person's current performance will be guided by masses of prior experience. Because current performance would not correspond exactly to any specific prior experience, cases of this sort are typically referred to as generic knowing. For example, read this sentence 'the cat meowed'. The word 'cat' will have been seen many times before and there is nothing unusual about the present context in which it occurs. Accordingly, many past experiences will come to mind and you will have the experience of understanding the 'literal meaning' of 'cat'.

There are two critical points in the above discussion worth repeating. Memory stores only one kind of information; namely, the actions performed in constructing an experience. However, there are many tasks persons can perform using that memory. Some tasks lead to a feeling of remembering (e.g., having seen a Manx cat), whereas others lead to a feeling of knowing (e.g., understanding the meaning of 'cat'). But this does not demonstrate that remembering and knowing are based on different memory systems. One and the same system can account for both types of experience, and there is no need to posit a cognitive system that automatically abstracts generic properties nor a memory system that stores representations of generic properties, including representations of the literal meaning of words.

According to SCAPE, the second function of memory is the evaluation of experience. Persons have no direct access to their cognitive processes (Nisbett & Wilson, 1977; Wilson & Nisbett, 1978) but instead must make attributions to account for their present behaviour. Only when attributions about behaviour are made does a person have a phenomenal or subjective experience. Put differently, the subjectivity of experience requires that persons adopt an attitude to their current processing. Thus, producing information about a stimulus is not remembering; rather, remembering is the subjective experience that present processing is due to having had a specific past experience that is stored in memory. An example may help clarify the distinction between production and evaluation of experience. Whittlesea (personal communication) notes that people tend to tickle cats and pat dogs; that is, they behave selectively towards cats and dogs. However, this does not mean that persons produce this behaviour by classifying cats and dogs into different categories. To categorize something is to judge that one's behaviour is due to knowledge of categories. Unless persons judge their behaviour in some way, behaviour is just behaviour and there is no associated, phenomenal experience.

If merely bringing representations from memory to mind is a non-experience, the issue arises as to what produces subjective experience. Whittlesea & Williams (2000, 2001) propose that if bringing representations to mind in order to accomplish some task results in a discrepancy between what is currently expected and what is occurring, persons engage in heuristic processing to attribute the source of the discrepancy. Such heuristic processing creates a psychological experience. Put differently, subjective, phenomenal experience only occurs when persons attribute their current ability to some source. Consider an example. If I get up in the morning and see my wife in the kitchen, my processing is fluent and as expected. Thus, I have no experience of recognizing her – I just simply see her and typically there is no phenomenal experience. However, if I am looking through some baby pictures in my wife's family's picture album and find myself processing one of the baby pictures more fluently than others and more fluently than I might have expected, I might attribute the unexpected fluency to familiarity. As a result, I might have the phenomenal experience of recognizing my wife.

In sum, according to SCAPE, memory produces effective behaviour. It is what persons do with memory rather than the nature of the stored representations themselves that distinguishes, for example, memory for categories versus memory for instances. Accordingly, most 'memorial' phenomena are not about the structure of memory but rather about the use of memory. Further, there is no direct access to the prior experiences that guide current processing. So, for example, if asked what 'dog' means I might give such-and-such a literal meaning, but giving the literal meaning is an act of production that results from interactions of the current task with the mass of representations of prior experience with that stimulus complex. Finally, bringing representations from memory to mind is a non-experience, whether those representations are brought to mind in an act of remembering or under-standing. Phenomenal experience only occurs when persons attribute the source of their processing to some source.

Implications of SCAPE for a model of talk

Central to SCAPE are the claims that memory stores the actions persons perform in constructing experience, and that persons have no direct access to their cognitive processes, including representations stored in memory. Thus, when persons come to use memory, they do so by acting on those stored representations. In other words, meaning is constructed from the actions persons perform on the world or the actions they perform on stored representations. Meaning is not encoded into and decoded out of representations. SCAPE, just as social pragmatics, is thus a constructivist view of meaning-making. It is also important to note that SCAPE is not a model of radical, anything-goes constructivism, but is rather a model of constructivism with constraints (Chapman, 1999; von Glasersfeld, 1984, 1988). In particular, the affordances of the stimulus and the context, the type of task, and the nature of past experiences that are cued by current processing (those past experiences are themselves constrained by stimulus, context and task) all set constraints on how experience will be constructed.

SCAPE also provides an account not only of the construction of meaning but also of the *co*-construction of meaning. In particular, meaning is always created and determined on the basis of the stimulus complex in interaction with representations of past similar experiences. When S interacts with A, A is thus an important component of context, as are the task S and A are engaged in and the sequential structure of their talk. Further, S's similar experiences with A in the past are cued by S's current processing. Accordingly, when S interacts with A, S's production and interpretation of behaviour is necessarily influenced by A (and similarly for A's interaction with S). What this implies is that the nature of memory is such that talk is automatically produced as recipient-designed and interpreted as recipient-designed. Thus, even though at this level creating and understanding talk is an individual and cognitive process, it is nevertheless a co-constructed process. This in no way undermines the claim that talk is also a social process since, as noted, it is both social and individual.

SCAPE is also an indexical model of meaning-making, as is social pragmatics. Given that meaning is always created and determined on the basis of the stimulus complex in interaction with representations of past similar experience, meaning-making is always indexical, it is always tied to the total speech situation. If the present word/utterance is non-distinctive in task and context, this cues vast numbers of past similar experiences in many contexts with the present stimulus. The result is production of 'literal' meaning. By contrast, if a word/utterance is distinctive in task or context, different past experiences are cued. The result is production of 'non-literal' meaning. SCAPE thus accounts for both 'literal' and 'non-literal' word/utterance meaning, though each is a construction and not an encoding/decoding.

The issue of why the notion of literal meaning has such a strangle-hold on conceptions of meaning can also be addressed by SCAPE. Most people have an intuitive view that words/sentences have a literal meaning. If asked to think about how they know the meaning of a word/sentence, persons would need to evaluate their performance, the ease with which they are able to understand words and sentences. It is likely that when they do this, they will use their intuitive view of meaning and, thereby, attribute their fluent, effortless processing to literal meaning. But, as has been emphasized, this does not mean that literal meanings are stored in memory, as all that is preserved in memory are the actions that were performed in constructing experiences. In other words, this evidence for literal meaning arises because persons confuse attributions for the source of the ability to understand talk with the nature of the representations of words stored in memory.

There are also some implications of SCAPE for the distinction between participants' and analysts' categories. In most talk, each participant simply produces a response to the other's contributions. Typically, processing is fluent, it is unlikely that there is any evaluation of the response and, thus, there is no phenomenal experience. (This is consistent with the feeling that, for the most part, talk just passes by, almost out of conscious awareness.) Understanding, however, is a subjective state that requires persons make a judgment about their current processing. According to SCAPE, the subjective experiences of understanding and failing to understand occur only when participants find their processing is not fluent and, thus, search for an attribution for that lack of fluency. One environment in which this is likely to occur is when repairs are initiated. Most of the time, however, participants just talk and the concept of 'understanding' is, on those occasions, an analyst's concept but not a participant's concept.

This distinction requires a precise interpretation of the next-turn proof procedure that manifest meaning is displayed in A's response to S's prior turn. On the basis of the next-turn proof procedure, an analyst might claim that A understands S to have done such-and-such. However, if A does not reflect on his own processing, it is not appropriate to attribute the subjective state of understanding to A. It is for this reason that in analyses of examples participants are described as manifestly *treating*, rather than understanding, a contribution in some specific way. In a similar vein, the analyst may view all talk as being based on interpretation (as with Gricean implicature). However, interpretation is a subjective state that occurs only when processing is not fluent. Thus, when the analyst argues that an inferential model is an appropriate model of talk, that claim is a claim about cognitive processing, not a claim about participants' meaning. The point of this discussion is that a model of talk will need to account both for those occasions when participants 'just talk' (i.e., produce behaviour but do not evaluate it) and those occasions when participants understand or interpret (i.e., evaluate their behaviour).

In sum, the discussion demonstrates that social pragmatics is *not* a form of behaviourism and is consistent with unitary models of memory. Accordingly, social pragmatics is a viable psychological account of talk.

8

Summary and Conclusions

Introduction and Chapter Overview

The chapter begins with a critical summary of each model of talk presented in the book. Next, implications of social pragmatics for models of persons, minds, and meaning are discussed. The final paragraph emphasizes the importance of talk for psychology.

MODELS OF TALK: A CRITICAL SUMMARY

Code Model theorists assume thoughts are a-linguistic representations of meaning located in individual brains, and that thought first occurs and then may be packaged into words/language. Thoughts are not directly observable to others, but the transmission of thoughts to others serves many useful purposes. Using their linguistic competence persons encode thoughts into words that the listener hears (talk) or sees (writing). The listener can then decode the speaker's thoughts out of the words, at which point the transmission of thoughts has been successfully achieved. On this view, talk is a cognitive activity of individual minds, and meaning is a mechanistic, encoding–decoding process. Observation of natural talk undermines the validity of all these assumptions.

One might hope the Code Model is nothing more than an historical curiosity of no relevance to present-day psychological research on language. That is a very optimistic position. Perusal of virtually any psycholinguistics text will confirm that the Code Model, supplemented by inferential processes that account for 'non-literal' meaning, remains psychology's most widely accepted view of language use/talk (the writings of Herb Clark, 1992, 1996, are welcome exceptions). The following assumptions, in particular, continue to retard development of a model of talk: the individualistic, inside-the-head view that renders talk epiphenomenal; the importance of literal meaning, along with an encoding–decoding view of the production and understanding of talk; the view that talk is a conduit for information transfer; the associated 'one function' view that persons talk to transmit information; and the equating of talk and writing.

As previously noted, psychologists with no specific interest in talk implicitly accept the Code Model when they use talk/writing to manipulate independent variables and measure dependent variables. Acceptance of the Code Model is seen also in recent attempts of neuro-psychologists to locate meaning in brains. The logic behind such an attempt is that if meaning is encoded into words and if words are represented in the brain, then it should be possible to locate specific words and specific word meaning in specific brain areas (Pulvermuller, 1999; for a social pragmatic criticism of that research agenda, see Turnbull & Carpendale, 1999a). In sum, the Code Model is psychology's default option, taken-for-granted model of language use/talk. It is hoped that calling attention to its many deficiencies may encourage psychologists to look for a better alternative.

Speech Act theorists conceptualize talk as action. Persons produce three types of actions when they talk; namely, locutionary (literal meaning of words spoken), illocutionary (the action produced by uttering a set of words with a determinate literal meaning; e.g., apology, refusal), and perlocutionary (intended and unintended effects on the listener) acts. The production of locutionary acts occurs through an encoding–decoding process involving the transformation of thoughts into language via linguistic competence. Speech Act theory also has an account of the relation between locutionary and illocutionary actions; namely, that speakers and listeners have stored in their brains a set of conditions for the felicitous performance of each type of illocutionary action. Production of some specific action involves using those conditions to encode that action into words and mental states, and recognizing that action involves using those conditions to decode the action from those words and mental states.

Emphasis on the various actions carried out by participants in talk is the most positive aspect of Speech Act theory. The contention that talk is action may seem peculiar since talk is often considered the very opposite of action. For example, the expression 'all talk and no action' seems to express the view that talk is not action. However, when a speaker uses such an expression, she does an action, perhaps accusing or blaming (e.g., 'He always claims he is going to write the great American novel, but he's all talk and no action'). This example also points to the importance of the total speech situation; that is, knowing what action someone is producing requires knowing how that action is produced and when, where, and to whom it is addressed.

One serious deficiency of (Searle's) Speech Act model is that it is a Code Model in which actions are encoded into and decoded from words. For Searle, all meaning in talk is ultimately based on the literal meaning of sentences or utterances, a meaning that is standard across all contexts. Speech Act theorists do not deny that there are contextual influences on meaning, but they do insist that such meanings are based in the first place on literal meaning. In particular, 'indirect' or 'non-literal' meanings (e.g., irony, metaphor) are assumed to arise from a process in which literal meaning is first determined, following which inferences are made to derive a meaning consistent with the context. On this view, contextual influences on meaning do not threaten the privileged place of literal meaning. By contrast, the many examples of natural talk presented in this book provide support for the essentially indexical nature of talk.

An insistence on the indexical nature of talk is also justified by a consideration of situated action, which underlies a second deficiency of Speech Act Theory. The question is whether talk, in whole or part, can be formalized; that is, is it possible to specify both a set of conditions that must be met in order to carry out each specific action and a rule that operates on those conditions? Whereas Speech Act theorists answer in the affirmative, a convincing argument can be made that classes of action and rules cannot be used to derive situated action because situated action relies on a host of unstated and unstatable conditions (Garfinkel, 1967; Suchman, 1987). Thus, situated action is always indexical (in accordance with Austin's emphasis on the importance of the total speech situation), and cannot be formalized. As a consequence, all formalistic views of talk must be rejected.

Since encoding–decoding models of talk run into insurmountable problems, a possible solution is to consider models based centrally on inference, such as Grice's Inferential Model. Grice views talk as embedded in and constitutive of purposeful social interaction involving specific persons in specific total speech situations. The main way of conveying and recognizing meaning in interaction is through production by S and recognition by A of an intention that was intentionally produced to be so recognized; that is, talk involves non-natural meaning. Non-natural meaning weakens the connection between what is said and what is done by saying it; that is, as long as S can get A to recognize the intention that was intentionally produced so as to be recognized, it does not matter what words S uses. The question then arises as to how participants in interaction can determine meaning.

In his second major contribution to a model of talk, Grice proposed that possible meanings are restricted by application of a set of constraints referred to as the Cooperative Principle (CP). Grice claimed that participants mutually assume that their contributions conform to the CP in being true, informative, relevant, and clear. Participants use the CP to draw conversational implicatures (a form of inference) to determine what S meant given what S said. The critical assumption is that participants make implicatures that preserve the assumption that the CP is being followed. Broadly, implicatures are drawn in two environments. Participants may assume that S is *observing* the CP and draw implicatures to fill in meaning in a restricted way. Alternatively, participants may assume that S is *exploiting* the CP; that is, S on the surface is ostentatiously violating the CP but S's intended meaning is consistent with the CP. In this type of situation, participants determine a meaning that is consistent with the CP. In either case, restricted inference is central to the production and recognition of action.

Grice makes a number of important contributions to a model of talk. One is the recognition that talk is embedded in and constitutive of social interaction and, thus, that talk is a cooperative activity requiring the coordinated and dovetailed actions of a specific speaker and specific addressee. Another is the central role of inference (implicature) in the construction of meaning. Finally, Grice brings to our attention that the coordination of social action requires participants to rely on certain mutual assumptions about their situation (e.g., the CP).

The main weakness of Grice's views is that, in spite of the importance of implicature, meaning-making is based on the encoding–decoding of literal meaning. In particular, Grice assumes that participants first mechanistically encode–decode literal meaning, then apply whatever inferences are required to satisfy, in context, the maxims of the CP, thereby deriving meaning. Observation of natural talk does not support this claim. Inference is involved at all levels of the determination of meaning, not just at the level of implicature.

Whereas the Code, Speech Act and Inferential models emphasize the transactional nature of talk, Brown and Levinson (B&L) argue for the importance of an interpersonal orientation. Specifically, B&L propose that participants want to have their desires desired (Positive face) and they want to be unimpeded (Negative face). Social interaction often has the potential to threaten face. If face is threatened or damaged, social interaction may cease or, at least, the efficiency with which participants can attain their transactional goals may be compromised. Accordingly, B&L argue that participants use strategies, referred to as 'facework', to decrease the threat to or repair damage to face. B&L made two additional and important assumptions; namely, the more an action threatens face, the more facework is required to restore face, and that the rational person does as much facework as required but no more.

To act rationally, as conceptualized by B&L, it is necessary that participants can compute the extent to which an action threatens face. B&L propose that face-threat is a linear, additive function of the relationship variables of Power and Social Distance, plus the degree of imposition of the action in question. In particular, face-threat increases as the Power of A over S increases, as the Distance between S and A increases, and as the degree of imposition increases. Depending on whether face-threat is low, medium or high, B&L describe various strategies for repairing/restoring damage to face.

There are many positive aspects of B&L's proposals. A model of talk that ignored interpersonal orientations would have great difficulty in accounting for much of the structure of talk. Many of those structures map directly onto facework strategies. Further, the strategic negotiation of face enters directly into and is influenced by the construction of talk; that is, talk and face are reflexively constituted. Finally, as is true of transactional meaning-making, the negotiation of face is an indexical accomplishment.

The main deficiency of the B&L model is that it equates social aspects of talk with face. There are, however, many social orientations; that is, there is more to the interpersonal dimension than face. A related concern is that most talk is rife with apparent facework, but often there is no manifest evidence participants are using those 'facework' structures to do facework. Thus, what is required are ways of restricting the notion of facework and warranting claims that such-and-such a structure is being used to do facework (MacMartin, Wood, & Kroger, 2001).

Conversation Analysts view talk as social interaction. As such, the structure of talk is the structure of interaction; namely, the sequential alternation of conditionally relevant turns by two or more participants. Sequential structures, particularly structures of adjacency, are the main resources participants use to construct interaction together. Intersubjectivity is a by-product of the sequential structure of turns at talk. The orderly structures of talk, which are manifest, are resources provided by a culture for the production and understanding of talk. Thus, talk is a social/sociological activity. Further, because interaction can only be achieved when participants trust that contributions to talk will be conditionally relevant, morality is built into the very possibility of talk/interaction. A most positive aspect of CA is that natural talk provides support for these claims.

CA was faulted on two fronts. First, although talk is a social activity, it is also an individual, psychological activity. Accordingly, a model of talk must include a psychological component. In particular, talk requires memorial processing, inference, and contextual access and use, plus psychological models of development and of language as a structured entity. The second deficiency of CA is methodological. The overwhelming tendency for practitioners of CA to avoid quantification, coding, and statistical analyses robs the psychological researcher of a set of useful tools for the analysis of human action.

By pulling together the positive features of existing models, a social pragmatic approach was developed. Social pragmatics can be summarized in seven points. First, talk is social interaction. Second, talk is an orderly activity. As Sacks (1984) put it, 'there is order at all points' (p. 22). Third, talk is achieved over sequences of turns; that is, there is an essential temporal aspect to talk. Fourth, talk is constitutive of social life, it is *not* epiphenomenal and it cannot be reduced to a set of cognitive states. Fifth, talk is both a social (e.g., co-constructed) and an individual (e.g., inferential) activity. Sixth, talk is multifunctional; that is, in every turn at talk, participants make claims about and negotiate both transactional and interpersonal meanings. Seventh, because the co-construction of talk requires that participants trust one another to be conditionally relevant, talk is a moral accomplishment.

Social pragmatics also has a research paradigm of use to psychologists. Of particular relevance are pragmatic elicitation techniques for generating natural talk in situations that allow various degrees of researcher control. The research paradigm allows for the quantification, coding, and statistical analyses of data where applicable.

Implications of Social Pragmatics

Though developed solely as a model of talk, the social pragmatic framework has implications for several important issues in psychology. In this section, I briefly explore implications of social pragmatics for conceptions of persons, minds, and meaning.

Models of persons and minds

Adoption of a social pragmatic perspective changes the way psychologists typically view the relation between and the nature of persons and minds. For the cognitively-oriented psychologist, the question of how people manage in the world (e.g., how they manage to perceive, understand, problem solve, etc.) is conceptualized as a question about what is going on *inside individual minds*. The cognitivist's answer to that question involves mental representations and processes. Accordingly, talk (social interaction) is conceived of as interaction between minds involving each participant's simulation of the other's mind. That simulation is based on an analogy with one's own mind. Jopling (1993) refers to this conception as the 'philosophy of subjectivity'. It should be noted that in the philosophy of subjectivity, other persons are reduced to other minds, where other minds are inferences from one's own mind.

The social pragmatist adopts a very different view based on what Jopling refers to as the 'philosophy of intersubjectivity'. Rather than asking what is going on inside minds when people do the many things they do, social pragmatists ask, instead, what is going on *between two or more people*. On this view, persons are *not* inferences based on an analogy from own to others' mind. Rather, other persons are manifest, out there, and different from ego. As Jopling puts it, 'we encounter persons, not minds' (p. 292). Being treated as a person and treating others as persons occurs from the earliest years of life. Even if we know that infants are not fully engaged in the social world, we nevertheless treat them *as* persons (see, for example, Meins, 1997, and Meins & Fernyhough, 1999 on mind-mindedness). Inanimate objects are treated in a very different way. Adopting the philosophy of inter-subjectivity locates persons as a psychological given rather than as an inference derived from mind. Social pragmatics returns the manifest person to the centre of psychological inquiry.

Models of meaning

In psychology, the dominant view of meaning accords with the Code Model. Mental representations correspond to 'entities' in the world and, thus, mental represen-tations encode meaning. Producing meaning and recognizing it involve individual persons mechanistically encoding and decoding meanings using a set of mental processes that operate according to rules. From that perspective, the best explanation of meaning-making is one that examines the mental representations that encode meaning and the mental processes that act on those encodings. And, further, meanings encoded into mental representations have a privileged status in that they are objective, absolute meanings.

That view of meaning runs into severe problems (Goldberg, 1991; Wittgenstein, 1953). Social pragmatics is based on an alternative, constructivist view of meaning that avoids those problems. As illustrated throughout this book, action is co-

constructed and negotiated over manifest and specific sequences of turns. Because meaning is negotiated over sequences of turns, meaning is always 'up for grabs' (Good, 1995). Words derive their meaning not from encoded representations but from the roles they play in action and interaction (Canfield, 1993; Turnbull & Carpendale, 1999b; Wittgenstein, 1953). Accordingly, rather than focusing their energies on locating meaning 'in' various structures (e.g., schemas, scripts), psychologists should examine the processes and resources persons use to (co)-construct meaning.

CONCLUSIONS

Talk is the primary way in which persons interact, it is the primary means by which children are socialized into a culture, it is the primary site in which identities are displayed and negotiated, and it contains within it the seeds of morality. Further, because turn-taking, initiating and changing topics, repairing problems, and terminating exchanges are required in all forms of social interaction, whatever is learned about talk has relevance to social interaction generally (Turnbull & Carpendale, 1999b). Accordingly, a model of talk is highly relevant for social, developmental and personality psychologists. Social pragmatics provides psychologists with a specific tool for investigating social interaction in its own right and for investigating the impact of social interaction on other psychological phenomena. Hopefully, social pragmatics may rescue talk from the marginal and marginalized role it plays in most psychological theorizing and research.

References

Atkinson, J. M., & Drew, P. (1979). *Order in court*. London: The Macmillan Press Ltd.

Atkinson, J. M., & Heritage, J. C. (Eds.) (1984). *Structures of social action: Studies in conversation analysis*. Cambridge: Cambridge University Press.

Austin, J. L. (1962). *How to do things with words*. Cambridge, MA: Harvard University Press.

Baker, G. P., & Hacker, P. M. S. (1984). *Language sense and nonsense: A critical investigation into modern theories of language*. Oxford: Basil Blackwell.

Baxter, L. A. (1984). An investigation of compliance gaining as politeness. *Human Communication Research, 10*, 427–456.

Bem, D. J., & McConnell, H. K. (1970). Testing the self-perception explanation of dissonance phenomena: On the salience of premanipulation attitudes. *Journal of Personality and Social Psychology, 14*, 23–31.

Billig, M. (1999). Whose terms? Whose ordinariness? Rhetoric and ideology in conversation analysis. *Discourse & Society, 10*, 543–582.

Bilmes, J. (1988a). Category and rule in conversation analysis. *IPrA Papers in Pragmatics, 2*, 25–59.

Bilmes, J. (1988b). The concept of preference in conversation analysis. *Language in Society, 17*, 161–181.

Bilmes, J. (1992). Mishearings. In G. Watson & R. M. Seiler (Eds.), *Text in context: Contributions to ethnomethodology* (pp. 79–98). Newbury Park, CA: Sage Publications.

Blum-Kulka, S. (1992). The metapragmatics of politeness in Israeli society. In R. Watts, R. J. Ide, & S. Ehlich (Eds.), *Politeness in language: Studies in its history* (pp. 255–281). Berlin: Mouton de Gruyter.

Blum-Kulka, S., House, J., & Kasper, G. (1989). *Cross-cultural pragmatics: Requests and apologies*. Norwood, NJ: Ablex Publishing Corporation.

Bradbury, T. N., Fincham, F. D., & Beach, S. R. H. (2000). Research on the nature and determinants of marital satisfaction: A decade in review. *Journal of Marriage and the Family, 62*, 964–980.

Brehm, S. S., Miller, R. S., Perlman, D., & Campbell, S. M. (2001). *Intimate relationships*. New York: McGraw Hill.

Brown, G., & Yule, G. (1983). *Discourse analysis*. Cambridge: Cambridge University Press.

Brown, P. (1995). Politeness strategies and the attribution of intention: the case of Tzeltal irony. In E. N. Goody (Ed.), *Social intelligence and interaction: Expressions and implications of the social bias in human intelligence* (pp. 153–174). Cambridge: Cambridge University Press.

Brown, P., & Levinson, S. (1987). *Politeness: Some universals in language usage*. Cambridge: Cambridge University Press.

Brown, R., & Gilman, A. (1989). Politeness theory and Shakespeare's four major tragedies. *Language in Society*, *18*, 159–212.

Budwig, N. (1995). *A developmental-functionalist approach to child language*. Mahwah, NJ: Erlbaum.

Button, G., Coulter, J., Lee, J. R. E., & Sharrock, W. (1995). *Computers, minds and conduct*. Cambridge: Polity Press.

Cahn, D. D. (1990). Intimates in conflict: A research review. In D. D. Cahn (Ed.), *Intimates in conflict: A communication perspective* (pp. 1–22). Hillsdale, NJ: Erlbaum.

Canfield, J. V. (1993). The living language: Wittgenstein and the empirical study of communication. *Language Sciences*, *15*, 165–193.

Cervantes, C. A., & Callanan, M. A. (1998). Labels and explanations in mother–child emotion talk: Age and gender differentiation. *Developmental Psychology*, *34*, 88–98.

Chapman, M. (1987). Inner processes and outward criteria: Wittgenstein's importance for psychology. In M. Chapman & R. A. Dixon (Eds.), *Meaning and the growth of understanding: Wittgenstein's significance for Developmental Psychology* (pp. 103–127). Berlin: Springer-Verlag.

Chapman, M. (1988). Contextuality and directionality of cognitive development. *Human Development*, *31*, 92–106.

Chapman, M. (1999). Constructivism and the problem of reality. *Journal of Applied Developmental Psychology*, *20*, 31–43.

Cherry, R. D. (1988). Politeness in written persuasion. *Journal of Pragmatics*, *12*, 63–81.

Chomsky, N. (1957). *Syntactic structures*. The Hague: Mouton.

Chomsky, N. (1965). *Aspects of a theory of syntax*. Cambridge, MA: MIT Press.

Chomsky, N. (1968). *Language and mind*. New York: Harcourt, Brace, and World, Inc.

Clark, H. H. (1992). *Arenas of language use*. Chicago, IL: University of Chicago Press.

Clark, H. H. (1996). *Using language*. Cambridge: Cambridge University Press.

Clark, H. H., & Schaefer, E. F. (1987). Collaborating on contributions to conversations. *Language and Cognitive Processes*, *2*, 19–41.

Clark, H. H., & Schaefer, E. F. (1992). Dealing with overhearers. In H. H. Clark (Ed.), *Arenas of language use* (pp. 248–297). Chicago, IL: University of Chicago Press.

Djik, T. A. van (Ed.) (1997). *Discourse studies: A multidisciplinary introduction: Vol. 2. Discourse as social interaction*. London: Sage.

Drew, P. (1995). Interaction sequences and anticipatory interactive planning. In E. N. Goody (Ed.), *Social intelligence and interaction: Expressions and implications of the social bias in human intelligence* (pp. 111–138). Cambridge: Cambridge University Press.

Drew, P., & Heritage, J. (Eds.) (1992). *Talk at work*. Cambridge: Cambridge University Press.

Drummond, K., & Hopper, R. (1993). Back-channels revisted: Acknowledgement tokens and speakership incipiency. *Research on Language and Social Interaction*, *26*, 157–177.

Dunn, J., Brown, J., Slomkowski, C., Tesla, C., & Youngblade, L. (1991). Young children's understanding of other people's feelings and beliefs: Individual differences and their antecedents. *Child Development*, *62*, 1352–1366.

Duranti, A., & Goodwin, C. (Eds.) (1992). *Rethinking context: Language as an interactive phenomenon*. Cambridge: Cambridge University Press.

Edwards, D., & Potter, J. (1992). *Discursive psychology*. London: Sage.

Ervin-Tripp, S. M. (1976). Is Sybil there? The structure of some American English directives. *Language in Society*, *5*, 25–66.

Fodor, J. A. (1968). *Psychological explanation: An introduction to the philosophy of psychology*. New York: Random House.

Fodor, J. A. (1983). *The modularity of mind: An essay on faculty psychology*. Cambridge, MA: Bradford Books, MIT Press.

Fox, B. A., Hayashi, M., & Jasperson, R. (1996). Resources and repair: a cross-linguistic study of syntax and repair. In E. Ochs, E. A. Schegloff, & S. A. Thompson, *Interaction and grammar* (pp. 185–237). Cambridge: Cambridge University Press.

Frisch, K. von (1966). *The dancing bees: an account of the life and senses of the honey bee*. London: Methuen.

Garfinkel, H. (1967). *Studies in ethnomethodology*. Englewood Cliffs, NJ: Prentice-Hall.

Garfinkel, H., & Wieder, D. L. (1992). Two incommensurable, asymmetrically alternate technologies of social analysis. In G. Watson & R. M. Seiler (Eds.), *Text in context: Contributions to ethnomethodology* (pp. 175–206). Newbury Park, CA: Sage Publications.

Gibbs, R. W., Jnr. (1983). Do people always process the literal meaning of indirect requests? *Journal of Experimental Psychology: Learning, Memory and Cognition*, *9*, 524–533.

Gilovich, T. (1990). Differential construal and the false consensus effect. *Journal of Personality and Social Psychology*, *59*, 623–634.

Glasersfeld, E. von (1984). An introduction to radical constructivism. In P. Watzlawick (Ed.), *The invented reality* (pp. 17–40). New York: Norton.

Glasersfeld, E. von (1988). The reluctance to change a way of thinking. *The Irish Journal of Psychology*, *9*, 83–90.

Goffman, E. (1959). *The presentation of self in everyday life*. Harmondsworth: Penguin.

Goffman, E. (1967). *Interaction ritual: Essays on face to face behavior*. Garden City, NJ: Doubleday and Company.

Goffman, E. (1971). *Relations in public: Microstudies of the public order*. New York: Harper and Row.

Goffman, E. (1983). The interaction order. *American Sociological Review*, *48*, 1–17.

Goldberg, B. (1991). Mechanism and meaning. In J. Hyman (Ed.), *Investigating psychology: Sciences of the mind after Wittgenstein* (pp. 48–66). New York: Routledge.

Good, D. (1995). Where does foresight end and hindsight begin? In E. Goody (Ed.), *Social intelligence and interaction: Expressions and implications of the social bias in human intelligence* (pp. 139–149). Cambridge: Cambridge University Press.

Goodwin, C., & Heritage, J. (1990). Conversation analysis. *Annual Review of Anthropology*, *19*, 283–307.

Goody, E. N. (Ed.) (1995). *Social intelligence and interaction: Expressions and implications of the social bias in human intelligence*. Cambridge: Cambridge University Press.

Greatbatch, D., & Dingwall, R. (1998). Talk and identity in divorce mediation. In C. Antaki & S. Widdicombe (Eds.), *Identities in talk* (pp. 121–132). London: Sage Publications.

Grice, H. P. (1957). Meaning. *Philosophical Review*, *66*, 377–388.

Grice, H. P. (1975). Logic and conversation. In P. Cole & J. L. Morgan (Eds.), *Syntax and semantics: Vol. 3. Speech acts* (pp. 41–58). New York: Academic Press.

Gumperz, J. J., & Levinson, S. C. (Eds.) (1996). *Rethinking linguistic relativity*. Cambridge: Cambridge University Press.

Hala, S., & Carpendale, J. I. (1997). All in the mind: Children's understanding of mental life. In S. Hala (Ed.), *The development of social cognition* (pp. 189–239). Hove, UK: Psychology Press.

Halliday, M. A. K. (1994). *An introduction to functional grammar*. London: Arnold.

Have, P. ten (1999). *Doing conversation analysis: A practical guide*. Thousand Oaks, CA: Sage Publications.

Heritage, J. (1984a). *Garfinkel and ethnomethodology*. Cambridge: Polity Press.

Heritage, J. (1984b). A change-of-state token and aspects of its sequential placement. In J. M. Atkinson & J. Heritage (Eds.), *Structures of social action: Studies in conversation analysis* (pp. 299–345). Cambridge: Cambridge University Press.

Heritage, J. (1999). Conversation analysis at century's end: practices of talk-in-interaction, their distributions, and their outcomes. *Research on Language and Social Interaction*, *32*, 69–76.

Horvath, A. (1981). *An exploratory concept of the therapeutic alliance and its measurement*. Unpublished doctoral dissertation, University of British Columbia.

Hutchby, I., & Wooffitt, R. (1998). *Conversation analysis*. Cambridge: Polity Press.

Ide, S. (1982). Japanese sociolinguistics: politeness and women's language. *Lingua, 57*, 357–385.

Innis, H. A. (1951/1991). *The bias of communication* (Rev. ed.). Toronto, ON: University of Toronto Press.

Jenkins, J. M., & Astington, J. W. (1996). Cognitive factors and family structure associated with theory of mind development in young children. *Developmental Psychology, 32*, 70–78.

Jopling, D. (1993). Cognitive science, other minds, and the philosophy of dialogue. In U. Neisser (Ed.), *The perceived self* (pp. 290–309). New York: Cambridge University Press.

Labov, W., & Fanshel, D. (1977). *Therapeutic discourse: Psychotherapy as conversation*. New York: Academic Press.

Lee, D. A., & Peck, J. J. (1995). Troubled waters: Argument as sociability revisited. *Language in Society, 24*, 29–53.

Lerner, G. H. (1996). Finding "face" in the preference structures of talk-in-interaction. *Social Psychology Quarterly, 59*, 303–321.

Levinson, S. C. (1983). *Pragmatics*. Cambridge: Cambridge University Press.

Levinson, S. C. (1988). Putting linguistics on a proper footing: Explorations in Goffman's concepts of participation. In P. Drew & A. Wootton (Eds.), *Erving Goffman: Exploring the interaction order* (pp. 161–227). Boston: Northeastern University Press.

Levinson, S. C. (1992). Activity types and language. In P. Drew & J. Heritage (Eds.), *Talk at work* (pp. 66–100). Cambridge: Cambridge University Press.

Levinson, S. C. (1995). Interactional biases in human thinking. In E. N. Goody (Ed.), *Social intelligence and interaction: Expressions and implications of the social bias in human intelligence* (pp. 221–260). Cambridge: Cambridge University Press.

Levinson, S. C. (2000). *Presumptive meanings: the theory of generalized conversational implicature*. Cambridge, MA: MIT Press.

Lewis, C., Freeman, N. H., Kyriakidou, C., Maridaki-Kassotiaki, K., & Berridge, D. M. (1996). Social influences on false belief access: Specific sibling influences or general apprenticeship? *Child Development, 67*, 2930–2947.

Lewis, D. K. (1969). *Convention*. Cambridge, MA: Harvard University Press.

McLuhan, M. (1964). *Understanding media: The extensions of man*. New York: McGraw-Hill.

MacMartin, C., Wood, L. A., & Kroger, R. O. (2001). Facework. In W. P. Robinson & H. Giles (Eds.), *The new handbook of language and social psychology* (pp. 221–237). Chichester, UK: Wiley.

Malinowski, B. (1923). The problems of meaning in primitive languages. In C. K. Ogden & I. A. Richards (Eds.), *The meaning of meaning* (pp. 296–346). London: Routledge & Kegan Paul.

Malone, M. J. (1997). *Worlds of talk*. Cambridge: Polity Press.

Margolin, G., & Wampold, B. E. (1981). Sequential analysis of conflict and accord in distressed and nondistressed marital partners. *Journal of Consulting and Clinical Psychology, 49*, 554–567.

Meins, E. (1997). *Security of attachment and the social development of cognition*. Hove, UK: Psychology Press.

Meins, E., & Fernyhough, C. (1999). Linguistic acquisitional style and mentalising development: The role of maternal mind-mindedness. *Cognitive Development, 14*, 363–380.

Montgomery, D. E. (1997). Wittgenstein's private language argument and children's understanding of mind. *Developmental Review, 17*, 291–320.

Muntigl, P. (2001). *Couples counseling and semogenesis*. Unpublished doctoral dissertation, Simon Fraser University.

Muntigl, P., & Turnbull, W. (1998). Conversational structure and facework in arguing. *Journal of Pragmatics, 29*, 225–256.

Neisser, U. (1967). *Cognitive psychology*. New York: Appleton-Century-Crofts.

Nisbett, R. E., & Wilson, T. D. (1977). Telling more than we can know: Verbal reports on mental processes. *Psychological Review, 84*, 231–259.

Ochs, E. (1988). *Culture and language development: Language acquisition and language socialization in a Samoan village*. Cambridge: Cambridge University Press.

Ochs, E. (1992). Indexing gender. In A. Duranti & C. Goodwin (Eds.), *Rethinking context: Language as an interactive phenomenon* (pp. 336–358). Cambridge: Cambridge University Press.

Ochs, E., Schegloff, E. A., & Thompson, S. A. (1996). *Interaction and grammar*. Cambridge: Cambridge University Press.

Ochs Keenan, E. (1975). The universality of conversational implicature. In R. Fasold and R. Shuy (Eds.), *Studies in language variation* (pp. 255–268). Washington, DC: Georgetown University Press.

Ong, W. J. (1982). *Orality and literacy*. New York: Methuen.

Owen, M. (1983). *Apologies and remedial interchanges*. Berlin: Walter de Gruyter & Co.

Penman, R. (1990). Facework and politeness: Multiple goals in courtroom discourse. *Journal of Language and Social Psychology, 9*, 15–38.

Perner, J., Ruffman, T., & Leekam, S. R. (1994). Theory of mind is contagious: You catch it from your sibs. *Child Development, 65*, 1228–1238.

Peters, R. S. (1958). *The concept of motivation*. London: Routledge & Kegan Paul.

Piaget, J. (1932/1965). *The moral judgment of the child*. New York: The Free Press.

Pomerantz, A. (1984). Agreeing and disagreeing with assessments: some features of preferred/dispreferred turn shapes. In J. M. Atkinson & J. Heritage (Eds.), *Structures of social action: Studies in conversation analysis* (pp. 57–101). Cambridge: Cambridge University Press.

Pomerantz, A. (1986). Extreme case formulations: A new way of legitimizing claims. *Human Studies*, *9*, 219–230.

Potter, J. (1996). *Representing reality : discourse, rhetoric and social construction*. London: Sage.

Potter, J., & Wetherell, M. (1987). *Discourse and social psychology*. London: Sage.

Potter, J., & Wetherell, M. (1995). Natural order: Why social psychologists should study (a constructed version of) natural language, and why they have not done so. *Journal of Language and Social Psychology*, *14*, 216–222.

Psathas, G. (1995). *Conversation analysis: The study of talk-in-interaction*. Thousand Oaks, CA: Sage.

Pulvermuller, F. (1999). Words in the brain's language. *Behavioral and Brain Sciences*, *22*, 253–336.

Rawls, A. (1989). Language, self, and social order: A reformulation of Goffman and Sacks. *Human Studies*, *12*, 147–192.

Rawls, A. (1990). Emergent sociality: A dialectic of commitment and order. *Symbolic Interaction*, *13*, 63–82.

Reddy, M. J. (1979). The conduit metaphor – a case of frame conflict in our language about language. In A. Ortony (Ed.), *Metaphor and thought* (pp. 284–324). New York: Cambridge University Press.

Robinson, I. (1975). *The new grammarian's funeral*. Cambridge: Cambridge University Press.

Sacks, H. (1984). Notes on methodology. In J. M. Atkinson & J. Heritage (Eds.), *Structures of social action* (pp. 21–27). Cambridge: Cambridge University Press.

Sacks, H. (1992). *Lectures on conversation* (Vols. 1 and 2). Oxford: Blackwell.

Sacks, H., Schegloff, E. A., & Jefferson, G. (1974). A simplest systematics for the organization of turn-taking for conversation. *Language*, *50*, 696–735.

Schegloff, E. A. (1984). On some questions and ambiguities in conversation. In J. M. Atkinson & J. Heritage (Eds.), *Structures of social action: Studies in conversation analysis* (pp. 28–52). Cambridge: Cambridge University Press.

Schegloff, E. A. (1993). Reflections on quantification in studies of conversation. *Research on Language and Social Interaction*, *26*, 99–128.

Schegloff, E. A. (1997). Whose text? Whose context? *Discourse and Society*, *8*, 165–187.

Schegloff, E. A., Jefferson, G., & Sacks, H. (1977). The preference for self-correction in the organization of repair in conversation. *Language*, *53*, 361–382.

Schegloff, E. A., & Sacks, H. (1973). Opening up closings. *Semiotica*, *7*, 289–327.

Schelling, T. C. (1960). *The strategy of conflict*. Cambridge, MA: Harvard University Press.

Schiffrin, D. (1984). Jewish argument as sociability. *Language in Society*, *13*, 311–335.

Schiffrin, D. (1994). *Approaches to discourse*. Oxford: Basil Blackwell.

Schober, M. F., & Clark, H. H. (1989). Understanding by addressees and over-hearers. *Cognitive Psychology*, *21*, 211–232.

Scollon, R., & Scollon, S. B. (1983). Face in interethnic communication. In J. C. Richards & R. W. Schmidt (Eds.), *Language and communication* (pp. 156–189). New York: Longmans.

Searle, J. R. (1969). *Speech acts*. Cambridge: Cambridge University Press.

Shannon, C. E., & Weaver, W. (1949). *The mathematical theory of information*. Urbana, IL: University of Illinois Press.

Sharrock, W., & Anderson, B. (1986). *The ethnomethodologists*. London: Tavistock.

Slugoski, B. R., & Turnbull, W. (1988). Cruel to be kind and kind to be cruel: Sarcasm, banter, and social relations. *Journal of Language and Social Psychology*, *7*, 101–121.

Sperber, D., & Wilson, D. (1986). *Relevance: Communication and cognition*. Cambridge, MA: Harvard University Press.

Stroud, B. (1996), Mind, meaning, and practice. In H. Sluga & D. G. Stern (Eds.), *The Cambridge Companion to Wittgenstein* (pp. 296–319). Cambridge: Cambridge University Press.

Stubbs, M. (1983). *Discourse analysis*. Oxford: Basil Blackwell.

Suchman, L. (1987). *Plans and situated action: The problem of human-machine communication*. Cambridge: Cambridge University Press.

Sudnow, D. (1972). *Studies in social interaction*. New York: Free Press.

Taylor, C. (1989). *Sources of the self: The making of the modern identity*. Cambridge, MA: Harvard University Press.

Terasaki, A. (1976). *Pre-announcement sequences in conversation*. Social Science Working Paper No. 99, Irvine, CA: School of Social Science, University of California.

Thomasello, M. (Ed.). (1998). *The new psychology of language: Functional and cognitive approaches*. Mahwah, NJ: Erlbaum.

Tracy, K. (1990). The many faces of facework. In H. Giles & W. P. Robinson (Eds.), *Handbook of language and social psychology* (pp. 209–226). Chichester: Wiley.

Tulving, E. (1995). Organization of memory: Quo vadis? In M. Gazzaniga (Ed.), *The cognitive neurosciences* (pp. 839–847). Cambridge, MA: MIT Press.

Turnbull, W. (1986). Everyday explanation: The pragmatics of puzzle resolution. *Journal for the Theory of Social Behaviour*, *16*, 141–160.

Turnbull, W. (1992). A conversation approach to explanation, with emphasis on politeness and accounting. In M. L. McLaughlin, M. J. Cody, & S. J. Read (Eds.), *Explaining oneself to others: Reason-giving in a social context* (pp. 105–130). Hillsdale, NJ: Erlbaum.

Turnbull, W. (2001). An appraisal of pragmatic elicitation techniques for the social psychological study of talk: The case of request refusals. *Pragmatics*, *11*, 31–61.

Turnbull, W., & Carpendale, J. I. M. (1999a). Locating meaning in interaction, not in the brain. *Behavioral and Brain Sciences*, 22, 304–305.

Turnbull, W., & Carpendale, J. I. M. (1999b). A social pragmatic model of talk: Implications for research on the development of children's social understanding. *Human Development*, 42, 328–355.

Turnbull, W., & Carpendale, J. I. M. (2001a). Talk and the development of social understanding. *Early Education & Development*, 12, 455–477.

Turnbull, W., & Carpendale, J. I. M. (2001b). *The morality of interaction*. Paper presented at the conference of the Association for Moral Education, Vancouver, BC, October, 2001.

Turnbull, W., & Carpendale, J. (2002). Constraint and cooperation in parent–child interaction. Paper presented at the annual convention of the Canadian Psychological Association, Vancouver, BC, June 2002.

Turnbull, W., & Saxton, K. L. (1997). Modal expressions as facework in refusals to comply with requests: I think I should say 'no' right now. *Journal of Pragmatics*, 27, 145–181.

Turnbull, W., & Slugoski, B. R. (1988). Conversational and linguistic processes in causal attribution. In D. Hilton (Ed.), *Contemporary science and natural explanation: Commonsense conceptions of causality* (pp. 66–93). New York: New York University Press.

Whittlesea, B. W. A. (1997). Production, evaluation, and preservation of experiences: Constructive processing in remembering and performance tasks. In D. Medin (Ed.), *Psychology of learning and motivation* (Vol. 37, pp. 211–264). San Diego, CA: Academic Press.

Whittlesea, B. W. A., & Williams, L. D. (2000). The source of feelings of familiarity: The discrepancy-attribution hypothesis. *Journal of Experimental Psychology: Learning, memory, and cognition*, 26, 547–565.

Whittlesea, B. W. A., & Williams, L. D. (2001). The discrepancy-attribution hypothesis: 1. The heuristic basis of feelings of familiarity. *Journal of Experimental Psychology: Learning, memory, and cognition*, 27, 3–13.

Wierzbicka, A. (1986). Does language reflect culture? Some evidence from Australian English. *Language in Society*, 15, 349–374.

Wilson, D., & Sperber, D. (1981). On Grice's theory of conversation. In P. Werth (Ed.), *Conversation and discourse* (pp. 155–178). London: Croom Helm.

Wilson, T. D., & Brekke, (1994). Mental contamination and mental correction: Unwanted influences on judgments and evaluations. *Psychological Bulletin*, 116, 117–142.

Wilson, T. D., & Nisbett, R. E. (1978). The accuracy of verbal reports about the effects of stimuli on evaluations of behavior. *Social Psychology*, 41, 118–130.

Wimmer, H. & Perner, J. (1983). Beliefs about beliefs: Representation and constraining function of wrong beliefs in young children's understanding of deception. *Cognition*, 13, 103–128.

Wittgenstein, L. (1953). *Philosophical investigations*. Oxford: Basil Blackwell.

Wittgenstein, L. (1970). *Zettel* (G. E. Anscombe Trans.). Berkeley, CA: University of California Press.

Wood, L. A. & Kroger, R. O. (1994). The analysis of facework in discourse: Review and proposal. *Journal of Language and Social Psychology*, *13*, 248–277.

Wood, L. A. & Kroger, R. O. (2000). *Doing discourse analysis: Methods for studying action in talk and text*. Thousand Oaks, CA: Sage Publications.

Wooffitt, R., & Clark, C. (1998). Mobilizing discourse and social identities in knowledge talk. In C. Antaki & S. Widdicombe (Eds.), *Identities in talk* (pp. 107–120). London: Sage Publications.

Wootton, A. J. (1997). *Interaction and the development of mind*. Cambridge: Cambridge University Press.

Zimmerman, D. H. (1998). Identity, context and interaction. In C. Antaki & S. Widdicombe (Eds.), *Identities in talk* (pp. 87–106). London: Sage Publications.

Name index

Subject index